Is the law fair
to the disabled?

WHO Library Cataloguing in Publication Data

Is the law fair to the disabled? : a European survey

    (WHO regional publications. European series ; No.29)

    1.Handicapped   2.Legislation   3.Europe
    I.Pinet, Genevieve   II.Series

    ISBN 92 890 1120 3   (LC Classification HD 7255)
    ISSN 0378-2255

World Health Organization
Regional Office for Europe
Copenhagen

Is the law fair to the disabled?

A European survey

Coordinated by

Geneviève Pinet
Regional Officer for Health Legislation
WHO Regional Office for Europe
Copenhagen, Denmark

WHO Regional Publications, European Series, No. 29

EUR/ICP/HLE 113

ISBN 92 890 1120 3
ISSN 0378–2255

PRINTED IN ENGLAND

CONTENTS

Foreword

This book records the findings of a survey on health and social legislation for the disabled, carried out as part of the health legislation programme of the WHO Regional Office for Europe. It is designed to report and assess progress since 1981, the International Year of Disabled Persons, and as such forms part of the activities of the United Nations Decade of Disabled Persons, 1983–1992. For many governments and international organizations, the International Year of Disabled Persons marked the starting point in the systematization of legislation for the disabled. This survey is WHO's contribution to that process.

The interests of the severely disabled are not easily acknowledged in the political process that leads towards laws and administrative practices. They are a minority group with few advantages and few to speak for them, especially in times of economic difficulty. Yet much can be done if the philosophy and thinking behind the legislative process are clear. Too little is known about the effects of legislative changes on the quality of life of those for whom the laws are passed in the first place. The legislation concerning disabled persons is vast and complex because its development has been piecemeal, including reactions to acute situations such as great wars.

The health and sociopolitical actions that have been taken on behalf of disabled persons have been unduly narrow, promoting the impression that disabled persons are sick, unable to work and a special group requiring help and pity from the non-disabled sections of society. Even deeper in people's social attitudes lies the belief that normality and good health are unitary concepts that leave no scope for individual variations.

The six major themes of the WHO strategy for health for all by the year 2000 are equity, health promotion, community participation, multisectoral cooperation, primary health care and international cooperation. These are essential concerns for disabled persons because, even in the most developed countries, they have largely been left out of the mutual social life of communities.

Health for all must mean that a positive healthy life is within the reach of severely disabled persons in the same sense as is possible for those who are not disabled. The European Region of WHO has formulated targets in support of its regional strategy for health for all. Target 3 states that, by the year 2000, disabled persons should have the physical, social and economic opportunities that allow them at least to lead a socially and economically fulfilling and mentally creative life. This target could be achieved if societies developed positive attitudes towards the disabled and drew up programmes to provide appropriate physical, social and economic opportunities for them to develop their capacity to lead a healthy life.

Social integration as the general aim for the disabled means, however, that all the targets of the strategy are important to them as fully qualified citizens of their societies, and not simply as disabled persons.

Despite all possible prevention and rehabilitation there will always be some people with permanent functional impairments and disabilities, but they need not be socially handicapped. People are handicapped only when they are denied the opportunities generally available in their community to enjoy family life, education, employment, housing, access to public facilities, freedom of movement and the accepted standard of living.

Full participation, equality and the social integration of disabled persons require all aspects of social life to be discussed from the point of view of disabled persons and the disabling factors in society. Legislation is one way — perhaps the most important — of promoting equality in society. Laws both reflect and affect societal values and the attitudes prevalent among the population at large.

As society becomes more and more complicated, disabled persons become more and more dependent on sociopolitical regulations, personal help, aids and devices. A new legislative strategy is needed. Most countries of the WHO European Region have already begun this process, and many are developing new strategies of legislation for the social integration of disabled persons. The total picture, however, is not very clear. This book tries to find some common trends in the disability and handicap legislation of countries with different economic and political systems. It highlights the advances in social policies for the disabled, and it reviews both the substantial legislation concerned with health and social welfare and the human rights issues behind the administration of these laws. It provides a framework for the systematic discussion of the strategies and targets for legislation for disabled persons, which may in a meaningful way combine the practices of public policy and the matters of everyday life.

We in the Regional Office for Europe hope that this joint effort will serve as a stimulus for further action in the field. Our initiative has met with a particularly responsible attitude and the full cooperation of the governments of the European Member States in providing the national contributions that constitute the core of the survey. These contributions have been prepared by the health and social administrations of 25 governments and represent a wealth of precise, up-to-date information.

I wish therefore to express my deep appreciation to the governments of the European Region for their keen interest in the WHO health legislation programme and for their rewarding cooperation with the Regional Office in performing this survey. In addition, thanks are due to Mr Ilpo Vilkkumaa of the National Insurance Institute, Helsinki for his contribution to the survey.

J.E. Asvall
WHO Regional Director for Europe

National contributors

Austria

Ministerialrat Dr J. Unger, Federal Ministry of Labour and Social Affairs, Vienna

Belgium

Ministry of Public Health and Environment, Brussels

Bulgaria

Fani Videnova, Legal Adviser, Ministry of Public Health, Sofia

Denmark

Lis Witso, International Relations Division, Ministry of Social Affairs, Copenhagen

Finland

Dr Raimo Miettinen, Director, Department of Rehabilitation Affairs, National Board of Social Welfare, Helsinki

France

Annick Morel, Administrative Officer, Directorate of Social Affairs, Ministry of Social Affairs and Employment, Paris

German Democratic Republic

Dr Bodo Barleben, Chief, Department for Rehabilitation, Ministry of Public Health, Berlin

Dr Joachim Mandel, Chief, Legal Department, Ministry of Public Health, Berlin

Federal Republic of Germany

Federal Ministry for Youth, Family Affairs, Women and Health, Bonn

Hungary

Dr György Kollath, Head, Department for Legislation and Administration, Ministry of Health, Budapest

Iceland

Jon Ingimarsson, Deputy Secretary-General, Ministry for Health and Social Security, Reykjavik

Ireland

Gerry Cullen, Welfare Unit, Department of Health, Dublin

Luxembourg

Raymond Mousty, Government Adviser, Ministry of Health, Luxembourg

Monaco

Denis L. Gastaud, Director, Directorate of Health and Social Affairs, Department of the Interior, Monaco

Netherlands

Marianne J.G. Aalders, Interministerial Steering Group on Policy for the Disabled, Ministry of Welfare, Health and Cultural Affairs, Leidschendam

Poland

Maria Suwalska, Senior Specialist, Department of Prevention, Medical Care and Rehabilitation, Ministry of Health and Social Welfare, Warsaw

Portugal

Pedro de Morais Barbosa, Legal Adviser, Office of Studies and Planning, Department of International Relations, Ministry of Health, Lisbon

Romania

Office of External Relations, Ministry of Health, Bucharest

San Marino

Ministry of Health and Social Security, San Marino

Spain

Legal Cabinet, Ministry of Health and Consumer Affairs, Madrid

Sweden

Gerd Ekholm, Head of Section, The National Council for the Disabled, Stockholm

Switzerland

Federal Social Insurance Office, Berne

Turkey

Department of External Relations, Ministry of Health and Social Assistance, Ankara
Ministry of Labour and Social Security, Ankara

Union of Soviet Socialist Republics

External Relations Board, Ministry of Health of the USSR, Moscow

United Kingdom

T.M. Thorn, Department of Health and Social Security, London

Yugoslavia

Branko Djukanovic, Senior Adviser, Head of the Social Welfare Group, Federal Committee for Labour, Health and Social Welfare, Belgrade

Introduction

The search for happiness and health is a fundamental human aspiration and, in a society with a sense of community among its members, disabilities concern all human beings, not only the disabled individual. Those who have to make the greatest efforts in their daily life to overcome various handicaps, do contribute to the enrichment of our society; their achievements are of value to all.

The United Nations during the past decade has devoted considerable attention to the rights of the disabled and has made several declarations dealing with human rights, some of a universal nature, some aiming at special groups of people, including the disabled.

In 1975, the United Nations General Assembly adopted the Declaration on the Rights of Disabled Persons, recommending that all relevant international organizations and agencies should include in their programmes provisions to ensure the effective implementation of the rights and principles of this Declaration.

The proclamation of 1981 as the International Year of Disabled Persons had a tremendous impact as a consciousness-raising campaign. It provided the opportunity to promote the recognition of the rights of disabled persons and the elimination of discrimination against them. It called the attention of the international community to the intolerable situation of more than 450 million disabled persons in the world. The goal of this movement is well summarized in the few words of its motto, "Full participation and equality".

Rehabilitation and the problems of preventing disability have been on the agenda of WHO both at headquarters and at the regional level. In the Regional Office for Europe various programmes, such as child health, cardiovascular diseases, accident prevention, health of the elderly, and mental health have undertaken activities that address disability prevention and rehabilitation. For the last few years a special programme has coordinated these activities.

1

In 1981, as a contribution to the International Year of Disabled Persons, the Regional Committee held its technical discussions on the subject of the medical and social problems of the disabled. On this occasion a first review of policy and legislation for the disabled was prepared by the health legislation unit. After these technical discussions the Regional Committee stressed the necessity to ensure a follow-up to the activities of the International Year of Disabled Persons.

By adopting the regional strategy in 1980 and the targets for health for all in 1984, the Member States of the Region agreed to promote the development of positive attitudes towards the disabled, and to set up programmes aimed at providing appropriate physical, social and economic opportunities for the disabled to develop their capacities to lead healthy lives. All human beings have an equal right to health; this is the fundamental principle of social policy that inspired the health for all movement and this is very close to the goal of equal opportunity and full participation previously mentioned. More specifically, these regional targets stress the need for better opportunities for the disabled (target 3), to reduce disease and disability (target 4) and to develop and strengthen the political and legislative support necessary to put these goals into practice (target 33). The willingness of the Member States of the European Region to increase their work on rehabilitation and disability prevention has been translated into action and has brought about a more concrete policy of social solidarity supported by legislation.

The United Nations General Assembly continued to give high priority to disabled persons by proclaiming 1983–1992 the Decade of Disabled Persons and adopting a World Programme of Action for its implementation. The immensity of the task proposed in this World Programme is a true challenge and, in particular, makes it necessary to evaluate progress towards its goals. The Programme itself states that monitoring and evaluation should be carried out regularly, and requests the specialized agencies of the United Nations, such as WHO, to participate in data collection for the purposes of evaluation. It is hoped that the present survey will make its contribution to this evaluation.

Aims and Scope

The purpose of this survey is to evaluate progress in health and social legislation for the disabled in the European Region since the International Year of Disabled Persons in 1981, providing examples of achievements as well as of difficulties met, and to throw light on the further legislative strategies envisaged by Member States in the spirit of the World Programme of Action concerning disabled persons and in the spirit of health for all in Europe.

The health and social legislation dealing with problems of impairment, disability and handicap partly stems from the early days of rehabilitation in the 1940s and 1950s, and partly reflects the concerns and opportunities for development of the days of steady economic growth in the 1960s and early 1970s. Although there was life in the policy for the disabled before 1981, that year marked an time of unprecedented enthusiasm and activity. For this survey, however, it would not have been meaningful, given the relatively slow pace of the legislative process, to restrict the research strictly to the years from 1981 onward. The period considered, therefore, starts around the mid-1970s when the United Nations decided that the year 1981 would be designated the International Year of Disabled Persons and goes on for some countries up to 1987.

The European Member States have shown a remarkable willingness to cooperate in this WHO initiative and have participated actively in the elaboration of this survey. The present book consists mainly of the reports received from 25 Member States: Austria, Belgium, Bulgaria, Denmark, Finland, France, the German Democratic Republic, the Federal Republic of Germany, Hungary, Iceland, Ireland, Luxembourg, Monaco, the Netherlands, Poland, Portugal, Romania, San Marino, Spain, Sweden, Switzerland, Turkey, the Union of Soviet Socialist Republics, the United Kingdom and Yugoslavia.

Special reports were also studied from the following international organizations, whose work has a considerable impact on national policies for the disabled: the Commission of the European Communities, the Council of Europe, the European Association for Special Education, the International Federation of Disabled Workers and Civilian Handicapped, the International Labour Organisation, the International Red Cross, the International Social Security Association, the United Nations Children's Fund, and the United Nations Economic Commission for Europe.

As part of the process of elaborating this survey, the Regional Office for Europe organized a Working Group on Health and Social Legislation for the Disabled, hosted by the German Democratic Republic in Dresden in November 1985. It gathered 31 experts from 25 countries, including the staff of ministries of health, social welfare and foreign affairs, members of national commissions for disability and rehabilitation, and members of the United Nations Centre for Social Development and Humanitarian Affairs and Rehabilitation

International. This was an opportunity for the authors of country reports to present and discuss their contributions, identify gaps in the information available, and compare their evaluation of legislative developments since the International Year of Disabled Persons. The country reports published here therefore date from around 1985, with some later contributions up to 1987. Although further developments will inevitably have taken place since then, the main aim of this survey was to assess the impetus that the International Year had given to action for the disabled and the trends that had developed by mid-decade.

A further gathering was organized six months later, in June 1986 in Vienna, by Rehabilitation International under the auspices of the United Nations Centre for Social Development and Humanitarian Affairs and in cooperation with the WHO Regional Office for Europe. This international expert meeting on legislation for the equalization of opportunities for people with disabilities was an important milestone in the promotion of social equity for such people.

Framework of the Survey

The problems of disabled persons are always so interrelated that any one aspect affects everything else. Therefore, in order to allow intercountry comparisons, the Regional Office proposed a common framework in which to present the content of the country reports, although not all the reports conform exactly to this format. The framework encompasses five areas.

General principles. This introductory section identifies how the rights of the disabled are recognized in various national policy declarations and instruments, such as national constitutions, plans and programmes of action, and their institutional framework.

National involvement in international action for the disabled. This section indicates how the countries participate in or support international initiatives in the field of disability at intergovernmental and nongovernmental levels.

Methodology. This section examines the type of legislative approach to the equality concept, for instance the integration of various disability issues in a number of different laws, or the adoption of a specific law to secure the rights of the disabled or to make provisions specific to a category of disabled person.

Main features of the legislation for the disabled. This section looks at the measures aimed at eliminating discrimination or social

4

prejudice against the disabled, facilitating social reintegration and full participation, preventing disability, and ensuring a system of income support for the disabled.

Evaluation of progress in national legislation. This section reviews the progress accomplished, mentioning examples of success and the constraints or difficulties encountered, reflecting on the impact of the measures implemented and considering the work ahead.

Highlights of the Survey

This book highlights three main aspects of national policies for the disabled: the positive developments experienced, the constraints met and the further work needed.

Positive developments

The year 1981 saw unprecedented enthusiasm and activity. Most countries spent the International Year of Disabled Persons working intensively to recognize the rights of the disabled to equal opportunity and full participation in the life of their societies.

First, all countries were motivated to find out about disabilities, the disabled and their families, and to plan and coordinate the work for the disabled in all areas of public policy. This was reflected in new national commissions or coordinating bodies, new laws concerned with the rights of the disabled, faster and more comprehensive implementation of existing measures, and many studies and statistical reports about the number of disabled people and their social condition.

Local self-government and decentralized decision-making, based on the principle of local democracy and increased citizen participation, have meant a great deal for developments in the field of disability and rehabilitation; they have resulted in a flexible system that can be smoothly adjusted in response to social developments. This was a successful step towards facilitating the integration of the disabled in society. The policy of shifting the emphasis in the distribution of resources from hospitals to primary health care also involved the services to the disabled. The increased use of framework legislation has supported this movement, allowing for flexibility, improvements in administration and ease of coordination.

Social integration, an essential requirement of the policy for the disabled, was promoted in many ways, for instance by the school administrations that agreed to accept more disabled children in normal schools, in the field of housing and in the important area of working life, where the public authorities are employing a significantly higher number of disabled persons than before 1981. Employment opportunities have also been improved, partly by extending the access to sheltered employment in private industry and partly by increasing the capacity in sheltered workshops run by the public authorities.

Progress has been made in the area of independent dwellings, as the extension of legislative, financial and practical measures has resulted in many more disabled persons than before living independently in their own homes, and new forms of residential accommodation and rehabilitation centres have been established.

One of the most important positive results of the International Year of Disabled Persons was the recognition of the disabled as experts in their own affairs. Some countries have made real progress in increasing the influence of the disabled and their organizations at all levels of legislative action.

The media were important in informing the general population about the difficulties encountered by the disabled. One very fortunate consequence of this promotional activity was the collection and distribution of information to the disabled about the services available to them.

The International Year made not only the public but also the authorities much more conscious of and sensitive to the problems facing the disabled. This has resulted in a far greater willingness to release funds for various forms of assistance to them. Increased awareness and, in many fields, amendments of existing laws have brought about improvements for the disabled.

Besides advances in general legislative questions, such as coordinating commissions, legislative information files, the continuing decentralization of services, and further progress in social integration in many areas of life, the position of disabled persons has improved in many ways since 1981: they now benefit from better transport, communication, social security and many other changes.

The progress achieved is reflected not so much in the updating of existing laws and the passing of new ones but primarily in the incorporation of new approaches, measures and methods, including new rights.

The developments in the legal field had a highly positive impact on the social integration of the disabled and on the creation of equal opportunities. Nevertheless, the success of policies aimed at improving the social integration of disabled people is very difficult to judge by any comprehensive and objective measures, even when governments seek to monitor the effect of their policies. Some countries

6

are carrying out national evaluations of the legislation for the disabled to find out, *inter alia,* how the intentions of the legislation have succeeded.

Difficulties and major constraints

Despite important breakthroughs, many difficulties still need to be overcome. The integration of disabled persons in their community is far from satisfactory in most countries. Nowhere have all the obstacles been overcome, despite the important steps taken by some countries to eliminate or reduce barriers to the full participation and equality of disabled persons. In many cases, disabled children and adults are still excluded from school because of their limited mobility or because those responsible for them are not sufficiently aware of their abilities and potential. Children with disabilities are too often confined to life in institutions that are more custodial than educational. Disabled persons are often denied employment or given menial and poorly paid jobs. Finally, the disabled are often denied the right to self-determination in their life and future development, as well as their chance to take part in the social life of their community. This deprivation is a result of physical, social and economic barriers that have often been caused by ignorance, fear or indifference. This socially inflicted deprivation is especially acute for the mentally handicapped. Prevention, particularly in the field of mental health, is insufficiently developed.

The difficulties mentioned by the Member States in their implementation of the social objectives of the World Programme of Action are primarily of an economic nature and relate to the financial options of the social community. They derive from the general economic slowdown that European countries are experiencing. So the major constraint on new measures is the need to consider the practical resource implications. Present economic circumstances necessitate careful control of public expenditure. For a government, additional resources can only be freed by switching them from other objectives, by greater efficiency or by the generation of greater national wealth through improved economic performance. In addition, resources are subject to growing pressures, for example through the growth in the number of elderly and disabled people because of demographic changes, and the growing cost and scope of new medical techniques. Policies for the disabled have suffered from inefficient services, including obsolete benefit systems. Constraints also come from old institutions not adapted to present needs, in particular, to those of the adult disabled, and located so far from city centres that they make social integration particularly difficult. In modern societies, terminating a service or a benefit that has lost its original meaning has proved almost impossible. When resources are scare, however, there should be methods of allocating them appropriately.

The objective of decentralization — to develop the interaction between different sectors of human services — has not always been achieved, even in the neighbouring sectors of health care and social services. In some countries the trend towards decentralization may have increased the inequality of services because of the different economic resources and the uneven availability of personnel. The health centres and hospitals may not have taken full account of psychological and social factors in the rehabilitation of disabled persons and the role of the family in the rehabilitation process is not duly appreciated.

There are still social isolation for and misapprehensions and unease about the disabled. The self-help groups are very active but encounter difficulties such as lack of subsidies and inadequate collaboration from health professionals and public authorities. Sometimes the fact that the various self-help groups have no general policy does not work in their favour.

Difficulties are beginning to arise with integration in the workplace. The situation is reported as satisfactory in protected workshops, but integration into normal professional life is complicated by the requirements of the labour market for higher qualifications and/or increased output. The disabled are also competing on the labour market with people already unemployed. Furthermore, the new technology that now dominates the market necessitates a qualification most disabled persons are not yet able to obtain. At the same time, the traditional sectors based on handicrafts are declining and giving place to the new technology. There is often a serious gap between the professional training provided to the disabled and the demand for their services on the labour market. The percentage of unemployed among the disabled is considerably higher than the percentage of unemployed in the total population.

It has also proved difficult to reach a coordinated policy for the disabled because responsibility is divided among too many varied authorities. This leads to a multiplicity of regulatory and legal arrangements resulting in poor quality, uncertain validity and gaps. The legislation that deals with questions of interest to the disabled is still very complicated and diffuse. This can lead to disputes over responsibility, long waiting times and a break in the continuity of the rehabilitation process. When framework legislation is used, it entails risks such as discrepancies between different local authorities in implementation and in resources available. In addition, laws and regulations are usually compiled for bureaucratic purposes, not for access by and information to the general public or the disabled. The involvement of many institutions increases the weight of administration and its burden upon the disabled; it sometimes also leads to a duplication of the medical examinations to which the disabled are submitted.

Even the most carefully drafted legislation will be ineffective if the political will is lacking to translate it into action. To be successful, legislation must not only be carried out but also be acceptable to the whole population. Law is the necessary basis of, but not the only guarantee for, the respect of human rights. There is always a gap between the text of the law and its implementation, and this gap fluctuates with different political and economic circumstances.

Further legislative strategy
A major effort is still needed to change the basic attitude of society towards the disabled. The work of informing all citizens must continue, with a view to arousing a greater awareness about disabled persons, their needs and difficulties, aspirations and abilities. Special programmes should be arranged to help disabled persons to develop their skills in daily living, in sport and in social interaction.

Despite the progress to date, there is still much scope for improvement in the design and effectiveness of services, particularly in their coordination, in the structure of income provision, and in the range of choices and opportunities for the disabled, and particularly those with severe or multiple handicaps, to improve their lives.

Further reforms of social security systems should take into proper account the situation of the disabled, and efforts should be made, for instance: to harmonize the type of allocation for income support for the disabled, to adapt the criteria for granting these allocations, to simplify the procedures for presenting requests to qualify for allocations and to revise the amount of allocations. A general reform of social security law will have an impact on conditions for the disabled, in terms of simplification and clarity, priority setting and permanent control of the budget.

Efforts have to be made to prevent the economic difficulties that require readjustments in publicly financed service, from affecting the efforts to integrate the disabled in society and to secure equal treatment for them on all social points. Ways must also be found to avoid cutting the public budgets for special services for disabled persons. Governments should sponsor a special drive to encourage the employment of the disabled. Measures to relieve the congestion

9

of the normal labour market could also contribute effectively to promoting the employment of the disabled.

It is important to seek further improvements through programmes of research that implement experiments and try out new ways of thinking, and through innovative projects that seek new ways of involving the disabled themselves and private organizations more in the responsibility for the integration process (for example, to stimulate the creativity of severely disabled persons). Public authorities should set aside special funds for pilot projects in the social field. Innovation can also be useful in testing new ways of working. Thus, some countries consider it possible to achieve many improvements without a large increase in appropriations, and have mentioned that the public authorities have not yet explored all the opportunities to improve the situation of the disabled, by setting up an appropriate infrastructure and by collaborating with private initiatives.

The power of legislation to prevent impairments, disabilities and handicaps should be used to the full in maternal and child health, in work protection, in environmental health and in other areas affecting health. Even the legislation that does not relate directly to the situation of the disabled can nevertheless contribute to the prevention, or at least the early detection, of a disability, for instance by improving school health services or workers' health services, and by improving the coordination of health and social services and of the different spheres of public and private activity.

It is still necessary to improve legislation on accommodation and the living environment. Although most recently constructed public buildings are designed to provide access for the disabled, in some countries there is no actual legislation imposing this requirement. This applies also to flats in residential buildings and to areas open to the public, such as pavements and underground parking areas. High priority should be given to the improved design of technical aids for the disabled. Public funding should cover the extra cost for the disabled of specially designed housing, transport, and tools for daily life, work and leisure. The availability of care in the home could also be extended to enable the disabled to remain as much as possible in their natural environment.

A continuous effort should be made to keep social laws abreast of social circumstances, and take account of changes in the needs of disabled persons and the actual capacities of the community. Efforts should concentrate on the coordination and clarification of measures, institutions and benefits for the disabled. This has often been said but not accomplished, and the disabled still have to face a very complex network of laws and institutions. A simpler and more comprehensive

10

instrument of law to back up the action carried out by the relevant authorities is still needed. In this connection teaching and research about the rights of the disabled should be developed among lawyers, health personnel and in organizations for disabled persons.

The disabled and their organizations should be encouraged to participate in all levels of the legislative process: in the planning, implementation and evaluation of laws. To this end, an easy-to-use information system describing the benefits and services for the disabled should be locally available to all, and information about pertinent legislation should be easily accessible. Most important of all will be the need to ensure that the disabled themselves exercise a decisive influence on the design of policies, programmes and legislation.

This introduction evokes only some of the salient points of this research. The complex field of health and social legislation for the disabled illustrates perhaps more than other issues the importance of intersectoral cooperation for health. The disabled person is an entity, even if his or her life has a variety of aspects and each of these aspects is the object of several policy and care sectors. There is no single status for disabled people but a diversity, depending on the origin and severity of their handicap, the place where a disability was caused and, above all, differences in assessing the effects of a disability. Disabled persons are estimated to represent 10% of the total population of each country, a fact that should impel the authorities to review, adapt and refine the policies that they have been applying up to now. The movement from an international convention or agreement to national laws, and then to local implementation of these laws is very slow and complex. Although each country has a specific and unique legal system, countries could be encouraged to take note of and learn from the actions that others are taking in health and social legislation for the disabled. Thus, together we in the Region can unite the high ideals of equality and full participation with the practicalities of everyday life.

Geneviève Pinet
Regional Officer for Health Legislation

Austria

General Principles

Rehabilitation and assistance for disabled persons have become an
integral part of Austrian social policy. On the occasion of the
International Year of Disabled Persons in 1981, the Federal Government of Austria issued a proclamation in which it accepted the rights
of disabled persons as set down in the United Nations Declaration on
the Rights of Disabled Persons. In this proclamation, the Federal
Government defined the focal points of its rehabilitation policy for
the coming years. Similar proclamations were issued by the provincial social consultants, who are responsible for assisting disabled
persons in the provinces, and by the League of Towns.

While the Austrian Constitution does not mention the problems
of disabled persons, it does guarantee equality before the law to all
citizens. The measures to be taken in the fields of disability and
rehabilitation fall within the competence partly of the Federation and
partly of the provinces, according to the Federal Constitution Act,
Article 15, paragraph 1.

The Federal Government is responsible for both legislation and
execution in the following areas, which are of essential importance
for assistance to disabled persons and their rehabilitation:

— under the Federal Constitution Act, Article 10: labour law (as
far as it does not fall under Article 12) and social insurance
(paragraph 1(11)); health care (except matters related to
deaths and burials) as well as local sanitary services and life-
saving services (paragraph 1(12)); military matters, and
welfare for war veterans and their survivors (paragraph 1(15));
population policy in so far as it concerns the granting of

13

children's allowances and the equalization of financial burdens in the interests of the family (paragraph 1(17));

— the Invalid Employment Act 1969, Article 1 (*Bundesgesetzblatt,* No. 22/1970) valid until 1989;

— the Welfare for Victims of Political Persecution Act, Article 1, 11th amendment (*Bundesgesetzblatt,* No. 77/1957).

The following areas are the subject of framework legislation by the Federation, with implementing legislation and execution by the provinces:

— under the Federal Constitution Act, Article 12, paragraph 1(1): assistance to persons in need, welfare for mothers, infants and youths, sanatoria and nursing homes;

— under the Federal Constitution Act, Article 14, paragraph 3(b): external organization of public compulsory schools.

In October 1977, the Federal Ministry for Social Administration presented its concept for the integration of disabled persons. This concept contains the principles for modern rehabilitation as the primary aim of all measures. It emphasizes the need for the creation of sufficient opportunities for the employment of disabled persons on the open labour market, the further development of sheltered workshops for disabled persons who, because of their state of health, cannot or cannot yet be employed on the open labour market, and better coordination of the activities of the different rehabilitation authorities.

To achieve coordination and cooperation among all the relevant rehabilitation authorities, administrative agreements have been drawn up by the federal and provincial rehabilitation authorities. These agreements provide for the elaboration of rehabilitation plans and contain regulations on the rehabilitation process when two or more rehabilitation authorities are concerned, on questions of medical examination, and on the costs to be borne by the rehabilitation authorities. On the basis of these agreements, teams of experts nominated by the different rehabilitation authorities have been set up in the provinces. When disabled persons require rehabilitation, these experts discuss each individual case and decide on the measures necessary.

Expert bodies with consultative status, which have been set up at the federal as well as at the provincial level, also serve the purpose of coordination.

A Federal Advisory Board for Disabled Persons was established at the Federal Ministry for Health and Environmental Protection in 1977. This Board counsels the Minister in all medical matters that concern the care of and assistance to disabled persons. The Board is composed of representatives of various federal ministries, interest groups, social insurance institutes and the provinces.

An Invalid Welfare Advisory Board was set up within the Federal Ministry for Social Administration to counsel the Ministry in matters of assistance to disabled persons and their rehabilitation. Organizations of disabled persons, the federal and provincial rehabilitation authorities, social insurance bodies and professional interest groups are represented on this Board, which meets whenever necessary.

On the initiative of the Conference of Provincial Social Consultants, a Provincial Coordinating Commission for Disability Matters was created in Vienna in 1977, in order to achieve better coordination among the authorities responsible for assistance to disabled persons and their rehabilitation in the province of Vienna. The Commission, which meets once a year, is composed of representatives of several departments of the municipal council, the main social insurance bodies, interest groups, and the federal authorities in the field of social administration.

National Involvement in International Action

Austria takes part in international activities for disabled persons within the framework of the United Nations, the Council of Europe and other international organizations. It fully recognizes the United Nations Declaration on the Rights of Disabled Persons and the World Programme of Action concerning disabled persons. Every year, Austria pays voluntary contributions to the United Nations Trust Fund.

Austria is one of the Signatory States of the European Social Charter. By ratifying the Charter, Austria accepted Article 15 as binding. This article regulates the right of physically and mentally disabled persons to vocational training, rehabilitation and social reintegration. To guarantee the effective implementation of this right, Austria is obliged to take measures to ensure the provision of vocational training opportunities, if necessary including public and private special facilities. It should also provide for the job placement of disabled persons, especially by creating special placement bodies, by providing sheltered employment free from competition and by giving incentives to employers to employ disabled persons.

International Labour Organisation Convention 159 on the Vocational Rehabilitation and Employment of the Disabled is completely covered by Austrian legislation and will be ratified in the near future.

Austria has also ratified the Florence Agreement of the United Nations Educational, Scientific and Cultural Organization on the import and export of equipment of educational, scientific and cultural value for disabled persons. The Nairobi protocol was not ratified, but parts of it will be included in the draft of a new customs law.

Organizations of disabled persons and the rehabilitation authorities are members of various nongovernmental organizations with whom they cooperate closely. These include Mobility International, the International Council on Social Welfare, the International Federation of Multiple Sclerosis Societies, the International Round Table for the Advancement of Counselling, the International Social Security Association, the World Federation of the Deaf, the World Council for the Welfare of the Blind, the International Federation of the Blind, and various sports organizations for disabled persons, such as the International Sports Organization for the Disabled and the International Blind Sports Association. Austria has particularly intensive cooperation with Rehabilitation International, whose president was until recently Mr Otto Geiecker, an Austrian.

Methodology — Types of Legislative Approach to the Equality Concept

Federal laws

Social insurance

Austrian social insurance covers health, accidents and pensions. The field of rehabilitation has recently been regulated by the 32nd amendment to the General Social Insurance Act (*Bundesgesetzblatt,* No. 704/1976). Similar regulations have also been included in the Social Insurance Act for the Self-Employed in Trade, Commerce and Industry and the Social Insurance Act for Farmers.

These laws stipulate that rehabilitation comprises medical, vocational and, as necessary, social measures aimed at encouraging disabled persons to regain their capacities so that they can permanently occupy a place in vocational and economic life, and in society, that is adapted to their capacities and needs. The social insurance regulations stipulate that the final decisions on rehabilitation measures must be made by the competent social insurance institute.

Labour promotion
The Labour Promotion Act (*Bundesgesetzblatt,* No. 31/1969) regulates the measures to be taken by employment agencies to achieve and maintain full employment and to prevent unemployment. These measures especially comprise vocational counselling, the placement of apprentices and, in other training places, subsidies to help people find work or training places or to maintain employment (especially training, retraining and additional training, job trials, preparation for a job and work training), as well as subsidies for the safety of workplaces. Persons with a physical or mental disability are given special consideration with regard to job placement and the granting of subsidies for the promotion of training or the maintenance of a workplace.

Equalization of burdens for families
The Equalization of Burdens for Families Act (*Bundesgesetzblatt,* No. 376/1967) regulates family, school travel and birth allowances. More favourable regulations apply to disabled persons. For example, an increased family allowance is granted for severely disabled children (consisting of an additional S 1300 (US $95) per month).

Army welfare
The Army Welfare Act (*Bundesgesetzblatt,* No. 27/1964) provides for benefits, such as pensions, special care and blind persons' supplements, vocational training, medical care and the provision of orthopaedic aids, for Austrian citizens whose health has been damaged in causal relation with ordinary or extraordinary military service.

Employment of invalids
The Invalid Employment Act (*Bundesgesetzblatt,* No. 22/1970) obliges all employers in Austria with 25 or more employees to employ at least one invalid entitled to preferential treatment for each 25 employees. Employers who do not fulfil this obligation have to pay a penalty. Furthermore, this law foresees many promotional measures to facilitate the vocational integration of disabled persons.

Welfare for war victims
The War Victims Welfare Act (*Bundesgesetzblatt,* No. 152/1957) provides for benefits, such as pensions, special care and blind persons' supplements, vocational training, medical care and the provision of orthopaedic aids, for Austrian citizens whose health has been damaged in causal relation with military service in the German army (*Wehrmacht*), the Austrian army during the First Republic or the armed forces of the Austro-Hungarian Monarchy, or as civilians in causal relation with war events.

National Fund for Special Assistance to Disabled Persons
In accordance with the National Fund Act (*Bundesgesetzblatt*, No. 259/1981), benefits for medical, vocational and social rehabilitation can be granted if no other possibilities of assistance exist and there is social hardship.

Welfare for victims of political persecution
In accordance with the Welfare for Victims of Political Persecution Act (*Bundesgesetzblatt*, No. 183/1947), victims of the fight for a free and democratic Austria and victims of political persecution are entitled to benefits. Decisions on the type and size of benefits take into consideration the regulations of the War Victims Welfare Act. Needy persons possessing an official notice are granted a pension. Furthermore, this law foresees various compensation measures, e.g. for imprisonment, restrictions of liberty or impediments to careers.

Assistance in the case of tuberculosis
In accordance with the Tuberculosis Act (*Bundesgesetzblatt*, No. 127/1968) persons suffering from tuberculosis have a right to medical care, nursing and treatment in hospitals, convalescent homes and sanatoria. To cover the costs of living for the sick person and his or her family, economic help can be granted (such as regular financial allowances and payment of rent). A person is entitled to assistance in the case of tuberculosis as long as he or she shows at least one certain sign of the disease. A certain category of disabled person is entitled to benefits under this Act.

School organization
The School Organization Act (*Bundesgesetzblatt*, No. 242/1962) stipulates that the different types of special school have to promote physically and mentally disabled children in a way appropriate to their types of disability, to do everything to provide them with an education corresponding to the one in the primary and secondary or polytechnic schools, and to prepare for their integration into vocational life. The curriculum has to include additional subjects of instruction appropriate to the pupil's disability, as well as therapeutic and functional exercises. The maximum number of pupils in the classes of the different types of special school is significantly lower than that in normal schools.

Compulsory education
The Compulsory Education Act (*Bundesgesetzblatt*, No. 241/1961) stipulates that education is compulsory for all children who are living permanently in Austria. Children of school age who are unable to

follow instruction in primary or secondary schools, owing to a mental or physical disability, but for whom education is nevertheless compulsory, have to attend a special school appropriate to their particular condition and learning capacities, or a primary or secondary school with special school classes attached.

Provincial laws

Assistance to disabled persons
Assistance to disabled persons in the provinces aims to guarantee, for those who have not been provided for under federal regulations, the best possible integration or reintegration into society and vocational life. Measures can consist of help with integration (medical care and the provision of orthopaedic aids, assistance with school training and education and assistance with vocational integration), sheltered work, occupational therapy, personal help and the payment of a special care allowance.

The provincial disability laws appear in the following issues of the *Landesgesetzblätter*: for Burgenland, No. 20/1966; Carinthia, No. 30/1981; Lower Austria, No. 9200 ex 1974; Upper Austria, No. 11/1971; Salzburg, No. 93/1981; Styria, No. 314/1964; Tyrol, No. 58/1983; Vorarlberg, No. 25/1964; and Vienna, No. 22/1966.

Blind persons' allowance
The blind persons' allowances laws provide for the payment of allowances to blind and severely visually impaired persons who do not already receive similar benefits under federal regulations.

The provincial blind persons' allowances laws appear in the following issues of the *Landesgesetzblätter*: for Burgenland, No. 11/1957; Carinthia, No. 39/1981; Lower Austria, No 9200 ex 1974; Upper Austria, No. 12/1977; Salzburg, No. 114/1966; Styria, No. 55/1956; Tyrol, No. 44/1965; Vorarlberg, No. 25/1964; and Vienna, No. 14/1969.

Social assistance
Social assistance is supposed to give the assistance of society to the persons who need it to lead a decent life. As a rule, it comprises assistance to secure the necessities of life, assistance in special circumstances and social services. Such assistance, including home help, home care, home cleaning, laundry service, meals-on-wheels, and visiting and counselling services, is especially important for disabled persons.

The provincial social assistance laws appear in the following issues of the *Landesgesetzblätter*: for Burgenland, No. 7/1975; Carinthia, No. 30/1981; Lower Austria, No. 9200 ex 1974; Upper

19

Austria, No. 66/1973; Salzburg, No. 19/1975; Styria, No. 1/1973; Tyrol, No. 105/1973; Vorarlberg, No. 26/1971; and Vienna, No. 11/1973.

The rights of disabled persons are regulated by the laws mentioned above. It is not possible to enact one special law to guarantee these rights because of the division of responsibilities between the Federation and the provinces.

Legal protection of the disabled

The legal provisions for a disabled person are based mainly on the cause of the disability. Laws for certain categories of disabled person, such as mentally disabled or blind persons, are an exception. By a federal law enacted on 2 February 1983 (*Bundesgesetzblatt,* No. 136/1983), trusteeship was introduced for persons who, because of their physical illness or mental handicap, are unable to settle their affairs on their own. This law replaces the interdiction decree with regulations that improve the legal protection of the mentally ill and handicapped, guaranteeing them legal assistance adapted to their needs. It should also serve to eliminate the stigmatization of and discrimination against such persons. The interdiction is replaced by the trusteeship, and within this framework legal assistance can be granted that will serve the wellbeing of the sick or disabled person.

Review of the Present State of National Legislation

Elimination of discrimination or social prejudice

Various public relations measures have been taken by the authorities, such as Campaign Together organized by the Federal Ministry for Education, Culture and Sports or the campaign Your Partner — the Disabled Person promoted by the employment agencies, in order to eliminate prejudices against disabled persons. All measures taken in the execution and interpretation of the laws also serve this goal.

To avoid discrimination against disabled persons, several special laws have been enacted or amended (such as the trusteeship law mentioned above). To protect disabled persons' rights and interests, the Broadcasting Act, for instance, provides for the nomination of a representative of disabled persons on the body representing radio and television customers.

The legal basis for the individual and specific care of disabled persons has been established. In the case of a disability, however, it is important to explore all the possibilities for assistance, not only the relevant laws providing supportive measures. Thus, in order to guarantee optimal rehabilitation, therapy groups are necessary for children; adults need vocational retraining, opportunities for holidays, adaptation of their dwellings and the elimination of constructional barriers; and social services for the elderly, such as meals-on-wheels, home help, laundry services and accommodation in old people's and nursing homes, are very important. Cooperation and coordination with private organizations or self-help groups in the implementation of special legal measures for disabled persons have proved to be useful for achieving optimal rehabilitation in the framework of the law. These self-help organizations, set up as a result of private initiatives, have cooperated in establishing special boards at several ministries to deal with the specific problems of so-called minority groups. Furthermore, the Office of the Ombudsman serves as a body for complaints in cases where no more legal action is possible.

Social reintegration and full participation

Nursing, medical rehabilitation and orthopaedic and technical aids are financed both during treatment in hospital and during treatment in special rehabilitation centres by health, pensions or accident insurance under the social insurance laws. There are rehabilitation centres for the treatment of myocardial infarction, metabolic diseases, physical impairments and mental impairments. Further centres are necessary for the after-treatment of head and brain injuries, strokes or mental impairments existing since birth.

The Austrian standard on constructional measures for physically disabled and aged persons (ÖNORM B 1600) was declared binding for public state-owned buildings by decree. It has also been partially included in the building regulations of the provinces. Furthermore, there are pavement regulations in towns (provincial capitals) and local construction consulting authorities in various villages. The Law for the Promotion of Residential Buildings provides further means to promote the construction of buildings adapted to the needs of disabled persons. (This covers buildings used by tourists as well as private buildings.) Special flats for disabled persons are being built by the local authorities. The rehabilitation authorities grant subsidies and loans for the adaptation of flats and houses to the needs of disabled persons.

Disabled persons are exempt from paying various fees for basic services (such as telephone, telephone for the deaf, radio, television and teletext). Transport services for disabled persons are subsidized under the social assistance or disability laws.

Vocational rehabilitation is guaranteed to a large extent by the legally regulated cooperation of the social insurance institutes and the employment agencies. In individual cases, however, the job placement of a disabled person may be difficult owing to the person's disability or the infrastructure of the enterprises (especially in rural areas). Measures for vocational rehabilitation are provided for under some of the federal laws mentioned above and in the provincial disability laws. Vocational training or retraining takes place in schools or universities, in facilities for adult education or in special training centres for disabled persons.

Sheltered workshops, the adaptation of workplaces to the needs of disabled persons and subsidies for the return to work facilitate integration in the open labour market. Some 11 sheltered workshops for the disabled have been established over the past few years. The Invalid Employment Act, which contains regulations for a quota system, will soon be amended. Unlike any other law, this has had both very positive and negative effects on the employment of disabled persons. While the financial benefits to be gained from employing a disabled person are an incentive, employers are afraid of the special protection disabled employees have against dismissal.

The following social services are available in towns: visiting services, meals-on-wheels, home help, family help, home nursing, visiting nursing, repair services, laundry services, home cleaning, occupational therapy at home, psychosocial outreach units, assistance in case of drug addiction, self-help groups, social support networks, personal assistance for adults, day-care centres, vocational therapy, physical therapy, neighbourhood help, transport services, trips into the country and others.

For compulsory education, there are additional facilities for special education and training facilities for certain groups of disabled person (such as the blind or deaf).

Reserved seat schemes in theatres and concert halls, as well as earphones for deaf persons have been provided in recent years, and adult evening schools with external branches for disabled persons offer a wide range of cultural activities. The activities of groups and organizations of disabled persons are promoted.

Sport, recreation and leisure matters are regulated under various laws and the labour regulations (collective agreements); promotional measures are taken by the provinces in the field of leisure and culture. Sports for disabled persons are extremely popular in Austria, and extensive moral and financial support is granted by public authorities.

Information is provided by means of a tape and record library, a magazine in braille, and teletext on television. Programmes on disability matters are broadcast from time to time.

The participation of disabled persons is guaranteed in the evaluation procedures for laws and through the collaboration of the

Austrian Committee on Rehabilitation with various boards, such as the National Fund for Special Assistance to Disabled Persons, the Equalization Tax Fund and the Invalid Welfare Advisory Board. In Vienna, a legal association of disabled persons has been set up under the Disability Act.

Self-help groups can be promoted according to the provincial disability laws and social assistance laws, as well as by social insurance institutes and private entities.

The aim is for the disabled to achieve independent living, but this is not always possible because of the degree of disability, the situation in the family and the lack of social services.

The prevention of disability

Measures for protection against various risks include the mother and child health card, infant welfare services, accident prevention services, labour inspection and safety-technical and medical services in the workplace, medical research in the framework of the university clinics and accident hospitals, brochures issued by the Ministries for Health and Environmental Protection, for Social Administration and for Family, Youth and Consumer Protection, vaccination campaigns, health examinations, and information campaigns (for example, on the risk of cancer from smoking).

Preventive measures are promoted by means of:

— television programmes giving information on dangers and risks;

— the development of pre- and postnatal examinations and improvement in the knowledge of the importance of vaccinations and on methods for the prevention of diseases;

— regular examinations in schools for the early detection of childhood impairments;

— health examinations, reporting procedures for epidemic and infectious diseases, the Tuberculosis Act, Vaccination Damage Act and other measures;

— supervision of the adherence to safety measures by the labour inspection, accident prevention service, Board for Traffic Safety and Austrian Standardization Institute; the marking of technical devices with the state safety examination stamp, and the obligation of the employer to install a safety–technical and medical service in companies with a certain number of employees;

— the training of personnel in safety techniques and occupational medicine through courses, seminars, symposia and the like (the right to participate is guaranteed by the Labour Constitution Act);

— the promotion of research on prophylactic measures and rehabilitation with support from public funds and the research promotion fund and by the legal obligation contained in the social insurance laws.

Systems of income support

The financial support measures in the field of social insurance (which includes protection against occupational accidents and diseases as well as health insurance and pensions insurance) are extensive; a pension from the accident insurance and from the pensions insurance may both be granted at the same time in a cumulative manner. There is no special disability insurance in Austria. For severely disabled children, the family allowances are doubled.

Health insurance

Sickness benefits are payable for the duration of incapacity to work because of illness for a maximum of 78 weeks; they amount to 50% of the last income for the first six weeks and 60% of this income for the remaining time off work, with supplements for dependant family members, the maximum amount allowable being 75% of the last income. In case of hospitalization, insured persons receive family or *per diem* allowances instead of sickness benefits. The family allowance amounts to one third of the previous income for the first six weeks, 40% for the following 20 weeks and 50% for the further time of entitlement; supplements are payable if the insured person has to care for two or more family members. Thus, the total amount of the increased family allowance can reach the amount of the sickness benefits. The *per diem* allowance (for entitled persons who do not have to care for family members) amounts to a quarter of the previous income for the first six weeks and 30% for the following time of entitlement.

Accident insurance

A pension from accident insurance is payable for the duration of a reduction in earning capacity of at least 20%, caused by an occupational accident or disease; if the earning capacity is reduced because of two or more accidents or diseases, the total reduction of earning capacity resulting from all cases must be of at least 20%. The reduction of earning capacity is evaluated theoretically (on the basis of the degree of disability and without reference to the occupations the insured person has had so far). The pension is calculated on the basis of the — real or assumed (completed) — income from the employment or self-employment under which the obligatory insurance was made, in the year before the occupational accident or the onset of the occupational disease; for certain categories of insured person, this is a set amount. A full pension (awarded for a reduction in earning capacity of 100%) amounts to two thirds of the calculation base; a partial pension corresponds to the degree of reduction in earning capacity. Disabled persons with a reduction in earning capacity of at least 50% are entitled to a supplement to the pension amounting to one fifth of their basic pension, as well as to a supplement of 10% of their pension for each child. If the occupational accident or disease has led to a permanent need for special care and assistance, a special care supplement, which amounts to half the full pension, is payable.

During training for vocational rehabilitation, a minimum income (comprising the pension, any income from employment or self-employment and a transitory benefit) of 60% of the calculation base is guaranteed to the disabled person. Supplements are granted for family members and the total income may at most reach the amount of the calculation base. If disabled persons cannot cover their living costs with this guaranteed income and any other possible income, they will be granted a subsidy for their own and their family's living costs as a voluntary benefit.

Pensions insurance
The pensions insurance grants pensions in the case of reduced working capacity (under the General Social Insurance Act) or permanent incapacity for gainful occupation (under the Social Insurance Act for Farmers and the Social Insurance Act for the Self-Employed in Trade, Commerce and Industry). Reduced working capacity is recognized if the insured person, because of his or her physical or mental state, has less than half of the working or earning capacity of a physically and mentally healthy person; distinctions are made according to the previous vocational training and the age of the insured person. Permanent incapacity for gainful occupation is recognized if the insured person, because of an illness or infirmity or a reduction of physical or mental capacities, is permanently incapable of maintaining regular employment or self-employment. Here too, distinctions are made according to the age of the person and the nature of the activity, for example, whether an undertaking can be maintained without the personal work of the insured person.

25

The size of the pension depends on the average income that was the basis for the calculation of contributions to the pensions insurance, during a period of up to 10 years of insurance coverage, and on the number of months of insurance coverage. For each 12 months of insurance coverage, 1.9% of the calculation base is granted up to the 360th month, and 1.5% from the 361st month onwards (maximum 79.5%). Supplements are payable if the claimant is over 50 years old.

In pensions insurance, too, special care supplements and supplements for children may be granted, corresponding to the benefits in accident insurance.

Income support under provincial laws
The social assistance offered by the provinces enables all persons who need the assistance of society to lead a decent life, even if they are not entitled to assistance from any other person or organization. This social assistance comes in the form of financial support to secure the necessities of life. While disabled persons are undergoing vocational rehabilitation, they are granted additional financial benefits. The influence of financial benefits on a disabled person's willingness to undergo rehabilitation differs from case to case.

According to the disability laws of the provinces, disabled persons who need special care and have attained a certain age are entitled to a special care allowance if they do not receive or are not entitled to similar benefits under any other federal legal regulations, such as the War Victims Welfare Act, the Welfare for Victims of Political Persecution Act or the Assistance to Crime Victims Act. The blind persons' allowances laws confer similar benefits under similar circumstances.

Evaluation of Progress in National Legislation

Without doubt, the legislative bodies' awareness of the problems of disabled persons was increased by the International Year of Disabled Persons, although only the National Fund Act was enacted in direct connection with the Year. Other laws, such as the one on trusteeship, were already drafted long before 1981. In many fields, however, amendments were made to existing laws that brought about improvements for disabled persons (including the School Organization Act, Compulsory Education Act, War Victims Welfare Act, Invalid Employment Act, General Social Insurance Act, Pupils' Allowances Act, Study Promotion Act, and Equalization of Burdens for Families Act). Important concerns of disabled persons were also taken into consideration in the new federal residential building laws

26

(Law for the Promotion of Residential Buildings (*Bundesgesetzblatt*, No. 482/1984) and Law for the Reconstruction of Residential Buildings (*Bundesgesetzblatt,* No. 483/1984)).

The Federal Ministry for Buildings and Technology has issued decrees concerning the implementation of the Austrian standard on constructional measures for physically disabled and aged persons (ÖNORM B 1600, first part) in the construction and renovation of state-owned buildings.

The worldwide economic crisis also had repercussions in Austria and led to a shortage of jobs, so it is difficult to evaluate what effect the growing interest in the problems of disabled persons has had on the persons concerned. The integration of disabled persons has, for instance, been promoted by the agreement of school administrations to accept more disabled children in normal schools. Furthermore, the public authorities are employing a significantly higher number of disabled persons than they did before 1981. In addition, integration is supported by the increasing participation of representatives of disabled persons in the evaluation of laws.

Special disability laws can only regulate the promotion and care of disabled persons. Therefore, special provisions concerning the interests of disabled persons must be included in other legal regulations. Both kinds of regulation must be adapted to or complement each other.

Social laws are permanently changing, and they must always be adapted to circumstances. The provincial legal regulations on assistance to disabled persons currently show wide variations and the benefits foreseen in these regulations are often much lower than the federal benefits. An adjustment is therefore being planned by means of the elaboration of a federal disability law and the conclusion of treaties between the Federation and the provinces.

27

Belgium

General Principles

Unlike the constitutions of some other countries, the Belgian Constitution contains no single article guaranteeing basic social rights, let alone the rights of the disabled. Nevertheless, Belgium has signed several international conventions that include provisions for disabled persons.

Belgium is in a special situation as a result of institutional reform and the redistribution of legislative and executive powers this has produced (Special Act of 8 August 1980 on institutional reform). There are at present three types of legislature: national legislature, responsible for the promulgation of laws; community legislature for the Flemish-, French- and German-speaking communities, responsible for promulgating decrees; and regional legislature for the Flemish, Walloon and Brussels regions, also responsible for promulgating decrees. These decrees have the force of law and are therefore equivalent to national legislation but are in force in a limited area. A community is understood to mean a subgroup of the population deemed to constitute a unit on the basis of an identical language and culture (the term community is therefore based on the personal characteristics of the population). A region is understood to mean a territorial subunit of the country that has been given the opportunity of developing its own socioeconomic policy (the term region therefore has a territorial significance). Community power is exercised by community councils (who have legislative power) and by community authorities (who have executive power). Regional power is exercised by regional councils (who have legislative power) and by regional authorities (who have executive power). The powers of the regions may, however, also be exercised by the appropriate community councils and authorities, as occurs in Flanders. The effect of this is that Flanders has a single Flemish Council and Flemish Executive Authority, which are competent for both the Flemish community and the Flemish region. In Wallonia, on the other hand, the community and regional powers are still separate. This new distribution of legislative and executive competence clearly involves a redistribution of powers between the national, regional and community authorities.

The national government is competent in respect of all matters that have not been explicitly assigned to the regions and communities.

The region is competent in all matters affecting the region that have been explicitly assigned to it for the implementation of its own socioeconomic policy. These include, *inter alia,* regional development and town planning, regional economic expansion, employment policy, housing policy, the removal and processing of solid waste, and water policy.

The community is competent in all matters of a cultural or personal nature, including intercommunity cooperation and international cooperation in these fields. While this chapter covers some cultural questions that include not only the preservation of the language, fine arts, and radio and television but also various aspects of education (intellectual, moral and social, and preschool, further and extracurricular), the questions with which this chapter is mainly concerned are those affecting the individual. All these questions thus come largely within the competence of the community. The concerns of the community that relate to conditions for the disabled fall into three main areas.

Public health policy includes:

— health care policy inside and outside health care institutions (with the exception of policies determined by constitutional legislation, the financing of operational work organized under constitutional legislation, sickness and disability insurance, basic regulations relating to programming, basic regulations relating to infrastructure financing including heavy medical equipment, national approval regulations (solely to the extent that these may have repercussions on operational work and sickness and disability insurance), and the determination of the conditions for and allocation of the status of a university hospital in accordance with current legislation on hospitals);

— health education and activities and services in the field of preventive medicine, with the exception of national preventive measures.

Social assistance includes:

— family policy, including all forms of aid and assistance to families and children;

— social assistance policy (with the exception of constitutional regulations for public social assistance centres, and the determination of the minimum wage and the conditions governing the granting and financing of the legally guaranteed wage, in accordance with legislation conferring the right to a minimum subsistence level);

— policy for the acceptance and integration of immigrants;

— policy for the disabled, including the training, retraining and professional rehabilitation of the disabled (with the exception of the rules for the financing of allowances to the disabled, including individual files, and the rules relating to financial subsidies payable to employers to promote the employment of the disabled);

— policy for the elderly (with the exception of the determination of the minimum income, the conditions of payment, and the financing of the legally guaranteed income for the elderly);

— the protection of the young (with the exception of matters relating to civil, criminal and judicial law);

— social assistance to convicted people in prison and after leaving prison (with the exception of the enforcement of the decision of the courts).

Applied scientific research includes: applied scientific research in the fields of competence exclusive to the community authorities.

Coordination mechanisms
Coordination mechanisms can be divided into two main categories: various councils, all of which have been established by royal decree (not by law), and nongovernmental organizations operating various services or centres.

Councils
The Higher National Council of the Disabled was established by the Royal Decree of 9 July 1981. It is responsible for examining all problems relating to the disabled that are within the competence of the national authorities, in accordance with the Special Act of

8 August 1980. It is empowered to issue opinions or make recommendations on this subject, including recommendations for the rationalization and coordination of legal texts and regulations. It consists of 18 members specially qualified by their participation in the work of organizations concerned with the disabled or by reason of their social or scientific activities.

The Higher Flemish Council for the Handicapped was established by the Royal Decree of 16 December 1981. It is empowered to issue opinions on all matters affecting disabled persons. It consists of a chairman, 20 regular members and 20 substitutes, who have the same special competences as the regular members of the Council.

The Consultative Community Council for the Disabled, for the French-speaking community, was established by the Royal Decree of 28 September 1981. Its function is to issue opinions on the broad lines of policy for the disabled and on its detailed implementation. It consists of a chairman and 17 specially qualified members, selected in the light of their knowledge of the problems raised by policies for the disabled or of the nature of their activities in organizations representing the disabled. It also includes representatives of the various ministries concerned with the problems of the disabled, representatives of the National Fund for the Social Rehabilitation of the Disabled, and representatives of the Medicosocial/Educational Care Fund for the Disabled.

Nongovernmental organizations
These organizations operate various centres or services working in a particular health care or welfare field. They all share the following aims: to watch over the interests of their member institutions and the people for whom they care, to represent the interests of their members *vis-à-vis* any authority that may be concerned, to keep their members informed (by holding conferences, establishing documentation centres, issuing information letters, sponsoring meetings and taking other measures), to ensure coordination and a common policy between member institutions and to make recommendations (for innovative action) to the competent authorities. They have the legal status of nonprofit associations and consist of members who are in general well acquainted with the relevant problems. Many of these organizations are concerned, among other activities, with the problems of disabled persons.

The Royal Decree of 5 July 1963 provides for official authorization to be given to some of these organizations to advise disabled persons, with a view to their admittance into the system of social rehabilitation.

National Involvement in International Action

Belgium is a signatory to a number of conventions guaranteeing basic rights and freedoms to all individuals and consequently to the disabled:

— the Universal Declaration of Human Rights (1948);

— the European Convention on Human Rights (1950);

— the First Additional Protocol to the European Convention on Human Rights (1952);

— the Fourth Additional Protocol recognizing specific rights and freedoms other than those already listed in the European Convention on Human Rights and in the First Additional Protocol to this Convention (1963);

— the European Social Charter (signed in 1961 but not yet ratified by the Belgian Parliament);

— the International Covenant on Civil and Political Rights (signed in 1966 but not yet ratified by the Belgian Parliament);

— the International Covenant on Economic, Social and Cultural Rights (signed in 1966 but not yet ratified by the Belgian Parliament).

European Community social integration programme for the disabled, 1981

Three specific measures in favour of the disabled were implemented within the European Community during the 1970s, in particular in the context of its social action programme: the 1974 Council Resolution regarding the vocational rehabilitation of the handicapped (this Resolution resulted in 1975 in the establishment of a network of rehabilitation centres); the participation of the European Social Fund in vocational training programmes and in the adaptation of employment positions to the disabled, and the implementation of pilot projects and preparatory studies; and the 1976 programme of pilot projects for the accommodation of the disabled.

It was the International Year of Disabled Persons in 1981, however, that imparted the necessary impetus to the European Community to undertake a more comprehensive and better coordinated programme. The Council Resolution on the social integration of handicapped people (21 December 1981), adopted by the government representatives of member states of the European Community, in conjunction with the Opinion of the Economic and Social Committee

(2 July 1981) on the situation and problems of the handicapped, led to the adoption in December 1981 of a social integration programme for disabled persons. To ensure the continuity of the measures taken in the context of this programme, the European Commission set up the Bureau for Action in Favour of Disabled People in May 1982. The Bureau's work programme includes the following principal elements:

— a network of rehabilitation centres (originally set up in 1975) intended to strengthen cooperation between rehabilitation and training institutions, and to encourage the collection and exchange of information on new methods and means of vocational training for the disabled;

— a series of policy declarations to ensure that sound policy decisions concerning the disabled are made in a systematic way;

— the establishment of a network of district projects to develop a model for the coordination of activities undertaken at the local level;

— an information base and cooperative support involving programmes designed to collect and make available all relevant legislative measures and other data on the disabled in the European Community.

District projects
The European Commission (through the European Social Fund) has provided half of the financial support for the district projects; the other half has come from the project sponsors and, in Belgium, by the National Fund for the Social Rehabilitation of the Disabled and the Flemish- and French-speaking communities. A total of 16 pilot projects has been set up by the European Commission since the beginning of 1984, covering a period of four years. The general aim of these projects is, according to the European Commission, to stimulate and assess the innovation process at the local level, paying particular attention to the coordination of services in respect of both planning and execution. The principal task of the people responsible for the implementation of the projects may be summarized as follows:

— to promote the social and economic integration of all disabled people, involving determination of their needs, continued coordination of the services provided under the legislation, coordination between governmental and nongovernmental organizations and their social partners, greater emphasis on

34

the use of all available resources (financial and other), participation of the disabled in decisions and activities relating to
them, and recommended guidelines for the future;

— to develop pilot and educational activities and study their consequences;

— to assess the experience gained and disseminate useful results.

In view of the aims of the European Social Fund, the main
emphasis has been placed in practice on pilot activities in the field of
vocational training and employment. One of the most attractive
aspects of district projects is their initiation and implementation at
local and regional levels, since this has given the disabled persons
concerned considerable discretion in selecting the forms and structures they want. Another distinguishing feature of district projects is
the direct contact between the disabled, the associations that represent them, local organizers, assistants and other staff.

The district project programme is based on the conviction that for
the people mainly concerned, namely the disabled themselves, genuine participation means the right of all to play an active and positive
part in the decisions that affect them personally. The disabled occupy
a central position in the network of projects implemented at the
district level. Moreover, these projects are directed not only at those
who are already disabled but also at those who are at risk and those
who occupy a rather marginal position in society.

Two of the 16 pilot projects are being implemented in Belgium,
one in Hasselt-Genk and the other in Liège.

The Hasselt-Genk project. One of the main aims of this project is to
study the approach and the methods for achieving effective cooperation and coordination between the different services working for the
disabled. Central to the project is the search for the structural and
cultural factors that affect, favourably or unfavourably, the integration of the disabled. These factors may be found both within
individual services and in the nature of the cooperation between
them. This task was included in a first contract concluded with the
Flemish community, which also covered the development of a system
of social indicators for assessing the degree of integration of the
disabled and the factors that influence it. In a second contract with the
Flemish community, this task was extended to cover a sociocultural
study of 200 disabled persons who may be recommended to attend a
specific vocational training course, a market survey of the forms of
employment open to the disabled in the district, and the basic
elements on which the vocational training should be based. This

vocational training is specifically intended for the disabled aged between 18 and 25 years (students, people in employment and the unemployed). In addition, the Minister for the Family and Welfare of the Flemish Community has asked for basic data and procedures to be compiled so that a single basic file can be drawn up for every disabled person. Over and above the work to be done at the request of the Flemish community, the Hasselt-Genk project includes a number of other tasks of rather more local or regional scope, relating to the coordination of services and institutions, vocational training, employment, public relations and communication.

The Liège project. This project is designed to promote the social and professional integration of the disabled in the Liège district. In pursuit of this aim, six working groups have been set up to monitor and support the project. These working groups are concerned with the employment of the disabled, technical resources, education and preparation for adult life, accommodation, transport and adaptation of the environment, and information, communication and public opinion. Their overall aim is to integrate disabled children into the normal educational system, to provide vocational training, and to promote their eventual employment. The members of these groups have been drawn from the management of organizations concerned with the disabled and the young, the media, the commercial sector, the social security sector, protected workshops, rehabilitation and vocational training centres, and trade unions.

The Handynet project
In relation to the establishment of an information base and cooperative support, the Bureau for Action in Favour of Disabled People is preparing a compendium of national legislation on the disabled, and a set of basic documentation (such as resolutions and communications) so as to provide a reliable documentation service on the disabled. The Bureau has also launched the Handynet project, the aim of which is to establish a Community data bank and automated data sets covering all aspects of the disabled individual.

The first module prepared under the Handynet project relates to technical aids. The Bureau has completed its general preparations, including the compilation of an exhaustive list of terms relating to technical aids in all the Community languages. This glossary is based on the Nordic system and is presented in the form of a thesaurus and a classification. It has been compiled in accordance with an agreement with the Nordic Committee on Disability and the International Organization for Standardization.

The Bureau has also been engaged in practical preparations for a first operational pilot project on the intercountry exchange of information on technical aids between a limited number of automated data banks. This pilot project, launched in 1986, directly involves some 12 centres located throughout the Community, and will enable an exact estimate to be made of the organizational and financial implications of the implementation of the full-scale project.

Feasibility studies have been requested to estimate the demand and existing opportunities for further Handynet modules, covering such fields as education, training and rehabilitation, employment, and the physical environment. The Bureau also intends, in cooperation with other Commission services, to undertake a study on the present state of the European market for technical aids, to extend the present glossary and to extract a specialist set of data on disability from the information currently available in the Commission. Steps will also be taken to ensure that Handynet develops in harmony with other Community systems covering both political and technical aspects.

Cooperation with other international organizations
Belgium has also collaborated with three other organizations that have recently taken measures of importance to the Community in the employment field. The Council of Europe has undertaken a major revision of its procedure for the regular comparison of national legislation on the rehabilitation and employment of the disabled, and issued a resolution on a coherent policy for the rehabilitation of the disabled in 1984.

The Centre for Educational Research and Innovation of the Organisation for Economic Co-operation and Development has a programme that deals in general with the training of disabled adults. There has been a shift of emphasis from the integration of disabled children in schools to the problems raised by their movement from academic to active life. In 1983, the International Labour Organisation adopted Convention 159 on the Vocational Rehabilitation and Employment of the Disabled. The ratification and implementation of this Convention in the European Community will afford significant support to measures taken at the Community level.

Review of the Present State of National Legislation

It is only relatively recently that social legislation in Belgium has included any real provisions regarding allowances for disabled persons. Previously, the disabled were not considered to be legal beneficiaries because, as nonworkers, they failed to pay any contributions. Although certain allowances were granted to pensioners, people suffering from long-term illnesses, victims of industrial injuries or occupational diseases, the unemployed and some children, these measures proved to be insufficient.

Gradually, work began on more expansive legislation for people who were deformed and crippled. During the 1960s, this resulted in two important acts, ensuring the improvement of facilities for the disabled: the Social Rehabilitation Act of 16 April 1963 and the Allowances for the Disabled Act of 27 June 1969. The latter was revised and simplified by the Act of 27 February 1987. Besides these acts, however, there are various other integration provisions, such as those for adapted education, admission to institutions, allowances for modifications to housing, special financing of medical care, artificial limbs or prostheses, equipment and all kinds of aids, social assistance, juridical protection, help from other people and exemptions from all sorts of duties or burdens. Thus, the overall picture is complex.

Details of provisions for the disabled in five areas — health care, education, provision of work, income and institutional care — together with a review of other special provisions, are given in the following sections.

Health care
Provided they pay certain contributions, disabled persons are eligible for health insurance, which provides them with the same rights to payment for health care as contributing employees. Under certain conditions, the disabled may be exempted from the "threshold fee" for various kinds of care.

For serious conditions such as poliomyelitis, cerebral palsy, multiple sclerosis, myopathy, congenital defects, chronic insufficiency of the kidneys and cystic fibrosis, the Ministry of Public Health may grant a special allowance to help cover the costs of admission to a special institution and rehabilitation.

The mentally disabled and patients with tuberculosis and cancer are eligible for an allowance from the Special Support Fund of the Ministry of Public Health, although the amount received will depend on the individual's own means of support.

Other institutions that help to bear the costs of health care for the disabled are the National Fund for Social Rehabilitation of the Disabled, the labour accident insurers, the Fund for Occupational Diseases and the National Work for War Invalids, all of which have different conditions and allowances.

Education

Education can be part of the rehabilitation process, which is the responsibility of the National Fund for Social Rehabilitation of the Disabled. This same Fund may also help towards the costs of special transport, school books and other materials, and tuition fees.

Adapted education is paid for or subsidized by the State and is designed to give an education to children who are physically or mentally incapable of going to a normal school. The State may also help towards the expenses of home teaching and the transport of pupils.

The social rehabilitation project

The social rehabilitation project tries to give the disabled steady and normal jobs, so as to enable them to reintegrate into society. Every disabled person with a physical incapacity for work of at least 30% or a mental incapacity of at least 20% can be considered for rehabilitation.

Entitlements

The expenses of medical treatment and rehabilitation are taken care of where they are not covered by health insurance. In principle, this is true for all kinds of treatment and equipment, although these have to be approved by the proper authorities.

The social rehabilitation project pays for special vocational guidance and afterwards for training in a school or vocational training centre, or with an employer. During this training, the disabled person receives allowances and complementary wages.

When the disabled person is appointed to a job, the social rehabilitation project may help by paying part of the wages and social contributions. The employer also receives compensation for any modifications that have to be made in the premises so as to accommodate the disabled person (for example, the installation of a telephone exchange that can be operated by a blind person). Additional help is given to meet the expenses of working clothes and tools.

Sheltered workshops are financed by the social rehabilitation project. The work is adapted to the capacities of the disabled, who receive special guidance. The social rehabilitation project pays for part of the wages and social contributions, as well as for the guidance personnel. The wages in a sheltered workshop are rather low in spite of the intervention of the National Fund, but a disabled person who works in a sheltered workshop is very often also entitled to family allowances and unemployment benefit.

The National Fund tries to improve the integration of the disabled and facilitate their contact with the environment by providing help towards the costs of a telephone, typewriter or other means of communication, adaptation of a car, other means of transport, transport for parents visiting their child, adaptation of a house or furniture, or other assistance.

How to qualify for entitlements

In order for a disabled person to enjoy any of the above benefits, the chances for rehabilitation should be real. This means that all the measures taken should enhance the possibility of employment. An engagement into domestic duties, for instance, is also considered a form of rehabilitation. It is not considered possible for the very severely disabled to take advantage of social rehabilitation.

A team of specialists decides on each individual case and eventually approves a rehabilitation programme. It is not possible to leave out any of the steps in this process of rehabilitation; the whole programme has to be accepted (or rejected). A disabled person who refuses to undergo the guidance investigations or the designed training loses all rights to the rest of the programme.

How to apply for entitlements

The disabled person should be registered with the National Fund for Social Rehabilitation of the Disabled. This registration is preceded by a medical examination for which the disabled person may choose a specialist. The National Fund reserves the right to request an additional examination to be undertaken by its own appointed doctor.

The disabled person should also apply for social rehabilitation allowances. On the basis of this application, certain medical, psychological, social and vocational guidance investigations are undertaken, which are free of charge, including transport expenses. Based on these investigations, a protocol is drawn up for the rehabilitation programme and the allowances that will be granted are determined.

Income

Lack of income is often the biggest problem for a disabled person. To overcome this, there are provisions in the social legislation for granting certain allowances to those who do not have enough means of support of their own.

Only recently, a law was passed that aims at the thorough revision, improvement and simplification of the former system of allowances. What used to be a complicated set of five different types of allowance has now been reduced to two:

— the income-replacing allowance is given to a disabled person who lacks a sufficient income as a result of limited earning abilities;

— the integration allowance is given to a disabled person who suffers from integration problems because of a lack of self-help.

The income-replacing allowance differs according to the situation of the beneficiary; the current annual allowance (valid on 1 February 1987) is BF 245 819 (US $6244) for a family, BF 184 363 (US $4683) for a single person, and BF 112 918 (US $2868) per person for people who live with others.

The integration allowance differs according to the degree of autonomy of the disabled:

— category I (slight reduction in autonomy):   BF 27 378 (US $695) per year;

— category II (intermediate loss of autonomy):   BF 93 293 (US $2370) per year;

— category III (severe loss of autonomy):   BF 149 071 (US $3786) per year;

— category IV (very severe loss of autonomy: BF 213 967 (US $5435) per year.

The new system has a simplified procedure so as to speed up the handling of applications. The age limit is fixed at between 21 years and 65 years for all beneficiaries and the required percentages of disability have been reduced to one standard, that is, a decrease in working ability of at least two thirds. Through the institution of a multidisciplinary and broad evaluation of the degree of invalidity, the new system comes much closer to the actual situation of each beneficiary than did the previous one. Only those resident in Belgium who are Belgian citizens, refugees, stateless or citizens of European Community countries or countries with which Belgium has made a treaty are entitled to these allowances. A short stay abroad of less than one month per year or admission to a foreign hospital is allowed.

Application for these allowances is made at the municipal hall in the town of residence. The application is then sent to the Office of the Ministry of Social Affairs. This Office then requests the person involved to undergo a medical examination by an official doctor, who determines the degree of invalidity. The Office also asks for an investigation into the means of support by the tax office before determining the entitlement.

Institutional care
Many disabled people require more comprehensive support in addition to allowances for their work situation, health or income. For

this purpose, there are homes, boarding establishments and other institutions. The Fund for Medical, Social and Paedagogical Care for the Disabled provides partly or totally the expenses of housing, maintenance, treatment, education and care. Care and attendance are principally meant for minors. Adults can also benefit if they are incapable of engaging in society without constant help.

The Fund subsidizes the institutions in such a way that the disabled person has only to pay for a small part of the cost of a nursing day. For a semi-boarding establishment, the disabled person has to pay an even smaller amount. The Fund also finances some special medical care, travel expenses and holiday residences.

The Fund provides help for residence in one of the following types of institution, which have to be recognized by the Ministry of Public Health:

— boarding or semi-boarding establishments for disabled children, called medicopaedagogical institutions;

— homes for disabled adults, who work during the day;

— day homes for unemployed disabled adults;

— nursing homes that ensure the continual care of disabled adults;

— homes for a short residence, where a less able person is admitted for three months at the most, owing to special circumstances.

The Fund also gives help to disabled people resident with foster families, provided that placement is undertaken by a recognized placement service.

Various special provisions for the disabled

Increased family allowance for disabled children
To claim an increased family allowance, the child should suffer from an inadequacy or a decrease of physical or mental capability of at least 66%, which results from one or more conditions.

Income tax and advance levy on income derived from real estate
Someone with a dependant whose disability amounts to at least 66% is entitled to tax relief. In the determination of the number of dependants for income tax assessment, children with a disability of at least 66% are considered as two people.

42

The advance levy on income derived from real estate is reduced by 10% per dependant and 20% per disabled dependant if:

— the house is inhabited by a man and/or a woman who is the head of a family; even a tenant — if he or she is head of a family — entitles the owner to request this tax relief, but the tenant has the right to claim the financial advantage of the tax relief, notwithstanding any contradictory clause in the lease contract;

— the head of the family has at least two living children of his or her own or two living adopted children; at least one of these should be a dependant or a child whose disability amounts to a minimum of 66%.

Transport facilities
The following people can claim a reduced value added tax (VAT) rate of 6%, or its complete refund, and exemption from registration tax on the purchase of a car (for use as a personal means of transport), its parts and its accessories:

— those who are completely blind;

— those whose upper limbs are completely paralysed or whose upper limbs have been amputated;

— those who suffer from a permanent invalidity of at least 50%, which is entirely caused by a defect of the lower limbs.

These benefits can also be claimed if the car has been registered under the name of the legal representatives of the disabled. The car may only be used for the personal transport of the disabled person. If family members use the car for other purposes, the financial advantage is lost. The reduced VAT rate also applies to orthopaedic equipment and wheelchairs.

The people listed above are also exempt from road tax on cars that are used as a means of personal transport only. Again, the cars must be registered under the name of the disabled person or the name of a legal representative and may not be used for other purposes.

A special parking permit is issued to disabled persons who suffer from an invalidity of at least 60% or from a permanent invalidity of at least 50% that entirely results from a defect of the lower limbs. The holder of this card is not necessarily the driver of the car, but the card should only be used when the holder is either transported in the car or driving it. This card permits parking for an indefinite period of time in places of limited parking time. It does not, however, automatically release the holder from the payment of parking fees through parking meters or ticket machines. Several municipalities, however, provide an exemption from this tax.

Some parking spots on the public road are reserved for vehicles used by disabled people. These parking spots are indicated by a blue rectangular P-sign, which displays the international symbol of the disabled. The disabled who wish to reserve such a parking spot in front of their house may apply to their municipality.

Various financial allowances for the disabled are available in the public transport sector:

— railways and long-distance buses: (*a*) a 50% reduction on the price of a second-class ticket, on presentation of a reduction card that is issued to widows, the disabled and orphans (this card is meant for visually and severely disabled people); (*b*) a special permit, valid for five years, that entitles the disabled person to travel with a companion on one single ticket (this permit is meant for severely disabled people who suffer from the loss of both arms or legs); (*c*) free transport in second class (the companion should purchase a ticket, however) for blind people or those with poor eyesight who can see 10% with one eye and 20% with the other;

— trams and buses: free transport for visually disabled people who possess a national reduction card for community transport.

On production of a medical certificate, certain disabled people are exempt from taxes on bicycles and mopeds, which are levied by the province. Disabled people can also obtain an exemption from the road tax on vehicles and motorbikes by making an application to the municipality before starting to use the vehicle.

Forms of communication
The blind or deaf and dumb, if suffering from a disability of at least 80% or if suffering from a permanent deficiency that makes it impossible to leave the house without the aid of another person, can be exempt from paying television and radio licence fees. This exemption is granted to the owners of radios or television sets provided that they make no direct or indirect financial profit from them. The exemption also applies to the parents of a disabled child who meets the requirements for exemption. The exemption also applies to car radios.

The Royal Decree of 26 February 1982 establishes a special telephone rate, and explicitly mentions the categories of beneficiary:

— those aged 70 or more who live by themselves or with two other people at the most, who must be at least 65 years old;

— disabled people who suffer from a disability of at least 80%, who are at least 18 years of age and live by themselves or with two people at the most, be they relatives in the first or second degree.

A maximum income has been fixed for both categories.

The Royal Decree of 12 January 1970 concerning the organization of the postal service states that Braille items for the blind and similar articles may be sent through the post free of charge.

Bulgaria

General Principles

All citizens of the People's Republic of Bulgaria enjoy full equality under the Constitution. The special rights of the disabled are enshrined in Articles 43 and 44. These consist of the right to socially useful work, free medical care, free education, short- and long-term material security and social assistance. All disabled persons are entitled to care irrespective of their sex, age, family status, or political or religious convictions.

The Social Assistance Order, approved in 1951, imposes on central and local social assistance services the responsibility of drawing up and implementing measures to assist those categories of persons who are not themselves — or with the assistance of their relatives — capable of taking their normal place in society and organizing their personal life and their work.

Social assistance is rendered by providing:

— special employment;

— professional training and retraining;

— special appliances and equipment, including invalid vehicles, to permit full integration of the disabled into the work environment and daily life;

— assistance in the home;

— accommodation in social assistance institutions and the necessary service facilities;

— financial allowances and assistance in kind;

— concessions for special categories of person.

Pursuant to the provisions of the Constitution and of the Social Assistance Order and in the spirit of the overall social policy of the People's Republic of Bulgaria, which is aimed at satisfying the requirements and raising the standard of living of the Bulgarian people to a progressively increasing extent, a number of regulations have been issued and social programmes drawn up to ensure the implementation of all forms of social care activities.

The main regulations and programmes are listed below:

— Decree No. 128/1963 by the Council of Ministers on measures to provide special employment for the partially disabled (*Government gazette*, No. 107/1963);

— Decree No. 38/1980 on special employment for the partially disabled (*Government gazette*, No. 57/1980);

— Instruction on special employment for the partially disabled (*Government gazette*, No. 101/1963);

— Work regulations in special enterprises and in units for specially employed persons (*Government gazette*, No. 55/1981);

— Rules on financial allowances and concessions (*Government gazette*, No. 100/1979);

— Rules for the organization and administration of social care institutions (*Government gazette*, No. 91/1965);

— Instruction No. 15 on the purchase of invalid vehicles (*Government gazette*, No. 93/1975);

— Instruction No. 19 on services for the elderly and disabled (*Government gazette*, No. 6/1976);

— Instruction No. 210 on the procedure and conditions governing the issue of orthopaedic devices and appliances (*Government gazette*, No. 7/1971);

— the December 1972 Programme of the Central Committee of the Bulgarian Communist Party and of the Council of Ministers for raising the standard of living of the people, with specific reference to social care measures;

— the April 1984 Programme of the Central Committee of the Bulgarian Communist Party, the Council of Ministers, the Bulgarian Central Trade Union Council, the National Council of Social Assistance Funds and the Central Committee of the Dmitrovskii Union of Communist Youth, providing for further social benefits and concessions for the disabled, the elderly, children exposed to serious medicosocial risks, and other groups;

— Decision No. 78/1980 of the Bulgarian Ministry of Health on the International Year of Disabled Persons, on the long-term programme of preventive medicine, treatment and rehabilitation, and also on the solution of the principal economic and psychosocial problems of the disabled in Bulgaria.

The aims of all these regulations and programmes are to restore the health of disabled persons, to enable them to make full use of their remaining capacity for work and to increase their material income, to ensure their independence in everyday life and create the necessary conditions for active recreation and relaxation, to enable them to organize their free time, develop their capabilities and talents in the fields of art and sport, and to provide them with the full support and assistance of society in dealing with the problems of everyday life.

Within the Ministry of Health, special care questions are the responsibility of the Social Care Directorate, and a wide range of social care activities is carried out by local services of the Ministry attached to people's councils, communities and municipal authorities, and activist groups in society. Many organizations participate in these activities, including the Bulgarian Red Cross, the National Council of the Fatherland Front, the Committee for the Advancement of Bulgarian Women, the Association of the Blind and the Association of the Deaf.

A number of other ministries and departments are concerned to a greater or lesser extent with social care problems, such as: the Ministry of Finance, in regard to such issues as the budgetary aspects of social care, financial allowances and the funding of the publication *Trud*; the Bulgarian Central Trade Union Council, in regard to special employment for the disabled under normal working conditions; the Committee on Labour and Social Affairs, in regard to social care, in particular the award of disability pensions; the Ministry of Production and Trade, in regard to the supply of major consumer goods; the Central Cooperative Union, in regard to the employment of the disabled under special working conditions; and the Ministry of Education in regard to the education of disabled children.

National Involvement in International Action

Bulgaria has ratified a number of international declarations and resolutions dealing with the protection and rights of the disabled. It has supported United Nations decisions on the International Year and Decade of Disabled Persons and has played an active part in the relevant United Nations commissions and in a number of international organizations such as the Food and Agriculture Organization of the United Nations, the United Nations Educational, Scientific and Cultural Organization, WHO and the United Nations Children's Fund.

The Higher Rehabilitation Council has been set up within the Ministry of Health to be responsible for coordinating rehabilitation measures in the fields of health, labour, education and social assistance. This Council represents Bulgaria on the European Rehabilitation Council and on the socialist countries' rehabilitation experts group.

The Association of the Blind and the Association of the Deaf of the People's Republic of Bulgaria are active at the international level, being members of the International Federation of the Blind and the World Federation of the Deaf, and the presidents of the national associations sit on the governing bodies of those organizations. They also participate in the corresponding support organizations.

Methodology — Types of Legislative Approach to the Equality Concept

In addition to the Constitution of the People's Republic of Bulgaria (*Government gazette*, No. 39/1971) and the Social Assistance Order (*Government gazette*, No. 77/1951) the problems of the disabled have been covered in a number of other acts, such as:

— the Public Education Act (*Government gazette*, No. 90/1954)

— the Communications Act (*Government gazette*, No. 27/1975)

— the Movement of Vehicles Act (*Government gazette*, No. 53/1973)

— the Population Promotion Act (*Government gazette*, No. 15/1968)

— the Health Act (*Government gazette*, No. 88/1973).

Review of the Present State of National Legislation

Elimination of discrimination or social prejudice
There is no discrimination or prejudice against the disabled in Bulgaria. The Bulgarian Constitution permits neither privileges nor

restrictions on the rights of citizens based on sex, nationality, origin, religion, race, education or social and material status. The State ensures the full equality of all citizens, providing them with the conditions and means of enjoying their rights and fulfilling their obligations.

Social reintegration and full participation

Care, medical rehabilitation and technical aids
In accordance with the Council of Ministers Decision No. 78/1980, the situation in regard to permanent disability is kept under review at the national level by a computerized information system, which provides statistics on, for example, the number of disabled persons, diagnoses of their conditions and the rehabilitation measures taken. This permits a comprehensive analysis of the different problems and aspects of disability, such as employment, vocational guidance, requirements for technical aids and medical rehabilitation.

The first priority, as part of the general rehabilitation procedure, is to meet the requirements for prostheses and to provide the disabled with the necessary orthopaedic appliances. This is covered under Instruction No. 210 of the Ministry of Health and of the Bulgarian Central Trade Union Council on the procedure and conditions for the issue of orthopaedic devices and appliances. The technical aids required (which range from wheelchairs to hearing aids) are either provided from domestic sources or imported. It would not be expedient to manufacture all types of technical aids in Bulgaria, where the proportion of disabled persons is not very high. Essential items are produced in the country, but most of the need for technical aids for rehabilitation is met by imports from abroad. Imported products are either exempt from all customs duties and taxes or charged at a very reduced rate. Technical aids are given to the disabled free of charge. In the case of insured persons, the costs are met by the State Social Insurance Fund, while the social assistance budget of people's councils bears the costs for uninsured persons.

Instruction No. 15 by the Ministries of Health, Finance, and Internal Trade and Services on the purchase of invalid vehicles provides for their supply to the disabled under favourable conditions. Disabled persons are given priority in the purchase of a vehicle, being entitled to a grant not exceeding 50% of the value of the vehicle and to a loan from the State Savings Bank at low interest and with a long repayment period. Owners do not pay state taxes or licence fees on these vehicles. The guarantee period for such vehicles is twice as long as that available on other vehicles. Under the Council of

51

Ministers Decision No. 15 of 30 May 1979, the disabled are eligible for a petrol allowance and priority use of vehicle-servicing facilities.

Housing and physical environment

Meeting the housing requirements of the disabled is an important form of social assistance in Bulgaria. Housing is provided on a priority basis from the accommodation available to local councils at the place of residence or from the housing available at the place of work. There are at present no legislative regulations on the building of accommodation suitable for the disabled, but the regulations on financial allowances and benefits provide for part or all of the expenses incurred in converting existing accommodation to be borne by the social assistance budget of people's councils in the form of a lump-sum payment.

Disabled persons receive special allowances for travel on public transport under Bulgarian legislation. The Movement of Vehicles Act and the rules governing its implementation require the provision of specially marked protected passages and the marking of elevated and underground crossings with the disabled symbol. Disabled persons are allowed privileged use of transport facilities, parking sites are reserved for them, and invalid vehicles are allowed access to zones prohibited to other drivers, with reserved parking free of charge.

All these concessions can be obtained on presentation of a special pass, issued by people's councils at the place of residence in accordance with the Ministry of Health Instruction No. 12 on the issue of passes to the disabled.

Communication and transport

Disabled persons enjoy a number of advantages in connection with communications and transport in Bulgaria. Instruction No. 3 on telephone communications, issued by the Ministry of Communication, gives priority to Group I and II disabled persons in the allocation of telephones. The Communications Act exempts the disabled from paying fees for radio and television licences and from postal charges in connection with the dispatch of Braille publications.

The rules on grants and benefits entitle certain categories of disabled persons to travel free on municipal transport in the area where they live or work; this applies also to those who accompany them (if they cannot travel alone).

Order No. 7 by the Council of Ministers, dated 8 November 1977, provides that war veterans and blind persons — and those accompanying them — shall be entitled to a 30% reduction in rail fares from Monday to Friday and a 50% reduction on boat fares every day of the week. In addition, Group I and II disabled persons, children suffering from serious physical or mental disability, and the persons accompanying them are entitled to two free return trips a year on the national railway and waterway systems.

Seats or compartments are reserved for the disabled on all forms of transport and marked with the international disabled symbol.

Working life and professional rehabilitation

Disabled persons enjoy special rights under Bulgarian labour legislation, guaranteeing them work and professional training. Work under normal or special conditions is provided for the disabled in accordance with the recommendations of an industrial medical expert commission. The recruitment of partially disabled persons is governed by the instructions on special employment issued by the Ministry of Health and the Bulgarian Central Trade Union Council, which require that up to 10% of all work vacancies and appointments in individual sectors of the national economy be reserved for the partially disabled.

Disabled persons recommended by industrial medical expert commissions for special employment (with reduced work norms, shorter working hours, home work or other arrangments) are directed to special enterprises or production cooperatives for the disabled, and special production units of the Association of the Blind and the Association of the Deaf. People working under special labour conditions are subject to 50% lower work norms (including reduced working hours and longer annual paid holidays) without any reduction in pay.

Many disabled persons work at home, selecting their own working regime. Under these circumstances, their work equipment, the transport of materials and the finished product, and any production expenses are paid by the enterprise that employs them. The work regime in enterprises of this type is governed by the rules for work in special enterprises and special employment units.

Social services

Under the Social Assistance Order (1951), central and local social assistance services are responsible for assisting those who cannot help themselves. In order to involve the population more closely in social assistance activities, various committees and commissions have been set up in addition to the state social assistance services. They include national and regional commissions on disability questions, regional councils on special employment and standing commissions on health and social assistance attached to people's councils.

Social activity offices have also been established, with the aim of inducing school and university students, retired people and others to assist on a short-term paid basis with the care and assistance of patients, disabled persons and the elderly. Social assistance institutions have been set up for disabled persons who have no close relatives or who for some reason cannot be cared for within their families.

Full support — bed, board and medical care — is provided for residents in social assistance institutions in accordance with the rules for the organization and administration of these institutions. Appropriate forms of occupational therapy are available for which the disabled receive pay. Cultural and educational activities are organized to enrich the quality of their lives and bring the disabled into contact with society. Disabled persons contribute according to their personal income towards the cost of their residence in social assistance institutions. No charge is made for Group I and II disabled persons with no source of personal income; war victims and those disabled in other conflicts are eligible for a 30% discount on the residential charges.

Education and professional training
Education at all levels — primary, intermediate, higher and advanced — is provided free of charge for all Bulgarian citizens. In addition, the State provides all students up to the level of the tenth class with textbooks and personal allowances; financial assistance is granted to students in reduced circumstances and scholarships are awarded for outstanding performance. All school and university students are entitled to accommodation in hostels or pensions for minimal payment; canteen meals are available.

In accordance with the National Education Act, special boarding-schools are provided for children suffering from physical or mental defects (such as hearing or visual defects and retarded mental development). These schools provide not only education but also vocational training. Social assistance institutions, which accept children with physical deficiencies, run their own intermediate special schools and economic technical training centres.

Children with defective hearing are taken in hand from an early age (12 months) and receive treatment at hearing and speech rehabilitation centres run by the Association of the Deaf, after which they are admitted to specialized or normal kindergartens and schools. At present, five schools are providing 872 places for children and young persons with defective hearing, six schools provide 632 places for children with speech defects and two

54

schools provide 257 places for the blind, thus fully satisfying the requirements for specialist training.

The vocational training and retraining of disabled persons who have no profession or who are obliged to change their profession are governed by the rules for the establishment of *Trud* educational/production enterprises. This system, run by the Ministry of Health, includes eight educational/production establishments, one specialized vocational school and two vocational schools with specialist teaching departments. More than 26 professions and specialist fields are covered in this way, including tailoring, knitting, printing, furniture making, shoe making, lathe work and mechanical engineering. Systematic vocational training and retraining is provided for disabled persons between the ages of 16 and 45 years, as well as for boys and girls who have completed special courses of instruction at schools for the deaf and mentally retarded. Two- or three-year courses of instruction are given, which count as work employment. During such courses disabled persons receive full board and accommodation and are issued with working clothes. Payment is based on performance, and pension rights are retained. About 900 disabled persons receive vocational training every year.

In addition, persons with defective vision are trained as masseurs and hydrotherapists in special parallel classes at the Intermediate Medical School in Sofia, and as computer programmers in mathematical schools in Sofia and Plovdiv; boys and girls with hearing defects are trained as dental technicians and clinical laboratory assistants, and as opticians and film technicians in the precision engineering technical college in Sofia.

Any disabled person wishing to acquire a higher level of education is entitled in principle to sit candidates' examinations at higher educational institutions in certain specialist fields.

Cultural activities

The national programme for the development of the human personality, approved by the Committee on Culture, includes a wide range of activities aimed at creating favourable conditions for nurturing the creative abilities of the disabled. These include various forms of club and circle activities in people's reading rooms, participation in regional and national art exhibitions and independent artistic activities at the regional and republic level.

Dance and pantomime groups among the deaf are widely known and enjoy international prestige, and professional mixed choirs include the participation of the blind.

55

Disabled children are also involved in various activities, participating in the Banner of Peace movement and in the annual Red Cross competition "What do you think of my creative work?". Anyone receiving a disability pension is entitled to a reduction in the price of cinema tickets.

Leisure and sport

In Decree No. 36/1972 of the Council of Ministers on the further development and popular integration of physical culture, sport and tourism, particular mention was made of the need to involve the disabled in sporting activities.

In order to encourage physical culture and sport among disabled persons, the Bulgarian Association for Physical Culture and Sport set up a section on sport among the disabled, which is represented at the local level throughout the country. Games for the disabled are held every year at the republic level, including contests of excellence in many fields, including weightlifting, basketball, swimming, table tennis, cycle racing, rowing expeditions on the Danube for blind rowers and car rallies for disabled drivers.

A wide range of sporting activities is carried out in the special enterprises and cooperatives for the disabled, at educational/production enterprises for the disabled and, in particular, under the auspices of the Association of the Deaf and the Association of the Blind, which are members of the corresponding international sporting organizations for the blind and the deaf.

Plans have been made and a large number of specific measures taken to enable disabled persons and their families to participate in daily recreation and enjoy their annual holidays. Recreational centres by the sea and in the mountains, run by the State and trade unions, are open to the disabled in the same way as to all Bulgarian citizens, as are balneotherapeutic sanatoria run by the Ministry of Health.

Information

The problems of the disabled, concern for their social care and their participation in the life of society receive wide attention in the mass media. Articles on the different aspects of disability are published in large sections of the daily press, in periodicals and in monthly journals. The subject is also covered on radio and television and in films. The Association of the Blind and the Association of the Deaf have their own publications — the newspaper *Quiet* and the journal *Redness at dawn*. Bulgarian television broadcasts daily a 15-minute programme especially for persons with defective hearing, and Bulgarian radio transmits a special daily broadcast for the Association of the Blind.

The prevention of disability

A fundamental element in Bulgarian legislation, the Labour Code, includes a separate section concerned with hygiene and safety at work, which details stringent legislative measures aimed at preventing unacceptable injuries due to accidents and occupational diseases. Enterprises are required to take all necessary precautions to ensure the safety of workplaces, to arrange compulsory instruction for workers in correct and safe working procedures, and to provide workers with personal protective clothing. The director and technical managers of an enterprise are held criminally liable for failure to ensure safe working conditions.

Special instructions have been issued for the protection of women and children from hazardous situations. The employment of young people under the age of 16 years is prohibited, and the under-18 age group may not be employed on night work. Workers under the age of 18 years and female workers of any age may not be given particularly heavy work or work that is liable to injure their health. Pregnant women, from the date that their pregnancy has been established, and mothers of children under the age of 10 months may not be employed on overtime or night duties.

The National Programme of Work Safety, Work Hygiene and Fire Protection, covering all forms of activity and all sectors of the national economy, was approved by the Government in 1980. This programme contains the main safety targets and programmed changes that already ensure that 71% of all production workers are employed under conditions that comply fully with modern health and safety requirements in the work environment. The costs of this programme amount to 2000 million leva (US $2300 million), half of which is to be spent on capital investment.

In order to reduce the number of traffic accidents, the Government has established a Central Commission on Traffic Safety and a state social commission to coordinate the activities of all departments concerned with this issue. A programme to increase safety and improve driving manners costing more than 3500 million leva (US $4025 million) was approved and brought into force during the period 1976–1985.

Systems of income support

The Bulgarian Constitution and the relevant legislative measures ensure the equality of all citizens of the country, while the disabled enjoy special rights under the Social Assistance Order. The legislation on disability pensions, contained in the Pensions Act, and its implementation regulations provide particularly favourable conditions for disabled persons.

People suffering from a complete or partial inability to work over a prolonged period, or without prospects of every working again, are eligible for a disability pension, as long as the disability originated at work or began not more than two years after the cessation of work. This condition does not apply to the congenitally blind or those who became blind before starting work, who are eligible for a pension based on a five-year working period, irrespective of their age.

Disabled persons are divided into three groups depending on the extent of their inability to work and their particular profession; the disability group is determined by an industrial medical expert commission in accordance with the rules approved by the Council of Ministers. Pensions are awarded for complete disability, inability to work or occupational disease, pathological conditions in general and civilian or service disabilities. The award of a disability pension in respect of a general pathological condition requires that the applicant shall have worked for a specified period depending on age:

— up to the age of 20 years: no specified period of work;

— up to the age of 25 years: three years' work;

— over the age of 25 years: five years' work.

All Group I and II disabled persons who have reached the age of 16 years are awarded a social pension amounting to 50% of the national average working wage, unless they are entitled to another pension. Group I disabled persons, entitled to outside assistance, are awarded a pension increment amounting to 35 leva (US $42).

Evaluation of Progress in National Legislation

Since the International Year of Disabled Persons, the Government of the People's Republic of Bulgaria has made a number of improvements and additions to the social legislation and the system of regulations dealing with the disabled. The increment to the disability pension, paid in addition to outside aid, has been increased 1.5 times, and the right to this increment has been extended to persons suffering from social, congenital and labour disabilities; disability pensions paid to agricultural workers as a result of injuries suffered at work or general pathological conditions have been increased by 32% and 38%, respectively. War veterans with disabilities now retain their full pension rights during employment and receive normal disability pensions. Persons suffering from specific diseases or on a minimum wage rate are entitled to free medicines when undergoing treatment at home. The monthly limits for social assistance payments have been increased by 30%; the allowances for the maintenance of children and young persons in special, convalescent and social institutions have been increased by 50%. Group I and II disabled persons and children with congenital conditions, as well as the persons accompanying them, are now entitled to two annual free trips on the railway and waterway systems. Finally, the monthly allowances in respect of children with congenital conditions have been doubled.

In connection with the International Year, the Council of Ministers approved a decree on the special employment of the partially disabled and on the extension of home work facilities to mothers with children up to the age of 6 years. This decree has greatly improved the conditions governing the special employment of disabled persons in the enterprises in which they suffered injury. The production categories and forms of work carried out in special enterprises and special employment units were also defined in the same decree. Various regulations guaranteeing the special employment of disabled persons on a rational basis have been updated since 1981, such as the rules governing the labour situation in special enterprises and special employment units, and the schedule of appointments and professions suitable for the disabled. At the same time the number of vacancies reserved for the disabled in enterprises and institutions was increased by 10% and the criteria for the classification of special enterprises were amended.

One question that remains to be dealt with by legislation relates to those who care for the seriously ill or disabled: the time spent on such care will have to be regarded as time spent at work for the purposes of calculating the working periods required to reach grade 3 in the labour system.

Revised versions of the Labour Code and Social Assistance Order are to be approved shortly, incorporating new and more favourable provisions to improve the lot of the disabled and accelerate their integration into society.

Denmark

General Principles

The constitutional basis for Denmark's legislation on the disabled is contained in Section 75, Subsection 2 of the Constitution, which states that any persons unable to support themselves or their dependants are entitled, where no other persons are responsible for their or their dependants' maintenance, to receive public assistance provided that they comply with the appropriate obligations imposed by statute.

On this basis, and as a general trend in the social and economic development of the last 100 years, Denmark has developed social legislation that includes legislation on the rights of the disabled, based on the principles of the welfare state, equality and participation in social life.

The legislation on the disabled originated in the general legislation on social support, education and medical care which was, at times, supplemented by special statutes concerning individual groups of disabled. These include the Public Assistance Act of 1933, which was supplemented by special statutes on the conditions of the deaf and the hard-of-hearing (1950), the blind (1956), and the mentally handicapped (1959). These special statutes provided for the setting up of special councils for each area, which have a democratic right to negotiate with the responsible governmental bodies and to co-determination as regards development within the area. The council members include representatives of the organizations for the disabled.

Whereas general social assistance in Denmark traditionally came under the responsibility of the local authorities, central government played an important direct role in the provision of economic, educational, vocational and social measures for the disabled. This governmental responsibility was codified in the Public Assistance Act and was also laid down in the special statutes for the deaf and hard-of-hearing, the blind and the mentally handicapped. A somewhat wider scope for rehabilitation was introduced by the Rehabilitation Act of 1960. The governmental administration of these laws was handled by the Ministry of Social Affairs and the special administrative units falling under that Ministry (since 1970, the Board of Social Welfare).

In connection with general social reform, however, the Social Assistance Act was adopted with effect from 1 April 1976, superseding much of the earlier legislation. A number of the statutes already in force on such groups as the disabled, children and the elderly were turned into a complete register of types of social assistance, based on the principle that assistance is to be granted according to need, irrespective of the source of the need.

In the period 1976–1980, responsibility for the services for the disabled was transferred from central government to the county and local authorities. This change resulted from local government reform in 1970, which produced local and regional units of a more efficient size and gave them the necessary legal, administrative and financial basis.

The purpose of this reorganization was to make local and regional authorities directly responsible to all citizens in their respective fields. The maintenance of an unchanged level of service for the disabled, among others, was secured through the transfer of resources, institutions and staff from central to county and local governments in the shape of lump-sum grants in accordance with objective criteria. The introduction of a special appeals system for the social sector aimed to ensure a uniform interpretation of national legislation.

Coordination of the work carried out by the county and local authorities is secured through planning, as laid down in the Act, for the administration of social and certain health matters. Under the financial provisions of the Social Assistance Act, funds are distributed to the central government and to the county and local authorities according to principles designed to ensure an impartial allocation of existing relief measures.

Following the shift in responsibility for the special care of the disabled from central to local and county authorities, the existing bodies that coordinated contacts between the different disability areas were replaced by the Central Council for the Disabled at the national level and a consumer council in the county authorities.

The Central Council for the Disabled is made up of representatives from organizations for the disabled and from central, county and local authorities. There are also representatives from the competent ministries responsible for housing, regional planning, traffic, training and education and employment.

The Council is intended to follow and assess social conditions for the disabled, including preventive measures. The Minister for Social Affairs and the other public authorities may consult the Council on matters of importance to the social conditions of the disabled, and the Council may take initiatives and submit proposals for changes in these areas. The county consumer councils, which — apart from representatives from organizations for the disabled — may include representatives from consumers in the counties, have similar responsibilities.

The setting up of similar councils at the local level is voluntary but many local authorities have set one up within the social sector.

National Involvement in International Action

In the International Year of Disabled Persons, 1981, Denmark carried out a number of activities at both government and private level, especially in the shape of informing and activating groups of citizens.

Denmark cooperates with other member states of the European Community on a network of rehabilitation centres and has also set up a four-year district project in Aarhus as part of the Community's programme for the social integration of the disabled (for further information on the European Community programme, see the details already mentioned under the Belgian contribution, pp. 33–37).

In addition, the Danish authorities try to include special consideration for the disabled in public and private development projects in developing countries.

Methodology — Types of Legislative Approach to the Equality Concept

The principle of equality between the disabled and other citizens has been implemented by making the relief measures of the Social Assistance Act equally accessible for the disabled and the old, children and other groups requiring assistance from the public authorities. It is, in principle, statutorily accepted that policies for the disabled should fall within the responsibility not only of the Ministry of

Social Affairs but of all ministries and administrative areas. Consequently, various ministries are represented by experts on the Central Council for the Disabled.

Denmark has thus abolished almost all the special legislation on services for the disabled by implementing the Social Assistance Act. The delegation of matters relating to the disabled to the regional and local authorities has also resulted in their administrative integration, which again is a means to further the individual integration of each disabled person.

The organizations for the disabled have played a major part in the debate on and the fight for equality for disabled persons in society. In Denmark — contrary to many other countries — this task has not been impeded by the fact that these organizations have direct responsibility for carrying through measures for the disabled.

Review of the Present State of National Legislation

Elimination of discrimination or social prejudice
The special legislation on discrimination against persons owing to race, colour, religion or other characteristics does not specifically include discrimination against disabled persons. The most important means of fighting discrimination and social prejudice against disabled persons in Denmark is the information regularly disseminated by organizations for the disabled, public authorities and trade organizations. Laws and regulations are systematically checked in order to remove discriminatory provisions.

Social reintegration and full participation
The abolition of almost all the special legislation on services for the disabled and the implementation of the principles of the Social Assistance Act on needs-tested assistance have placed disabled persons in an equal position with other citizens. Legislation on health and education is also marked by the same concern for equality. A special law on adult education for the disabled provides an opportunity to show special consideration.

The aim of the measures for disabled persons is to enable them to create a life as near to normal as possible. This is done through the granting of anticipatory and compensatory benefits, by making housing conditions as normal as possible and by helping to provide different types of employment.

The Social Assistance Act contains the principle that there should be as little intervention as possible in the autonomy of the individual, early action in case of impending social crisis and the greatest possible re-establishment of the independence of the individual. The means for this process are contained in the sections of the Social Assistance Act dealing with advice and supervision, cash assistance, practical assistance in the home, aids and institutions under the local and county authorities.

Advice is provided by the social welfare committee of the local authorities and the social centres of the county authorities. A number of special welfare consultants are concerned with the major disabilities: blindness, deafness, hardness of hearing, physical disability and mental disability.

Practical assistance in the home must be provided by all local authorities and the aim is to help disabled and old persons to carry on a normal life at home. Such assistance may be granted in a transitional period or as permanent home help.

Aids for the disabled and the old are usually provided free of charge if the costs are over a certain minimum amount. Part payment of the purchase price of cars for the disabled may be given under special conditions. If a dwelling needs special adaptation because of the inhabitant's disability, this work is undertaken free of charge by the local authorities.

Support of an advisory, financial and technical nature is granted for the vocational training of disabled persons, either within the general educational system or through specific types of training. This also applies to persons who, for physical or mental reasons, are unable to obtain or keep a normal occupation in the open labour market. They may be offered employment either in sheltered workshops operated by the public authorities or in private businesses supported by the public authorities. The restoration of working capacity and other sorts of rehabilitation measures are also undertaken in special rehabilitation institutions and in private undertakings subject to public support.

In order to help persons who, owing to a handicap or social problems, need more specific help than may be given while they live alone, both the county and the local authorities run various residential institutions that cater for different categories of person in need of temporary or continuing help. The aim is to make these institutions as small as practicably possible and to equip them with every possible amenity for private life and individual development.

With regard to the physical environment, the question of the handicap-oriented layout of houses and other facilities is under continuous consideration by the Central Council for the Disabled and by a special body set up by the organizations for the disabled.

Telephones especially equipped for the hard-of-hearing are paid for through the general telephone rental and not by the disabled themselves.

As far as transport is concerned, there are several measures to compensate for the difficulties of the disabled, partly by way of financial support and special transport arrangements at the local level, and partly through institutional treatment.

The disabled have equal access to leisure facilities, including sport, cultural, social and political activities. To the extent that handicap prevents the disabled from participating with the non-disabled, there are a number of special activities for disabled persons only. A special organization is engaged in arranging sports events for the disabled on a national and international level. In principle, the disabled have equal rights to participation in social and political life. For those who participate in activities in institutions or who live in institutions, there are democratic structures and co-determination in the internal life of the institutions.

The prevention of disability

Preventive measures are carried out mainly in connection with the legislation on health, the working environment and traffic. Besides technical and financial measures, prevention also includes publicity within the school system and the vocational training system, and general information provided by the State and the public authorities.

Under social legislation, both the social security schemes and the system of social welfare contain important preventive elements, such as early action in the event of a social crisis in the family and in the individual; day-care institutions and other sorts of day-care scheme have also been of fundamental importance in the prevention of social handicaps.

Systems of income support

The most important scheme for the maintenance of income for the disabled with reduced working capacity is the legislation on social pensions, which provides for anticipatory old-age pensions for the disabled. The amount of pension is related to the degree of disability. In principle, the old-age pension is the same for everybody, but different supplements are available to meet special needs.

Persons who are disabled as a result of industrial injuries are covered by special legislation.

Disabled persons who work in sheltered workshops are paid in accordance with special guidelines issued by the Ministry of Social Affairs and the Board of Social Welfare. In addition, there are special rules on the phased reduction in pension as the amount of earned income rises.

Disabled persons who live on their own are granted a rent allowance according to fixed rules, as are other social groups.

Persons who live in publicly run institutions have part of their pension withheld to pay for their stay in that institution, and a fixed amount is paid for personal necessities.

Evaluation of Progress in National Legislation

Since the International Year of Disabled Persons, 1981, Denmark has continued its endeavours to further the equality of treatment and the integration into society of the disabled, and to improve the facilities for granting help to individuals living on their own and to groups of disabled persons.

Employment opportunities have been improved partly by extending the access to sheltered employment in private industry, and partly by increasing the capacity in sheltered workshops run by the public authorities.

By 1980, responsibility for the services for the disabled had been transferred from the central to the local and regional authorities. This shift has been recognized as a successful step towards facilitating the integration of the disabled into society. Another step forward is the general acknowledgement of the fact that matters relating to disability should be dealt with in the sector where they arise (such as housing, traffic and education) and should not automatically come under the social welfare authorities.

Within the area of housing, the last 15–20 years have seen the extension of legislative, financial and practical measures that have resulted in many more disabled persons than before living independently in their own homes.

The difficulties experienced over the last few years have derived from the general economic slow-down that has hit Denmark, as well as many other countries. Efforts have been made, however, to prevent these economic difficulties — which have called for readjustments in publicly financed services — from affecting the work of integrating the disabled into society and securing equality of treatment for them on all social points.

Successful efforts have been made to avoid cutbacks in public budgets for special services for disabled persons. Such efforts have included new ways of thinking and innovative projects that have aimed at finding new ways of helping the disabled. To a large extent these have involved the disabled themselves and private organizations in the responsibility for the integration process. The public authorities have set aside special funds for pilot projects in the social field.

Future work in this field will include greater activation of private organizations and individuals, including the disabled themselves, and the testing of new ways of working. It is considered possible to achieve many improvements without any increase in spending.

Finland

General Principles

The integration of disabled persons into society is the general aim of Finnish social policy. It is hoped to achieve this aim by the following strategies to organize the services and economic support for disabled persons and their families. The responsibility for arranging these services lies with local government and municipalities, which have wide self-determination in Finland (the State subsidizes all social and health services equally). The principal form of services for disabled persons is the same as for the rest of the population; special services for disabled persons are always secondary and used only when the general services are not applicable. Much of the implementation of services for disabled persons is arranged by nongovernmental organizations for the disabled.

The Finnish Constitution does not mention disabled persons, but it ensures that all Finnish citizens have equal rights and obligations.

Since 1972, there has been a continuous five-year planning system within the health services, and, since 1984, within the social services as well. Most of the services that disabled persons need daily are planned according to a three-tier system comprising central, regional and local levels. Education and employment policies have their own shorter-term plans. There is no special planning system for a policy for the disabled.

A National Committee of Disabled Persons was set up in 1985. It has an equal representation of disabled persons and government officials. The National Committee of Rehabilitation Affairs coordinates rehabilitation and other services for disabled persons.

National Involvement in International Action

Finland has ratified the International Labour Conference Convention 159 on the Vocational Rehabilitation and Employment of the Disabled, 1983. An *ad hoc* group will formulate a national policy for the vocational rehabilitation and employment of disabled persons. Finland also adheres to the United Nations World Programme of Action to implement the Decade of Disabled Persons. The Programme has been translated into Finnish and will be widely distributed. Finland also participates actively in the WHO strategy for attaining health for all by the year 2000.

In addition, the Charter for the 80s issued by Rehabilitation International has been translated into Finnish.

Methodology — Types of Legislative Approach to the Equality Concept

The basic laws on the health and social services, education and employment should satisfy most of the needs of disabled persons. In the more difficult cases, the secondary laws serving the smaller group of handicapped persons are applied. As the mainstream services achieve expertise in catering for handicapped persons, integration will advance accordingly.

There are two special laws for disabled persons: the Disabled Persons Welfare Act (1946) and the Act on Special Services for Mentally Retarded (1977). The Disabled Persons Welfare Act covers all disabled groups other than the mentally handicapped, although the latter group may be given services under the Act.

No special law on equality, participation or human rights for disabled persons is planned in Finland at the moment. These aims should be achieved by developing the implementation of the existing laws.

Review of the Present State of National Legislation

Elimination of discrimination or social prejudice
Since the 1970s, many local councils for the disabled have been established to coordinate with municipal governments. Their function has been to bring forward the views of disabled persons about the accessibility of public buildings, streets and other facilities. These councils have also reviewed local services from the point of view of the needs of the disabled.

In Finnish society the position of organizations for disabled persons has always been very strong. Most of them are so-called patient organizations in which all the members are disabled. Many of these organizations arrange rehabilitation services for the groups they represent. This activity has increased the influence of the organizations within the field of social and health services as equal partners with health professionals.

In matters of medical care there is a state official, or patient ombudsman, who deals with complaints arising from alleged misconduct on the part of doctors and hospitals. Some of the large hospitals have a patient ombudsman of their own. The Finnish Hospital League has also published regulations concerning complaints made by patients.

Social reintegration and full participation

Up to the end of 1983, the medical rehabilitation of the disabled was regulated by the Disabled Persons Welfare Act. Since 1 January 1984 medical rehabilitation has become an integral part of medical care through local health centres and hospitals, according to the Primary Health Care Act and the Communal General Hospitals Act. Medical rehabilitation consists of the following groups of services, delivered according to need:

— various kinds of therapy (such as physiotherapy, speech therapy, psychotherapy, occupational therapy);

— care in medical rehabilitation institutes;

— assessment of rehabilitation needs;

— psychosocial rehabilitation;

— rehabilitation counselling;

— technical aids;

— other similar activities.

Through the local social services, disabled persons may obtain the technical aids and structural changes in their houses or flats that are necessary for them to live independently in their own homes. The Building Act demands that public facilities be built so that they are accessible to disabled persons. The local councils for the disabled are very efficient in monitoring development in this respect. The most severely disabled persons live in their own rented flats in service houses where they pay the rent themselves, the extra services being paid for by the local municipality.

In three quarters of the municipalities, there is a transport service for disabled persons. The service belongs to the local social services for the disabled and is subsidized by the State. Such transport services are not available in some of the smallest municipalities.

Responsibility for the employment of the disabled is divided between the Ministry of Social Affairs and Health and the Ministry of Employment. The Disabled Persons Welfare Act regulates assessment centres and sheltered workshops, even though most of the clients and workers come to these services through local employment offices. Early vocational rehabilitation is not sufficiently developed, however, since the Occupational Health Care Act (1978) requires the employer only to inform the disabled worker of the possibility of rehabilitation, not to arrange it. Much vocational rehabilitation is arranged by the Social Insurance Institute or the Insurance Companies' Rehabilitation Centre.

The Disabled Persons Welfare Act concerns the provision of social services and is in principle secondary to the Social Services Act (1984), which aims to guarantee all disadvantaged groups certain basic services, such as the costs of personal help while living in one's own home, psychological guidance for children and day centres for disabled persons.

The integration of schooling for disabled children is in its final stages. The basic education of mentally handicapped children has been transferred from the social service authorities to the local educational authorities, and a similar transfer will take place in the case of physically disabled children whose primary schools are still financed through the social services budget. The content of their education has always been under the authority of the National Board of Education.

The strength of the organizations for the disabled in Finland may have contributed to the amount of sports and other leisure activities among disabled persons.

Receiving information is a grave problem for the blind and the deaf. During the International Year of Disabled Persons, some local authorities started to collect news bulletins of local events and send them out through the telephone services. There are now many similar telephone services around the country. Other groups of disabled persons besides the blind find this service useful. Many national and regional newspapers exist in taped versions for the blind. The National Association of the Deaf has very rapidly developed a countrywide video service that sends out all kinds of information and educational material. There are now about 1000 sets of equipment in constant use. An interpreter service for the deaf has been growing over the last few years. Some local authorities have recruited special employees to work as interpreters. The National Association of the Deaf has 15 regional counsellors who are also interpreters, but most interpreters work part-time. The churches have done spiritual work among the deaf for many years.

The Finnish Red Cross, the Finnish Invalid Association and various other organizations have for some time organized support groups for disabled persons. The organizations for the disabled use their own members as a "trusted friend": these groups are experimenting with various forms of self-help.

The prevention of disability

The prevention of disability is practised in various contexts under different laws. The Primary Health Care Act is concerned with health education, maternal and child care, and primary care in cases of chronic illness. The Communal General Hospitals Act and the Mental Patients Act stress the importance of prevention in a primary, secondary and tertiary sense. The Occupational Health Care Act and labour protection legislation also contain measures that should prevent disability.

Maternal health care is an essential part of the preventive work of primary health care centres. This service has its roots in the *Goutte de lait* movement, which started in Finland in the early 1920s. Well-mother and well-baby clinics gained legal status through the promulgation of two important acts in 1944, the Municipal Public Health Nurses' Act and the Municipal Midwives Act. In 1972 this efficient nationwide preventive system was amalgamated with the primary health care centres.

The well-mother clinics are attended by 99% of pregnant women. The use of the clinics' services is not obligatory, but for the woman to get her maternity benefit (Fmk 550 (US $125)), she must attend a well-mother clinic or consult a private doctor before the end of the fourth month of pregnancy. On average, pregnant women attend a well-mother clinic 12 times before the delivery of their babies.

During the first and second visits to the well-mother clinic, the expectant mothers are screened for syphilis, rhesus antibodies, ABO antibodies and rubella antibodies. Women over the age of 38 years are referred for amniocentesis in order to detect Down's syndrome. In four Finnish provinces alpha-fetoprotein screening is performed; countrywide screening is not considered necessary, as neural tube defects are rare in Finland.

The well-mother clinics have been very effective in achieving their main objectives: health promotion and family counselling. For example, the proportion of smoking mothers is less than 15%, and the number of breastfeeding mothers has more than doubled in a 10-year period. Today more than 60% of mothers breastfeed for at least three months, and about 30% breastfeed for more than six months. The number of babies with low birth weight (under 2500 g) has declined in 10 years from about 5% to about 4%. Special emphasis is placed on total abstention from alcohol and drugs during pregnancy.

In addition to the screening procedures provided by the well-mother clinics in many districts, all pregnant women are offered the opportunity of attending ultrasound screening in early pregnancy. After delivery, mothers who are rubella-antibody negative are vaccinated against rubella.

The well-baby clinics provide services for all children from birth to 7 years of age. From this age onwards, the care is provided through school health services. There is a comprehensive system for the developmental monitoring of the child. In cases of suspected deviation from normal development, the child is referred for specialist examination. The services of the well-baby clinics are meant for all families and children. They therefore pay special attention to families with disabled children. General vaccinations reach over 90% of Finnish children. As an important contribution to disability prevention, children receive vaccination against measles, mumps and rubella at the age of 18 months, with a booster vaccination at the age of 6 years.

In order to coordinate research on congenital malformations, the National Board of Health has kept a national register of congenital malformations since the early 1970s.

Owing to the previous geographical isolation of certain districts and villages, there are several rare genetic diseases that exist only in Finland. Many of these result in permanent mental and/or physical handicap. The university hospitals of Helsinki and Oulu have special research units for these hereditary diseases.

The public is educated in matters of disability mainly by the more than 100 organizations for the disabled. The International Year of Disabled Persons was a very important event in this respect. Information is usually given in the form of publicity campaigns through television, radio and the daily press.

A Finnish speciality is the Slot Machine Association, which allots annually Fmk 250 (US $57 million), to various organizations within the social and health sector. The organizations for the disabled receive about one quarter of the total sum annually.

The insurance companies have a great interest in accident prevention in traffic, at work and in the home. The Social Insurance Institute spends yearly a fixed proportion (2%) of sickness insurance

74

premiums on preventive work and rehabilitation. The prevention of home and leisure-time accidents has been strengthened by establishing the National Committee on Home Accidents under the National Board of Health. The National Board of Labour Protection keeps cumulative, descriptive statistics on serious work accidents with the purpose of developing safer methods of work. The Work Protection Fund finances a great number of research projects on accident prevention. The Institute of Occupational Health is the centre for scientific studies on occupational diseases. The Institute is financed by the State, through the Ministry of Social Affairs and Health. A similar governmental institute is the Public Health Institute which concentrates on the prevention of common diseases.

Systems of income support
The organization of Finnish social insurance is unusual. Much of the social insurance is handled by private insurance companies and funds. The working population enjoys both the governmental social insurance schemes (run by the Social Insurance Institute) and privately owned insurance schemes.

The Social Insurance Institute administers the national sickness insurance and the national pension insurance schemes. The national sickness insurance scheme (under the Sickness Insurance Act,, 1963, as amended) provides refunds of medical expenses and compensation for loss of earnings due to sickness and maternity, besides helping to pay for health services for students and employees and financing preventive care and rehabilitation services. Sickness insurance refunds are earnings related, but independent of the insurance record.

Earnings-related pensions for employees in the private sector are handled by insurance companies. They are financed partly from premiums paid by employers and partly by public funds.

People aged from 16 to 64 years who, owing to illness, disability or injury, are unable to do their normal work or similar work suitable to their age and skills are entitled to a national invalidity pension that will assure them a reasonable income. Pensioners requiring continuous assistance are entitled to helplessness supplements.

On 1 January 1985, a two-part system of unemployment insurance was established. The benefits are a flat-rate basic daily allowance and an earnings-related additional allowance to workers who are members of an unemployment fund.

The benefits of earnings-related pension insurance (based on the Employees Pensions Act and Temporary Employees Act) are similar to the benefits of the Social Insurance Institute, the latter forming a flat-rate basic level.

The Social Insurance Institute administers the scheme of national child care allowances, which provides a child care allowance payable to severely disabled children under 16 living at home. The allowance is higher in cases of extreme helplessness.

The local social services provide last resort social assistance for people whose means are not sufficient to assure their livelihood or care. The minimum standard today is 50% of the level of the national pension.

Disabled persons derive their income security from the social insurance described above. In the case of accidents, income is guaranteed by the appropriate laws. The only form of income security administered by social welfare is a disability allowance payable to blind persons and other severely disabled persons who are active in working life.

Evaluation of Progress in National Legislation

A substantial achievement of Finnish national planning has been the shift of emphasis in the distribution of resources from highly technical hospitals to primary health care. This had to be achieved without infringing the autonomy of the municipal governments. The last stages of this development involved the services to the disabled. Since 1 January 1984, the Disabled Persons Welfare Act has been financed by the communal sector; it was previously totally state financed. Power of decision in individual cases was given to local social and health authorities. The planning and budgeting of the services for the disabled were extended through the sector of health and social services.

The decentralization of the services appears to have had mixed success so far. The waiting times for various services have shortened, but in some cases the expertise and the continuity of the services have not been upheld. The stated aim of developing interaction between different sectors of human services has not been achieved, even in the neighbouring sectors of health care and social services. The rehabilitation of the disabled is still arranged under many different laws. This leads in some cases to disputes over responsibility, long waiting times and lack of continuity in the rehabilitation process. The organizations for the disabled have complained that the local social services vary too much owing to differences in economic resources. The health centres and hospitals are also criticized for their neglect of psychological and social factors in the rehabilitation of disabled persons. The role of the family in the rehabilitation of disabled children is not duly appreciated.

The most important tasks facing the health authorities in the field of legislation are as follows:

— coordinating legislation for the welfare and rehabilitation of the disabled, taking into account the different purposes of primary health care, local services, occupational health, work protection, employment education and social insurance;

— developing a coordinated system of decision-making and referrals at the local level, based on expert group work and patient participation;

— guaranteeing a reasonable and continuous income during the whole span of the rehabilitation process, during which vocational rehabilitation may last 6–10 years;

— developing the necessary codes of practice and laws to promote early rehabilitation in the workplace, and improving the opportunities for disabled persons to form an increased proportion of the active labour force.

France

General Principles

The comprehensive Disability Act of 30 June 1975 is the cornerstone of French legislation on behalf of disabled persons. It states clearly in Article 1 that their integration in the educational system and in professional and social life is a national obligation. To promote this integration, the Act sets out various services in cash and in kind that are available for all disabled persons irrespective of the nature and origin of their impairment. This legislation is carefully tied in with measures taken to assist previously employed disabled persons (the disabled under the social security system and victims of work accidents).

Coordination mechanisms

Various organizations have been set up to coordinate the measures taken by the public authorities to assist the disabled.

The National Consultative Council for Disabled Persons, set up in 1976, has to be consulted about all measures taken by the public authorities in this sector. All those concerned are represented on the Council: the competent authorities, associations of or for disabled persons, associations and unions representing employers and employees, and the relevant research and study organizations.

Three further councils have been established to cover specific fields. One of these is concerned with the transport of disabled persons (the Liaison Committee on the Transport of Disabled Persons), another deals with the employment of disabled persons (the Higher Council for the Professional and Social Reclassification of Disabled Workers), while the third looks after the integration of the disabled and their dependants into their urban environment and habitat.

National Involvement in International Action

France acceded to the European Convention on Social and Medical Assistance on 30 October 1957 and to the European Social Charter on 9 March 1973. These instruments affirm the rights of disabled persons to social and medical assistance and establish the principle of the reciprocity of benefits between signatory countries.

France has also taken part, within the Committee on the Rehabilitation and Resettlement of the Disabled set up on the basis of the Partial Agreement of 1959, in the drafting of a coherent policy for the rehabilitation of disabled people, and was signatory in September 1984 to a resolution on this subject.

France has also actively implemented the European Community's programme of action on the social reintegration of disabled persons (for further information on this programme, see the details already mentioned under the Belgian contribution, pp. 33–37). In particular, two district projects have been set up in France, one in Dijon and one in Montpellier, as part of the European Community network.

Methodology — Types of Legislative Approach to the Equality Concept

Remedies and compensation for personal disabilities have progressively improved under the French social security system. This is at present covered under four separate but coexistent areas: accidents at work, veterans and war victims, disability covered by social security and disability under the Act of 30 June 1975.

Accidents at work
The first item of major legislation (1898) deals with the protection of victims of work accidents. Its main aim is to eliminate the need for the worker to establish liability by proving incorrect or negligent action on the part of the employer. It establishes the principle of a legal remedy for accident victims (benefits in cash and in kind), in the form of compensation for the disability suffered, compensation for the professional implications of the accident (based on a professional scale), and damages linked to the degree of occupational risk.

Assessment of the degree of disability is based on a scale that was last revised on 30 December 1982. Compensation is granted for any disability within the range 1–100% with the award of a permanent pension varying in proportion to the degree of disability.

Veterans and war victims
Compensation for physical injury caused by war to both civilians and members of the armed forces has been covered in a very wide range of legal enactments, starting with that of 31 March 1919 and supplemented in 1921, 1923 and 1924. This legislation covers pension rights, retraining in specialist centres and employment in businesses and in the public service. The right to a pension and the degree of disability are assessed on the basis of a scale revised on three occasions (1898, 1915 and 1918) and codified in 1951.

Disabled persons covered by social security
The third major item of social legislation covers disability insurance (under the 1930 Act which was recast from 1945 onwards). This affords protection to persons insured under the social insurance system, based on their remuneration, who are rendered unfit for work for a period in excess of three years. A person insured under the social insurance system, who suffers a two-thirds reduction in his or her working or earning capacity, is deemed to be disabled. The degree of disability is not based on a quantitative scale, but rather on the insured person's residual working capacity, general state, age, physical and mental faculties, and suitability for professional training.

Disability Act of 30 June 1975
This Act establishes the principle of benefits for persons who are not covered under other legislation. It reformulated from this point of view the various types of allowance previously paid in the form of social assistance or by the family allowance offices. The scope of the Act is, however, more far-reaching. It affirms the rights of disabled persons to education, work and leisure, irrespective of the origin of their disability, and is a homogeneous and consistent instrument (covering also specialist establishments) dealing with the problems of the disabled. Orientation commissions[a] were established in each *département*: departmental commissions on the special education of children, and technical commissions on the vocational guidance and reclassification of adults. These commissions were given the competence to recognize disability and authorize the

---

[a] These commissions consist of the following elements: a secretariat; a technical team that examines the file prepared by medical specialists, social workers and others depending on the nature of the particular problem (for example, whether the person concerned is an adult or a child); and the commission itself, which is responsible for taking decisions.

granting of all forms of benefit provided by the law (allowances and vocational guidance in specialist establishments). Under the Act of 30 June 1975 assessment of the disabled is based on the scale applicable to veterans and war victims.

Review of the Present State of National Legislation

Social reintegration and full participation

Care, medical rehabilitation, technical aids
The social security system is responsible for the care and treatment of the disabled. The following items are covered:

— medical, surgical and pharmaceutical charges;

— functional rehabilitation, provided by public or private establishments with the necessary resources, or health centres in the hospital system, either privately run or administered by the social security services;

— the provision of technical aids is the responsibility of technical aid centres under the Ministry of Veterans which cover purchase costs (reimbursed at a rate laid down by the competent authorities, and including the costs of repair, renewal and if necessary modification), dispatch costs and the attendance costs incurred by the disabled persons themselves;

— the transport costs incurred by disabled persons travelling between their normal residence and the medical care centre.

Education
The present trend is towards a change in the orientation of the educational regulations to emphasize the academic and social integration of disabled children. Special education for disabled children is at present provided in most cases in two types of establishment: health and medicosocial units financed by the social security system, and specialist schools or classes run by the Ministry of National Education.

Health or medicosocial units. The social security system assumes full responsibility for the costs incurred by disabled minors in health or medicosocial units. Parents are not required to contribute to the costs of accommodating or educating their children in such units.

Severely disabled small children from birth to 3 years of age are generally accommodated in day nurseries where they are given the medical care required. Disabled children and young persons between the ages of 3 and 20 receive medical care in specialist medicosocial establishments that provide both education and professional training. They are staffed by multidisciplinary teams of medical specialists (mainly psychiatrists), psychologists, specialist educators and re-educators (experts in psychomotor and speech disorders), depending on the nature of the particular disability. These establishments specialize in particular disabilities and in certain degrees of severity of the handicap (establishments catering for mental, sensory and motor disorders, and for minor, medium or severe deficiencies). They accept patients on a boarding, semi-boarding or outpatient basis and are 83% run by private associations. These institutions have a total capacity of 133 000 vacancies.

Specialist schools or classes. In parallel with the provision of medical care, the Ministry of National Education set up specialist schools or classes as early as 1909 for "retarded, semi-educable children". These establishments, essentially devoted to education, provide teaching that is tailored in method and content to the needs of such children. No medical or paramedical services are provided.

The options are:

— classes to improve academic performance, operating at primary school level;

— special education sections attached to secondary schools, intended to provide academic and vocational training for disabled adolescents within the group aged 12 to 17 years;

— national secondary schools, specializing in individual types of disability, some of which may be linked with a health care service that operates within the framework of the school.

These classes and institutions have a total capacity of 220 000 vacancies.

Vocational training
The vocational training of disabled young persons is provided by the special education sections of secondary schools referred to above, the medicosocial training units also referred to above, and periods of apprenticeship served with an employer, in which case the usual training period may be increased by 12 months (to three years instead of two years).

Professional rehabilitation
Professional rehabilitation courses for disabled workers are run mainly by professional re-education centres (13 000 vacancies) which

are funded by the social security system. These establishments provide training up to qualification level, conferring the right to professional apprenticeship certificates and, on occasion, technical diplomas. Disabled workers accepted for training at these centres enjoy the status of professional trainees and are paid a minimum wage equivalent to 90% of the monthly minimum interprofessional wage.

Working life

Protected labour establishments. Two types of establishment have traditionally accepted disabled persons unable to work in a normal environment:

— assistance-through-work centres for disabled persons whose working capacity is less than one third of the normal; these institutions have two aims, (*a*) production (the profits from which accrue to the commercial operations account) and (*b*) medicosocial support (financed by a daily wage paid by social assistance); these centres had 58 000 vacancies in 1985;

— protected workshops employing less seriously affected persons, which enjoy the status of an enterprise but receive a make-up subsidy from the Ministry of Labour; at present these workshops have 5000 vacancies.

Normal work environment. Teams responsible for the preparation for and follow-up of professional reclassification (64 teams existed in 1985) assist disabled workers who are looking for employment in a normal work environment. These teams normally consist of one job-finder and one social assistant.

Various measures have been taken to facilitate employment in a normal work environment:

— firms with a staff of more than 10 workers are required by law to allocate 10% of their vacancies to war victims and disabled workers;

— financial grants are made to employers for the modification of workplaces, the adaptation of machines or equipment, the individual fitting out of workplaces and arrangement of access to such workplaces, and to compensate for additional instructional expenses, such assistance being restricted to the period during which the additional instruction is necessary;

— legislation on reserved employment in the public sector requires each section of the administration (apart from the recruitment service) to accept war victims and disabled workers on a scale that is specified by ministerial decree.

In addition to these special measures, recruitment by public competition is open to disabled persons. Special arrangements for the examination procedure are authorized in such cases.

Housing and physical environment

Availability of protected accommodation. Persons who are too dependent to live alone are housed in special accommodation or institutions. Two types of special accommodation are available: apartments or hostels that receive, at the end of the day or for the weekend, disabled persons working in assistance-through-work centres, in protected workshops or in a normal work environment; and permanent hostels that accommodate a more dependent population no longer able to work but retaining a measure of intellectual or social independence. In 1984, some 34 397 vacancies were available in special accommodation. These units are financed by departmental social assistance, while the disabled persons themselves contribute to their accommodation costs. The rates of contribution to accommodation costs, which are proportional to the disabled person's resources, are laid down in regulations. The contribution paid by disabled persons must leave them a minimum income.

Disabled persons who are entirely dependent are accommodated in special institutions financed by the social security system. In 1985, some 100 of these special homes had been authorized, providing a total capacity of 3921 vacancies.

Accessibility of independent accommodation. Various legal texts, in particular the Decree of 4 August 1980, have been adopted in implementation of Article 49 of the Act of 30 June 1975, in order to ensure that new communal dwellings and the apartments contained in them are accessible to disabled persons. The Decree of 1980 requires in particular the installation of a lift in dwellings with more than three storeys above the ground floor, and the provision of wheelchair access to the lift in all communal residential accommodation for which building permits have been sought from 1 January 1983 onwards. The aim is to offer a progressively wider choice of new accommodation that is accessible and easily adapted to the special needs of the disabled. Since the provisions of this Decree are generally applicable and mandatory, the granting of state building grants is subject to compliance with these regulations. Article 4 of the Decree provides, however, for these requirements to be waived where the characteristics of the terrain or the presence of existing structures hamper their implementation. Such waivers may be granted after consultation with a departmental accessibility commission, on which associations for the disabled designated by the Prefect are represented.

Technical aids. Payments for equipment intended to mitigate functional deficiencies are made by social security services on an optional basis.

In 1980 the National Family Allowances Office, acting pursuant to Article 54 of the Disability Act of 30 June 1975, allocated FF 30 million (US $4.7 million) to finance personal assistance grants for the modification of existing flats. These grants have not been drawn on to the same extent in all cases, and the unused balances have been made generally available for different forms of social action funded by family allowances offices (such as to provide furniture and improve the home environment).

Local sickness insurance offices are empowered under certain conditions to pay exceptional benefits for equipment that is not normally reimbursable. They have assistance funds for this purpose, as specified in the Order of 22 July 1954. The Health and Social Action Commission of the Salaried Worker's National Maternity Insurance Office may also contribute to the installation of specific equipment.

In 1982 an exceptional allocation of FF 15 million (US $2.35 million) from the European Social Fund enabled the local sickness insurance offices to help about 3000 persons to acquire specific items of equipment.

The environment. As provided for in the 1975 Act, various regulations have been brought into effect since 1978 to ensure that disabled persons have access to urban establishments. The Decree of 1 February 1978 specified the measures to be taken to ensure that disabled persons with reduced mobility can gain access to newly constructed installations open to the public; departure from these regulations is authorized in the event of serious material difficulties, but only after hearing the opinion of the accessibility commission referred to above. The Decree of 9 December 1978 laid down the measures to be taken for the progressive modification of existing public structures (the road system, buildings and installations) belonging to public organizations.

Communications and transport
A sustained effort has been made to guarantee the disabled access to public transport. The metropolitan railways recently constructed in

Lille and Lyon, for example, are fully or partially accessible to disabled persons. A programme is being put into effect on all railway networks to reposition platforms so as to reduce the width of the gap between platform and trains. New carriages on trains include a compartment and toilet easily accessible to disabled persons. All major French airports are designed to provide full access for the disabled.

Various tariff reductions are granted to disabled persons. Many local authorities responsible for urban transport have granted free or reduced cost travel to the disabled and an accompanying person. The same privileges are granted on the national railway (permanent reductions for war victims, free transport for persons accompanying either 100% disabled war victims or disabled persons certified to require the attendance of another person, and a 50% reduction for persons accompanying either the blind or holders of disability cards).

Special services (run by private enterprise or the public authority) are available in many French towns to be called on by persons with reduced mobility. These services are in general subsidized by local authority grants.

Leisure and sport

Sporting activities for disabled persons are run by two main sporting federations: the Handi-Sport Federation for disabled persons suffering from motor and sensory disorders, and the French Federation of Adapted Sport for the mentally handicapped.

The present trend is to incorporate in the training syllabuses of physical training centres an increased emphasis on the specific problems of disabled persons, so as to permit their participation in normal sporting activities.

Access to and participation in cultural performances during leisure hours have received considerable emphasis as a means of ensuring the full participation of disabled persons in cultural life. A programme entitled Handicap and Culture, organized in 1982 and 1983, was followed up in a number of regional campaigns.

Promotion of self-help groups

Associations for the disabled are highly organized in France, some having been in existence for more than 50 years; 25 of these are represented on the national scale. They receive subsidies in general for some of their functions from the Ministry of Social Affairs.

The prevention of disability

General regulations on prevention

The health and social protection of pregnant women and of children up to the age of 6 has been in force in France since 1945. Mother and child protection centres, which have been set up in districts and sectors covering between 8000 and 20 000 inhabitants, provide facilities for prenatal and postnatal examination and consultations on infant problems. Pregnant women are entitled to five prenatal examinations completely free of charge. Facilities for the prenatal diagnosis of various metabolic diseases have been available free of charge since 1982. Similar examinations for chromosome abnormalities were introduced in 1984 for three additional conditions (haemophilia, thalassaemia and sickle-cell anaemia). Perinatal prevention programmes have been implemented in five regions. Children now have 20 obligatory examinations from birth up to the age of 6 years, including 9 during the first year of life.

Various other measures have recently been adopted to avert the risk of a potential handicap resulting from various diseases. For example, a campaign against rubella was launched in November 1983, consisting of the vaccination of children of both sexes in conjunction with measles vaccination from the age of 12 months onwards, so as to reduce virus reservoirs and afford indirect protection to pregnant women, and the systematic vaccination of girls and young women where screening tests show this to be necessary.

It has been estimated that the mean annual sales of vaccines doubled in 1985.

Consultations with genetic counsellors have been extended throughout France, so as to provide better medical supervision of at-risk families.

Periodic campaigns on accident prevention (covering domestic accidents, accidents on the public highway and traffic accidents) have been run by the ministries concerned. These campaigns are aimed both at parents and at children in schools.

In the more specific field of traffic accidents, the Act of December 1983, aimed at intensifying the campaign against excessive consumption of alcohol by vehicle drivers, has opened the way for the adoption of modern means of detecting excessive alcohol consumption. It has also strengthened the relevant penalties and lowered the threshold of a criminal offence. Appreciable results were recorded in 1984 when the number of serious injuries due to road accidents fell by 8%.

Research

The National Study and Research Centre on Disabilities and Handicaps was set up in 1975. Its task is to advise the Minister for Social Affairs on a wide range of problems linked with the prevention, care and rehabilitation of the disabled and the handicapped.

A Research and Study Centre on Technical Aids was established in May 1984 by the Secretary of State for Veterans. In addition to research, its terms of reference include the performance of tests, the compilation of relevant documentation and practical instruction in this field.

In 1983, after a meeting of 18 working groups, the National Institute of Health and Medical Research in Paris published a report entitled *Réduire le handicap* [Minimizing the effect of a handicap], which laid down the lines of research to be pursued in this sector.

Research undertaken in conjunction with industry has been financed since 1981 by the Scientific Committee on Aid to the Disabled of the Department of Biological and Medical Engineering of the Ministry of Research and Technology, the aim being to develop electronic communication or environmental control devices (remote alarms) for persons with sensory or motor disorders.

Systems of income support

Allowances for the parents of disabled children

The special education allowance is an allowance paid to the family to compensate for the excess costs incurred in the education of disabled children. This allowance, which is paid for children and adolescents up to the age of 20 years, is subject to technical conditions that have to be assessed by departmental special education commissions, namely an 80% incapacity level or a 50–80% incapacity level if a child is undergoing special education. If the child has been found a place in a special boarding establishment, sponsored by the social security system, the special family allowance is payable only for holidays or time spent at home. Provision has been made for two graduated increments to the allowance if particularly substantial expenses are incurred over the child's education, or if the child needs the attendance of another person. Since 1 June 1985, the basic amount of the allowance has been FF 512.64 (US $80.5) monthly, the category 1 increment FF 1153.44 (US $181) monthly, and the category 2 increment FF 384.48 (US $60) monthly. Only one of the two increments can be added to the basic allowance.

Benefits payable to adults

Disabled persons under social security. These draw disability pensions (based on contributions) that vary according to their degree of dependence. If a person is capable of working but has lost two thirds of his or her earning capacity as a result of disability, a category 1 pension amounting to 30% of his or her previous salary is paid. The pension paid to disabled persons who are incapable of working (category 2 disabled) amounts to 50% of the previous salary. Disabled persons who are completely incapable of engaging in professional activity and who are, furthermore, dependent on the assistance of another person to carry out the everyday actions of life are paid a category 2 pension with an increment for their assistant. Disability pensions may not be less than a minimum amount, possibly supplemented by a compensation allowance in order to bring the total benefit to an amount fixed on 1 June 1985 at FF 2470 (US $388) monthly. Persons entitled to disability pension are entitled to benefits in kind under the Sickness and Maternity Insurance system: the costs incurred are fully reimbursable.

Victims of work accidents. Calculation of the pensions payable to the victims of work accidents are governed by complex rules. The compensation payable depends on the degree of incapacity (being reduced or increased if it is less than or greater than 50%) and on the basic salary earned during the 12 months preceding incapacitation. Victims of work accidents, whose incapacity for work is at least 66.66%, are entitled to receive benefits in kind under the Sickness and Maternity Insurance system, provided that they have not been re-employed in remunerative activity.

The 1975 Act: two new allowances for adults. The aim of the cash benefits instituted in 1975 was to cover the needs of disabled persons who, never having worked, were not entitled either to disability pensions or to pensions arising out of accidents at work. This constitutes therefore a subsidiary form of assistance.

Two types of benefit were created for the first time in the 1975 Act: the disabled adult allowance and the compensation allowance. These allowances replaced a heterogeneous collection of allowances that had been previously paid by social assistance or the family allowance fund. The recasting of the system also made it possible to eliminate any reference to the obligation on the family to provide support for disabled persons in order to establish eligibility for these benefits. The substitution of collective responsibility for that of mutual aid within the family in providing support for disabled persons was a bold step forward.

90

The disabled adult allowance is a minimum social allowance payable to adult disabled persons. It is financed by the national budget and administered by the family allowance offices. Payment of this allowance is subject to fulfilment of the following technical conditions, certified by the Technical Commission for Adult Vocational Guidance and Professional Reclassification (COTOREP): an 80% disability level or, alternatively, the inability to obtain employment as a result of a handicap. In order to draw the allowance, the person must also comply with the following administrative requirements: to be a French national or a citizen of a country that has a bilateral convention with France, to be resident in France, to have a net taxable income below a variable level depending on the family situation, not to be drawing any equivalent disability or old age pension, and not to be eligible for family allowances. Persons drawing the allowance are eligible for sickness and maternity benefits, based on social contributions payable by the State. The amount of the allowance corresponds to the minimum disability pension, or FF 2470 (US $388) monthly as at 1 June 1985. The level below which the allowance becomes payable is FF 28 460 (US $4468) per year for a single person and FF 56 920 (US $8936) for a married couple, these amounts being increased by FF 14 230 (US $2234) for a dependent child. The allowance is at present being drawn by 500 000 persons.

The compensation allowance has the double aim of providing the seriously disabled with the assistance of another person and of compensating for excess costs incurred in connection with their professional activities. Payment of the allowance is dependent on the recognition by COTOREP of an 80% incapacity for work, and the inability to carry out alone the essential actions of everyday life or the necessity to incur additional expenses as a result of the disability in the exercise of a professional activity. Payment is also subject to the condition of residence in France (a 15-year residence period being required for foreign nationals from countries that have not signed a convention with France), and an available resources condition (whereby the net taxable income of the person concerned has to be below a determined level). Furthermore, the person concerned should no longer be eligible for family allowances and should not be drawing any equivalent benefit from the social security system. The allowance varies, as a function of the state of dependence of the person concerned, between FF 1650 (US $259) and FF 4125 (US $648) monthly. The income levels here are identical with those applicable to the disabled adult allowance (plus the amount of that allowance granted). This allowance is additional to the disabled adult allowance. Compensation allowance is at present being drawn by 170 000 persons.

Remuneration for work performed
The Act of 30 June 1975 fixed a "minimum" professional wage, which was guaranteed to disabled workers employed in a normal work environment, in protected workshops or in assistance-through-work centres. Disabled workers are also eligible for bonuses.

The guaranteed wage, which was fixed in relation to the minimum interprofessional wage (SMIC), was as follows: in a normal work environment, 100% of the SMIC with a maximum of 130% of the SMIC; in a protected workshop, 90% of the SMIC; and in an assistance-through-work centre, 70% of the SMIC.

The guaranteed wage consists of two elements: the amount paid by the employer (whether a normal firm, protected workshop or assistance-through-work centre); and the additional payment by the State, restricted in the different work environments to: 30% of the SMIC in a normal firm, 56.66% in a protected workshop and 55% in an assistance-through-work centre. The employers' social insurance contributions on this additional amount are payable by the State.

To be eligible for this guaranteed wage, a person must have been recognized as a disabled worker and received vocational guidance from COTOREP. At present 70 000 persons are drawing the guaranteed wage, including 58 000 workers in assistance-through-work centres.

Other provisions
A lodging allowance is paid by the family allowance offices to disabled persons who comply with the technical conditions for the disabled adult allowance, provided that their accommodation complies with certain criteria in respect of surface area and comfort.

A disability card, providing entitlement to various tax advantages (an additional half-quota allowance on income tax), is also issued by COTOREP to persons with a disability level of at least 80%.

Evaluation of Progress in National Legislation

A reorientation of the current regulations to favour disabled persons has become necessary, in order to stimulate more effectively the keeping of disabled children within the family and in school, the professional integration of disabled workers, and the social integration of disabled adults. Institutional accommodation is geographically unevenly spread, and does not cater adequately for those who require it. The measurement of disability is still unsatisfactory but the problem is receiving close attention.

The keeping of disabled children within the family and in school

To complement the conventional institutional policy, France has now developed a system of services and benefits to support families caring for a disabled child. Efforts are being made at the same time to modify the operation of the specialist institutions and develop effective means of integrating disabled children in normal schools.

Home services

Keeping small disabled children at home necessitates the provision both of support for the parents and of early medical care and re-education facilities.

Support for the parents is provided as soon as the presence of the disability is notified, at the time of birth or at the mother and child protection centre, which is in general responsible for prevention and early detection. The greatest possible emphasis is placed on this stage, which is decisive if parents are to accept the difficulties involved in caring for their disabled child.

Parental guidance and the re-education of the child from birth to the age of six years is provided subsequently by early medicosocial action centres (CAMPS). These centres, which were set up by the Act of 30 June 1975, perform a threefold function.

1. They provide outpatient care on the basis of a multidisciplinary team (consisting of doctors, specialists, re-educators, psychologists and specialist education staff) and the early care necessary to prevent any deterioration of the condition and to mitigate as far as possible functional incapacities.

2. They advise parents in their role as educators, guiding and assisting them in solving their problems. The persons providing the necessary treatment for the child may operate in the home or in the centre itself.

3. They provide an effective link with nursery schools where the child can be accepted in a normal environment.

The number of CAMPS at present in existence is 137, most covering different forms of disability, although some specialize in particular disabilities (most frequently visual and auditory deficiencies). They are funded by the social security system (80%) and by *départements* (20%) from the disease prevention budget.

Medical care and education services in the home are also available to the parents of children from the age of three years onwards, where the latter have not been admitted to specialist establishments. Any necessary care and re-education is provided on this basis. These services may be supplemented by so-called life helps who assist seriously handicapped children to perform the essential actions of everyday life. The services of life helps are financed jointly by the national budget, by local authorities and by the parents, who draw special family allowances for this purpose.

Changes in the function of establishments for the disabled
At the same time, the move toward allocating establishments to particular categories of disabled children has been encouraged. Their operation on an external and semi-boarding basis has now made it possible in many cases for disabled children and adolescents to remain in the home, in particular those with mental handicaps. This has led in turn to a clearer definition of the policy for accepting children with multiple handicaps on a semi-boarding basis, including their temporary acceptance as full boarders. The recently adopted policy for integration of disabled children in schools is intended to give parents a genuine choice about their education by extending the range of available solutions.

Integration in school
The integration of disabled children in normal schools is by no means a recent development. Several normal schools have for a long time been accepting pupils with psychomotor, mental or sensory defects. At the same time, specialist establishments have been able to establish close links with normal schools in the vicinity, so as to implement partial integration measures for their children. On the basis of the experience gained, however, two interministerial circulars of 29 January 1982 and 1983 have now introduced three essentially new elements: integration as a priority aim, integration as a pragmatic step and integration as an educational project requiring continuous support.

The principle of voluntarism, the reliance on voluntary action rather than compulsion, adopted by the public authorities, has radically transformed the aims of specialist establishments and normal schools. The integration of disabled children into a normal school environment as a priority aim for all elements in the system has three important implications:

— in normal schools, integration will necessitate changes in the educational system towards a greater tolerance and a more sympathetic allowance for differences;

— it will mean at the same time that medico-educational establishments will have to be opened up to the outside world, thus avoiding the confinement and restricted access that have resulted in children spending their whole school career in a specialist institution;

— it will serve as an example to the social service as a whole; the school is of course the primary collective structure in the system of socialization, and the acceptance in schools of children who are different, in the way that disabled children are, will provide a driving force for change in the collective mentality.

The integration of disabled children in schools is to be regarded as a pragmatic step and not a dogmatic principle. It is to be implemented without compulsion, the result of a clearly expressed choice by the child, his or her family and the educational team, arrived at in conjunction with the specialists responsible for guiding the child and following up progress.

It is essential to look carefully for the type of education that is most appropriate, not only to the disability but also to the character of the child, taking into account family environment, existing specialist establishments and normal schools, and the competence and motivation of the teacher concerned.

Integration is not a general formula that can be adopted indiscriminately for all disabled children. It can also be implemented in very many ways according to the different stages of development of the child. These include integration on a very flexible basis, involving only some aspects of the normal school curriculum; collective integration in small numbers at a time when changes are being made in the educational and therapeutic regime, necessitating periods of preparation and observation; and individual integration in a normal class.

Integration has to be regarded as a continuous process that can be modified to meet changes in each individual situation. The voluntary aspect of integration on both sides makes it clear that the integration of the disabled in a school does not immediately signify assimilation. The disabled child has to be accepted at school with all his or her differences.

Finally, each disabled child to be integrated in a normal school will need special support. There is no room for "in at the deep end" policies whereby a disabled child is simply placed in an ordinary class without any modification of the teaching regime or any form of medico-educational support.

Resources required in support of school integration
Three specific requirements have to be met for the integration of the disabled child in a school: specialist staff, material resources and a suitably modified teaching system.

The specialist support provided for each child during integration into a normal school has to be considered in advance and jointly by the teaching team, the specialist staff, guidance teams and the families who must together prepare a plan of education. It will also be followed closely by the administrative authorities, in particular departmental directors of health and social affairs and school inspectors, who will coordinate the measures to be taken and ensure that agreement is reached between all the partners, for example, the heads of schools and specialist establishments, the associations responsible for running specialist establishments, associations representing the parents of normal and disabled children, and the local authorities.

When sufficient progress has been made with this joint preparatory work, the results are formulated in an agreement, which is binding on the different parties concerned in the integration operation. The agreement lays down in detail the procedure for cooperation between schools and specialist institutions.

Specialist support may be provided within the school by the staff of medico-educational establishments or by health care and educational services. It may also be provided outside the framework of the school in mental health centres or by private practitioners. The integration of disabled children in schools will therefore involve breaking down the barriers between normal schools and specialist establishments and also between the services responsible for their management.

The accessibility of school premises is one of the prerequisites for integration, especially in the case of children with motor defects. The Decree of 1 February 1978 imposed the requirement that all new installations open to the public should be accessible to the disabled. This policy has been implemented progressively in the case of existing public buildings by virtue of the Decree of 9 December 1978.

The material teaching resources required for the acceptance of children with motor or sensory handicaps are provided by the school itself. The necessary re-education techniques, on the other hand, are the responsibility of the social security system.

The individual integration of disabled children in a normal class can only be achieved in small classes. The teacher will sometimes need specialist assistance (in the form of life helps for children with motor defects and sign language interpreters for the deaf). The child may need a private tutor outside school hours to enable him or her to acquire the necessary knowledge to achieve a proper academic result.

Professional integration of disabled workers

In normal firms
Various measures were adopted in 1983 and 1984 to promote the professional integration of disabled workers into a normal work environment:

— individual professional adaptation contracts financially supported by the national employment fund, whereby the State assumes responsibility for 80% of the wages of the disabled worker in a normal work environment over a period of six months, provided that the employer undertakes to continue the employment for a corresponding further period;

— long-term professional integration contracts between the State and firms, permitting firms special access to government aid provided that they undertake to recruit disabled workers on contracts of several years' duration;

— the experimental training and integration of workers in assistance-through-work centres, providing the basis for nine-month adaptation periods in a normal work environment;

— relaxation of the conditions governing the payment of installation grants to independent workers;

— simplification of the procedures for the payment of grants for the modification of workplaces, and compensation for additional charges incurred on job training, where disabled workers are employed in normal production shops.

To promote professional integration and thus save expenditure on assistance, some protected work establishments have developed — so far on a marginal basis — graduated forms of integration into the normal work environment. Two specific approaches can be pinpointed:

— the permanent collective posting of workers from an assistance-through-work centre, with their eventual incorporation in a firm, so that they represent an extension of the centre in the normal work environment;

— the posting of individual workers from an assistance-through-work centre to a firm, whereby the workers remain the responsibility of the protected work establishment, which pays them

97

and discusses regularly with them their professional situation and any problems that arise.

This range of experience and the new procedures adopted for the integration of the disabled in schools bring out clearly the importance of a flexible approach and the decompartmentalization of the relevant institutions. There is no longer any question of an "inside" and an "outside" in regard to the integration of the disabled, but merely a range of different formulae, enabling changes to be made that offer opportunities and permit progress — although this involves of course the possibility of regress also.

In the public service
To promote the acceptance of disabled persons for reclassification, the conditions regarding admission to the public service have been modified as follows:

- deletion of the upper age limits for access to grades and levels of employment in the public service, as specified in Article 27 of the Act of 11 January 1984, setting out the statutory provisions governing the national civil service, and Article 35 of the Act of 26 January 1984, setting out the statutory provisions governing the civil service in local authorities;

- more flexible conditions in regard to physical fitness for admission to employment in the public sector, introduced by Article 50 of the Act of 13 July 1983, setting out the rights and obligations of civil servants, and Article 35 of the Act of 26 January 1984, referred to above;

- special provisions to facilitate the reclassification of civil servants who have become disabled, introduced by Article 63 of the Act of 11 January 1984 and in accordance with the Act of 26 January 1984 (these regulations provide that civil servants who have become unsuitable for their existing post as a result of a deterioration in their physical health may be reclassified in another section of the civil service at a higher, equivalent or identical level);

- the provisions of the Act of 11 and 26 January 1984, which give priority to civil servants with a recognized disability who have requested a transfer;

- improved access to reserved employment by deletion of the age limit for applicants for reserved employment in the public sector (Decree of 26 December 1983 amending Article R 323-100 of the Labour Code);

— the establishment of a classification list for admission to reserved employment (in the Act of 7 June 1983 and the Decree of 26 December 1983) and reduction of the period allowed to the administrative authorities to appoint candidates to reserved employment (in the Act of 7 June 1983).

Experimental rules for the recruitment of disabled workers have also been introduced by the Ministry of Posts and Telecommunications. The procedure in this case consists of their engagement as assistants for a probation period of four months with the possibility of two four-month extensions. During the probation period, disabled workers may be regraded to posts more suited to their capacity. Those whose work has been satisfactory after a full probation period of 12 months sit an establishment examination or undergo a professional test for appointment to a permanent post in the sector in which they have served during the probation period. Since 1981, some 1030 disabled workers have been recruited in this way.

Social integration of disabled adults

Support services in the home
Life helps were introduced in 1981, partly financed from the national budget and intended to provide support for severely disabled persons in the home and to assist them in the performance of the essential activities of everyday life. The number of life helps employed has now reached 1864. They frequently operate in conjunction with other services (such as home helps).

Adaptation of accommodation
A pilot campaign in connection with the accommodation of disabled persons was initiated in 1983 as part of the measures adopted to encourage the maintenance of disabled persons in their own homes in accordance with the general principles of the interim plan. This campaign, which was financed by the State from the budget of the Ministry of Social Affairs and National Solidarity, had two specific aims: (*a*) the improvement and adaptation of accommodation to meet the needs of disabled persons; and (*b*) the modification of accommodation as a means of mitigating functional deficiencies. To implement the aims of this campaign, the national authorities concluded agreements with three separate organizations in 1982. They received grants for the purpose of examining the relevant files and proposing any necessary improvements. This pilot campaign was restricted mainly to persons with motor defects living in old-style accommodation, who were not in professional employment and received only

a low income, assistance being provided in principle in direct relation to their disability.

The adaptation of their accommodation has not only provided disabled persons with a very much higher standard of comfort but also enabled them to continue to live at home under satisfactory conditions rather than being admitted to a specialist institution.

The pilot campaign was superseded in 1984 by changes in the conditions governing eligibility for different forms of assistance for improvements to the home. Disabled persons who own their own homes are now entitled to draw two grants simultaneously for the modification and the improved accessibility of their accommodation (taken together, the two grants amount to a total of FF 28 000 (US $4396)). The same advantages are available to low-income disabled tenants.

Development of the protected home environment

A number of changes are now taking place in the conventional pattern — which still predominates — of the accommodation of disabled persons in communal units. New types of home are being introduced in both rural and urban environments. This applies to all forms of accommodation, including those catering for the severely disabled who are incapable of working. Preference is now given under the new policy to small units (housing 20–30 persons) rather than to large-scale establishments.

The attempt to foster the independence of disabled persons within these homes has resulted in a departure from the conventional way of meeting the costs of accommodation. Income-related participation has been replaced by a fixed-rate payment corresponding to the accommodation costs. The choice of leisure activities is left to the discretion of the persons concerned who thus learn to organize their free time and manage their own budget. Since the transfer of responsibility for social assistance from 1 January 1984, this rationalization of the administrative procedure has been left to the discretion of the departmental authorities.

Even the underlying concept of homes for the disabled is changing. There has been a movement away from conventional communal units in the direction of semi-communal living conditions (in flats) for small groups of people, or more or less self-sufficient bed-sitters for those who wish to live independently. The same approach has been adopted in the renting of flats or bed-sitters to mentally handicapped adults, with the provision of some degree of attendant services.

Difficulties encountered and current lines of development

Adaptation of the institutional structure to meet current needs
The French institutional structure for the accommodation of disabled persons was built up during the 1950s and 1960s to cater mainly for disabled children. It now has surplus capacity for this purpose, and some of this will have to be converted to meet the requirements of disabled adults, where there is today a very substantial need. This redeployment of resources raises a number of problems, however, mainly owing to:

— the unsatisfactory geographical distribution of these establishments (the clearly marked imbalance favours *départements* in the south of France at the expense of those in the east);

— the unsuitability of the establishments (many institutions for disabled children were not designed for access by persons of reduced mobility);

— the first generation of specialist buildings being located away from urban centres, which is in flat contradiction of the current policy of social integration.

What is needed now is a balanced development of institutions for disabled adults over the whole of France, so as to overcome the constraints of their current unsatisfactory distribution. This will necessitate regional and on occasion national planning, involving also reconversion at the local level, with an unsettling effect on the staff employed in these unsuitable establishments.

Development of social and professional integration
In spite of the efforts that have been made, disabled persons in France are still accommodated very largely on an institutional basis. The change of approach that has emerged will now have to be maintained against the background of serious economic and budgetary stringency and the decentralization initiated in 1982. As it affects disabled persons, the Act on the Transfer of Competence of 22 July 1983 has made the *départements* responsible for measures relating to the accommodation of the disabled (with the exception of the accommodation of the severely disabled in specialist establishments) and for encouraging their continued residence at home.

Assessment of disability
The 1975 Act makes no reference to an overall assessment of a person's disability. It merely refers to a permanent incapacity at least

101

equivalent to a percentage laid down by decree. The Decree of 16 December 1975 lays down that use shall be made of the disability scale applicable to veterans when assessing this permanent incapacity. The veteran's scale is, however, essentially a measurement of deficiencies. Furthermore, it is incomplete in that it takes no account of certain disabling conditions such as psychological disorders or mental deficiency, and congenital or metabolic diseases in children that give rise to a chronic and disabling condition. It will therefore be necessary to combine the deficiency measurement provided by the veteran's scale with other parameters set out in the WHO *International classification of impairments, disabilities, and handicaps,* namely the resulting incapacity and the social or professional disadvantages in the environment resulting from the deficiency or the handicap. These questions are at present under active consideration.

Future developments
The integration of disabled persons into academic, professional and social life is a significant indicator of the way in which a society accepts and deals with differences from the norm. The changes of attitude and the measures adopted in France during the past 10 years make it clear that the aim for the future must be a progressive renunciation of conventional methods with their emphasis on the institutional approach. This will involve a close and flexible cooperation between specialists in the field of disability and communities of the healthy, and a greater readiness on both sides for contact between the national community and the specialist institutions.

German Democratic Republic

General Principles

The care and responsibility assumed by the State for the complete integration of disabled citizens into socialist society is a reflection of the humanitarian nature of the socialist order. Ever since its foundation in 1949, the German Democratic Republic has given particular priority to this task. One of the particular aims of social policy in the German Democratic Republic is to assist citizens who are physically or mentally handicapped without any reservations whatever.

The basic aim of the sociopolitical activities on behalf of disabled citizens, as laid out in the programme of the Socialist Unity Party, is to promote the integration of disabled citizens into social life, mainly by providing suitable educational and work opportunities and by comprehensive rehabilitation measures.

The Constitution of the German Democratic Republic sets out the principle that the rights enjoyed by all healthy citizens of the German Democratic Republic shall also apply, without restriction, to any citizen suffering from a physical or mental handicap. This applies in particular to the right to work and the right to education, accommodation and development of the personality. This principle, enshrined in the Constitution, has become a social reality. It is a direct instruction to all state organs, undertakings and social organizations to initiate and carry through all activities necessary for the full integration of disabled citizens into social life. This is to be achieved in particular by the full utilization of all means of medical and professional rehabilitation as well as by an optimal arrangement of living and rehabilitation conditions.

The equality of disabled and healthy citizens before the law provides an essential guarantee that disabled citizens can participate actively in the life of society, thus ensuring to the full their fundamental human right to the development of their personality.

103

The Constitution is implemented in detail and supplemented by a wide range of special legal texts relating to the care and rehabilitation of the disabled. These legal texts cover the essential components of rehabilitation, namely the medical, educational, professional and social aspects. Taken as a whole, they form an important part of the health legislation of the German Democratic Republic. They provide official organizations, undertakings and services responsible for the care and rehabilitation of the disabled, with mandatory guidance on how to interpret their responsibility in the various fields of rehabilitation. They require the harmonized and coordinated cooperation of all institutions to ensure that full use is made of the available facilities and resources in the achievement of optimal results in the interests of disabled citizens.

The Constitution and the special legal texts provide the basis for the competent authorities to lay down special regulations in favour of disabled persons resident within their jurisdiction. The Ministry of Health has a key role to play here, since it is responsible for the uniform implementation of rehabilitation measures. At the same time, it coordinates the preparation and implementation of these measures with other central organs of the State, such as the Ministry of Education, the State Secretariat for Labour and Wages, the State Secretariat for Professional Education, the Ministry of Building and the Ministry of Transport. The Ministry of Health is responsible for ensuring that all the different rehabilitation measures are mutually harmonized and supplement each other. It is also responsible for preparing the necessary legislative measures. State rehabilitation commissions have been set up to operate in the different regions, and they are attached to divisions of the health and social services of regional and district councils. These commissions are advisory organs of the councils and are also empowered, in the interests of disabled citizens, to take decisions in various fields of rehabilitation for which they have been made responsible under the legislation. Special working groups have been set up to take over selected tasks (such as the responsibility for disabled children and young persons).

State organs are empowered to take decisions both of a general nature (such as those relating to the construction of suitable dwellings for the disabled), and also at the individual level (such as providing financial support for the procurement of consumer goods in the technical field and for the provision of technical aids, and assistance with rents).

Coordination mechanisms

The responsibility of the State for the care of the disabled is fully integrated with the activities of social organizations. This applies in

104

particular to the Free Trade Union Federation and its social insurance institution for workers and salaried employees. This is an important element in the trade union representation of workers' interests, providing material and financial resources within the framework of a compulsory and voluntary insurance system, thus ensuring the constitutional right of workers, pensioners and members of their families to material security during illness, in the case of accidents at work, during pregnancy, in the case of disability and in old age, and for surviving family members.

The Association for the Blind and Visually Disabled and the Association for the Deaf (and those with seriously impaired hearing) also have an important place among responsible organizations in the German Democratic Republic. They stand ready to assist disabled citizens in word and in deed and they participate actively in organizing the care of the disabled. This applies to all aspects of rehabilitation for these specific groups. Some of the other social organizations in this field are the Gymnastics and Sports Association, which does particularly important work through the Association for Disabled Sport, and the Red Cross, which assists disabled persons with medical rehabilitation. These social organizations maintain regular contact with state organs.

Mention should also be made of the National Rehabilitation Society, which consists of various sections and working groups, and elaborates scientific principles in support of official activities to promote the care of the disabled.

Methodology — Types of Legislative Approach to the Equality Concept

Since the foundation of the German Democratic Republic, special legislation has been passed specifying the content and orientation of medical, educational, professional and social rehabilitation. A number of general regulations are also applicable to all groups of disabled persons, harmonizing the different aspects of rehabilitation.

One of the general legal texts is the Labour Code of 16 June 1977 (*Gesetzblatt I*, No. 18, p. 185) which, in conjunction with the Constitution, guarantees all disabled citizens the right to work. This right to work is implemented by the obligation on enterprises, imposed in a special legal regulation supplementing the Labour Code, to reserve a specified proportion of vacancies for disabled citizens. This obligation goes further in requiring enterprises to provide more sheltered workplaces and to extend systematically the opportunities for disabled citizens to work in a protected environment. Workshops with favourable conditions are provided for rehabilitated persons in the health and social services, in administrative divisions or individual workplaces in industry, in agriculture and in other sectors.

The employment of disabled workers may only be terminated under very restricted conditions, so that disabled workers enjoy a large measure of protection against dismissal (Article 59 of the Labour Code). Such persons must be regularly examined by the industrial medical service, in order to determine how far they are capable of meeting the requirements of their work in the light of their disability. If they are not fit to do so, they must be transferred to other work appropriate to their actual physical capacity.

Another fundamental regulation, laying down the principal tasks of state organs in regard to the care and rehabilitation of the disabled, is the recent law dealing with local elected bodies and their executive organs in the German Democratic Republic of 4 July 1985 (*Gesetzblatt*, No. 18, p. 213). This law expressly spells out the responsibility of elected organs of the people in regions and districts for promoting the active participation of disabled citizens in social and professional life (Articles 37 and 55).

The Order of the Council of Ministers of 29 July 1976 on further improving the social support of disabled and severely disabled citizens (*Gesetzblatt*, No. 33, p. 411) occupies an important place in the category of basic regulations on rehabilitation. This Order places particular emphasis on the concern of the socialist State that appropriate social measures should be taken to permit the progressively greater participation of disabled and severely disabled citizens and their families in social life, and to provide for them a special degree of care. The content of the Order pays particular attention to the care, promotion, education and training of disabled children and young persons and to the complex questions involved in professional rehabilitation.

The responsibility of the authorities extends also to the provision of suitable accommodation and far-reaching measures of social support and assistance.

Review of the Present State of National Legislation

The legislation on the aims of medical rehabilitation has been considerably extended and updated in recent years. Two characteristic features of these regulations may be emphasized.

1. The aim of all medical rehabilitation is, as far as possible, to restore a person's health and to restrict the adverse consequences of a disease or accident.

106

2. Great emphasis is placed on prophylactic measures. The aim here is to detect as early as possible the risk of injury to health and to initiate measures to prevent any adverse consequences. This includes not only immediate medical treatment in the early stage of a disease, but also regular preventive and monitoring studies. Prophylaxis occupies a very important place in socialist health policy, the aims of which extend well beyond medical rehabilitation.

In the German Democratic Republic, prophylactic health protection has been systematically extended in recent years, covering in particular the protection of the health of mothers, children and young persons. A special legal regulation (the Order of 11 April 1979 on the health inspection of children and young persons, *Gesetzblatt I*, No. 12, p. 91) lays down the requirement for regular group and individual examinations in schools, kindergartens and crèches, specifies the medical and social aspects of primary care in permanent or temporary medical centres, imposes the requirement for regular protective vaccinations, and prescribes continuing dental care and periodic evaluation of the health and growth of children and young persons.

Depending on the degree and extent of their disability, disabled children are catered for in networks of medical centres, where they are cared for by experienced paediatricians. Educational and professional questions, which are important for the development of the personality of the child or young person, play an important part in this aspect of the care of the disabled, which in turn forms part of the complex rehabilitation process. Special schools are provided for disabled children of school age, where they receive an education fully equivalent to that of normal children and young persons. The parents of disabled children are given advice on the choice of a profession, in conformity with the child's wishes and interests and with the nature and extent of the disability.

The aims and content of medical rehabilitation are based on the principle that the nature and extent of the disability require different types of treatment; this is taken into account in the relevant regulations. For example, a regulation issued by the Minister of Health some years ago specifies the health service institutions in which the different rehabilitation phases are to be carried out. Everything shall be done to extend rehabilitation activities, where possible, to a sufficient extent to enable the average disabled person to live his or her life without outside help. In order to understand clearly the complex nature of rehabilitation, one can look, for example, at the importance for the disabled of eliminating physical impediments — a problem that representatives of the building industry in the German Democratic Republic are proving progressively more successful at solving.

Special rehabilitation measures apply to the blind. A distinction is made here between blindness occurring at an advanced age and congenital blindness. All citizens suffering from blindness can, in general, enjoy the advantages of elementary rehabilitation courses for the blind. These courses last about three months and are available free of charge. They cover professional guidance, taking into account the individual capabilities and wishes of blind persons, their ability to read and write (in Braille), the building up of orientation capacity and development in the direction of maximum independence. Further aspects studied are familiarization with and the use of specific working, learning and other aids, and the ability to put leisure to good use in cultural and sporting activities. These measures are also covered in a special regulation, issued by the Minister of Health as early as May 1969.

Education and vocational training
The strict implementation of prophylactic measures has led to the early detection of disabled children and young persons. This is the basis for planned educational measures that distinguish between children who are suitable for school education and those who are not. Special schools are available for the former category, while the latter attend day centres, weekly attendance centres or homes in which they are taught elementary facts, again with the aim of achieving as great a degree of independence as possible.

Particular attention is paid in the German Democratic Republic to the choice of profession by young persons suffering from a physical or mental handicap, a choice that takes into account both the nature and extent of the disability and the wishes and interests of the person concerned. To facilitate the choice of a future profession, details of the nature of various professional activities are circulated in schools to enable disabled young persons to arrive at a correct decision in a matter of such critical importance for their future life. This decision is further facilitated not only by the provision of information on a wide range of selected professional activities but also by the existence of a whole series of training establishments, in particular rehabilitation centres for professional training. At the same time, firms are required to provide adequate numbers of training vacancies for persons suffering from physical or mental handicaps. A special regulation provides that disabled young persons who have completed their school career are given priority over their healthy contemporaries when applying for training vacancies in firms. This applies, in

108

particular, to young persons with visual or hearing defects or to the physically disabled. Further support is given to disabled youngsters in exempting them from particular training curricula for which they do not have the necessary health requirements. This in no way restricts the general aim of imparting to disabled young persons the necessary training to enable them to do satisfactory work in their chosen profession, thus making a substantial contribution to the development of their personality.

Working life and professional rehabilitation

In the case of persons already exercising a profession who have become disabled as a result of illness or accident, rehabilitation measures are aimed at ensuring their re-establishment in their profession as soon as possible. The rehabilitation commissions attached to the health and social services in regional and district councils play their part in this complex rehabilitation work. In addition, rehabilitation commissions are set up in enterprises in order to provide further support for the State's cardinal responsibility for the important humanitarian task of rehabilitation. One of their functions is to watch over the professional rehabilitation of disabled adults, primarily by ensuring that they perform a type of work to suit their health and capacity, and by providing medically relevant rehabilitation measures for workers whose health and capacity have been adversely affected by chronic disease or the effects of a serious accident.

Industrial medical officers play an active part in the work of rehabilitation commissions, submitting special proposals for medical care such as attendance at medical centres, courses of treatment, occupational therapy and physiotherapy. Enterprise rehabilitation commissions have another obligatory task that they have been able to perform very successfully, namely promoting sympathy and understanding for disabled workers among their healthy colleagues, and establishing the basis for their incorporation into the work collective. They are also concerned with the living conditions of disabled workers, assisting them to obtain suitable accommodation and ensuring that they obtain the financial benefits to which they are legally entitled.

If the disabled worker is no longer able to continue work in his or her previous profession, it is the responsibility both of rehabilitation commissions in regional and district councils as well as of enterprise rehabilitation commissions to take steps to ensure that he or she is in a position to undertake other professional activities. Relevant proposals are made for suitable training or upgrading.

Social rehabilitation

In the German Democratic Republic, the principle has been put into practice that, in addition to medical, educational and professional rehabilitation, social rehabilitation is of critical importance for re-integration into society and, in consequence, for the development of the personality of the disabled person. Great emphasis is placed on social rehabilitation measures aimed at ensuring that the disabled citizen has adequate mobility. Vehicles for the disabled are therefore available and facilities are provided such as ramps in public buildings, in dwellings, in commercial premises and on pavement kerbs. This category of assistance also includes unimpeded access to public transport and the systematic expansion of facilities to enable disabled persons to travel with their wheelchairs on buses, trams and trains.

Satisfactory living conditions are indispensable for successful social rehabilitation. In the German Democratic Republic, suitable dwellings have been built specially for disabled persons who are confined to a wheelchair. The guiding principle is that disabled persons should enjoy free access to all parts of the dwelling, in particular bathrooms and toilets. The disabled are also entitled to rent relief within the social rehabilitation system, and the costs of heating, domestic hot water and other services may be met by the competent authorities. At the same time, a wide range of useful services is available to disabled persons, such as laundry, the cleaning of carpets and curtains, the repair of domestic appliances, window cleaning, furniture cleaning and domestic help. Welfare workers can ac-company disabled persons to the doctor if they so desire, provide assistance in completing documents, in booking holidays and in obtaining tickets for travel. The disabled are given priority in the allocation of telephones to facilitate communication with others.

An aspect of fundamental importance is the provision of the technical aids on which the disabled person depends day in and day out. Industry is being progressively adapted to provide these aids in the German Democratic Republic. Entitled persons suffering from severe physical handicaps are provided free of charge, by the social insurance service, with a mechanically operated invalid vehicle or an electrically operated folding chair, and all repair charges on these vehicles are taken care of. Workers who wish to purchase their own car, instead of a mechanically operated invalid vehicle, are entitled to an appropriate allowance for the necessary modification of the car.

Holidays play a very important part in social rehabilitation. The disabled are entitled to special holiday facilities in the German Democratic Republic, which have the great advantage of providing not only recreation but also further medical rehabilitation. Special holiday vacancies are available for disabled children, for example on the Baltic Sea and in the mountains.

Communication in all its aspects is an essential component of the successful social integration of disabled citizens. Cultural activities for the disabled are also encouraged, for example by means of special music clubs in cultural centres. Particular efforts are made to ensure that the disabled are brought into contact with normal persons, and this promotes a sympathetic attitude to the disabled on the part of the healthy population. Readiness to help, courtesy and attention are to an increasing extent the characteristic features of the behaviour of the population as a whole to the physically or mentally handicapped. It is a great help in this connection if the average healthy person is aware of what can be done to help the disabled, what they need and to what extent they would like to have active assistance.

Sport, recreation and leisure — all important factors in the life of a healthy person — are of critical importance in the context of social rehabilitation activities. The competent authorities in the German Democratic Republic are required, in conjunction with social organizations such as the Gymnastics and Sports Association, to provide the necessary material conditions for the disabled to perform sporting activities and to organize their leisure time so as to enhance the quality of life. At the same time, a patronizing attitude has to be avoided at all costs. The aim of a health policy is to provide assistance and support, the ultimate intention being always to enable the disabled to achieve a large measure of independence, to make their own decisions and to assume responsibility for running their own lives.

Systems of income support

The general principle applies under social insurance legislation that disabled persons are entitled to free medical care for the whole period of treatment for sickness or the results of an accident. Disabled persons are not required to pay the sometimes substantial costs of medical rehabilitation. The medical care they receive is governed only by the state of medical knowledge and the available health service facilities. The medicines required for their treatment are also provided free of charge.

The disabled are also entitled to financial payments (sickness benefit or disability pension) in accordance with the Social Insurance Order. Sickness benefit is payable from the first day of illness or from the date of the accident. It amounts initially to 90% of the working wage, being recalculated on a different basis after a lapse of six weeks, when it amounts on average to 70% or more. Sickness benefit is payable for a period of 78 weeks. After this, if the effects of the disease are still apparent, the disability procedure is initiated, the principle being that the disabled worker, if unable to return to work, receives a disability pension based on the number of working years and the mean wage received. A disability pension is also payable to disabled persons from the age of 18 onwards if, as a result of injury, they are not entitled to claim a disability pension on the basis of previous work. The Social Insurance Order has been updated several times. The most recent version dates from 17 November 1977 (*Gesetzblatt I*, No. 35, p. 373).

In addition to free medical care and free medicines, disabled persons are also entitled in principle to the free provision of prostheses, orthotic devices, orthopaedic footwear and other aids. During 1981 the social insurance service paid more than M 31 million (US $16.5 million) for orthopaedic footwear alone, which covered the provision of 245 000 pairs of fitted orthopaedic shoes.

In addition to the above benefits, social insurance payments also cover spectacles, contact lenses and magnifying glasses. Visual aids with special glasses, such as cataract lenses and contact lenses, are provided for persons with highly defective vision. The costs are again borne in full by the social insurance service — they amounted in 1981 to over M 127 million (US $68 million) for visual aids alone.

Persons with defective hearing receive special assistance in the form of hearing aids, which cost the social insurance service M 16 million (US $8.5 million) during 1981. The persons concerned were not required to pay anything for their hearing aids. Any repair costs are charged to the social insurance service, which also provides batteries and battery-charging equipment. Deaf persons have the assistance of special interpreters, who are trained both in speech and sign languages and are very often closely trusted by the deaf since they assist in clarifying many questions in connection with medical, educational, professional or social rehabilitation.

The social insurance service makes a wide range of financial payments to special groups of disabled persons. In addition to disability pensions, these include expenses incurred for medical care, the amount being governed by the level of care required. Payment is made in four categories. Special care allowances are paid for such seriously disabled persons as, for example, paraplegics with a transverse lesion of the spinal cord or persons suffering from multiple disability.

Further financial benefits for the disabled
In addition to statutory social insurance payments, disabled and severely disabled persons are entitled to a number of other

concessions, such as a tax rebate on earned income. Public transport fares are substantially reduced and rebates are available on telephone charges. If disabled persons require the use of a car and are physically and mentally capable of driving, they are exempted from payment of a vehicle licence fee or pay a substantially reduced fee and are entitled to a grant for the purchase of the car. Disabled persons are also entitled to lump-sum assistance payments (for example, for the purchase of furniture or the repair of accommodation) among many other forms of assistance.

Evaluation of Progress in National Legislation

Rehabilitation activities in the German Democratic Republic have already made great progress. Current efforts are directed at further coordinating the various resources and facilities available, and establishing closer contact between them to ensure that rehabilitation activities have the optimal impact on the disabled. This applies both to the activities of rehabilitation establishments and rehabilitation commissions in the health and social services attached to regional and district councils, and of enterprise rehabilitation commissions, and also to the further extension of sociopolitical measures in favour of the disabled, with the aim of intensifying and reinforcing the progress made in the rehabilitation field.

Federal Republic of Germany[a]

General Principles

Under the Constitution, the Federal Government has a social obligation to assist all its citizens to take their place in professional life and society. Efforts to integrate the disabled in professional life and society are particularly necessary in the present period of economic and financial stringency. The concept of a social right to assistance is reflected in Article 10 of the First Book of the Social Code, which states that any person suffering from a physical, mental or emotional disability or exposed to the risk of such a disability shall be entitled to the help that she or he needs in order to:

— avert, eliminate, improve, prevent any deterioration in or mitigate the consequences of such a disability;

— guarantee him or her a place in society, in particular in a work environment appropriate to his or her inclinations and capabilities.

This form of social right cannot be the responsibility of a single institution within the articulated social service system of the Federal Republic of Germany. It is incumbent on the whole community and in particular the social service institutions to provide every disabled person or those threatened with disability with the aid and services they require to achieve the aims set out in this chapter.

---

[a] This country contribution is based on a report by the Federal Government on the present state of the disabled and on rehabilitation measures (document 10/1233, 4 April 1984).

National Involvement in International Action

The celebration of the International Year of Disabled Persons in 1981 and the various related activities have meant that, not only in official circles but in many fields of social life, the population as a whole has learnt to concern itself more than before with the special problems and needs of their disabled fellow citizens. This has led to a very much greater awareness and understanding of the problems of the disabled. These changes have been occurring not only in the Federal Republic of Germany, but in a similar fashion in other countries as well. An international exchange of experience and views is therefore desirable and indeed essential not only at government level, but also between associations of the disabled and other bodies who are active in the field. In addition to a large number of bilateral contacts with other countries, the Federal Republic of Germany supports the great efforts made by international organizations to improve the situation of the disabled. As part of the European Community's social integration programme for the disabled, approved in December 1981, the Federal Republic of Germany has set up two district projects (in Berlin (West) and in Gelsenkirchen). (For further details about this programme, see those mentioned under the Belgian contribution, pp. 33–37.) The Council of Europe adopted a resolution in 1984 on a coherent policy for the rehabilitation of the disabled, in which previous pertinent resolutions of this body are summarized, revised and brought up to date. The General Conference of the International Labour Organisation adopted Convention 159 on the Vocational Rehabilitation and Employment of the Disabled in 1983. The Federal Republic of Germany will be actively participating in the implementation throughout the world of the concept of the full partnership and equality of all handicapped persons, within the framework of the United Nations World Programme of Action concerning disabled persons and the Decade of Disabled Persons 1983–1992.

Methodology — Types of Legislative Approach to the Equality Concept

Assistance and benefits aimed at the integration of the disabled and the potentially disabled into the work environment and society necessitate an appropriate legislative background. A uniform but highly differentiated system of social and other regulations has been built up in recent years, including in particular the Rehabilitation–Adaptation Act, the Severely Disabled Act and the Federal Social

116

Assistance Act, as well as a wide range of supplementary provisions in other acts and orders. These laws are based on the idea that intervention must begin as early as possible. This approach is reflected in the priority given to rehabilitation over disability pensions in Article 7 of the Rehabilitation–Adaptation Act, and also forms the basis of the formulation in Article 10 of the First Book of the Social Code. The principle should be to make every effort to reduce to a minimum the scope and effects of the disability, in accordance with the potential and needs of the individual case, and as far as possible not to provide compensation for effects that can be avoided.

Preventive care, the treatment of acute cases and medical rehabilitation share the same aims and require similar measures. That is why the list of services in Article 10 of the Rehabilitation–Adaptation Act and also in Article 29, paragraph 1, No. 1, of the First Book of the Social Code are broadly equivalent to the assistance provided to the sick in the statutory sickness insurance system. All those responsible for providing medical services — not only the sickness insurance system, but also pension and accident insurance and the services responsible for social compensation and social aid — are also responsible for medical rehabilitation. A line of demarcation can thus only rarely be drawn between the services to be rendered, but the Rehabilitation–Adaptation Act does indicate various ways of dealing with disputes over competence among the relevant authorities.

Review of the Present State of National Legislation

The integration into the work environment and society of the disabled and the potentially disabled is the main aim of rehabilitation. Financial benefits and social assistance form the central element in the rehabilitation process. It is however essential, in the interests of a far-reaching and effective integration into society, that these benefits and forms of assistance should be supplemented by a disability-oriented rearrangement of the conditions of life to which the disabled are exposed and that they have to master, for example, in relation to transport or communication with others, and by the necessary readiness on the part both of the disabled themselves and of society to do everything possible to achieve their integration.

For most disabled persons their own social environment, in particular their families and friends, provides the best basis and form of assistance for their integration into society. One of the principal aims of the comprehensive rehabilitation process must therefore be to emphasize the importance of retaining and developing the existing social environment. Provided that effective assistance, including the necessary care, nursing and services, is available on an outpatient basis, the existing social environment gives the disabled the opportunity of adapting their own conditions of life, independently and under their own responsibility. In many cases, on the other hand, assistance with integration can only be rendered by admission to an institution. Care should be taken in these cases to ensure that the existing social environment is still retained, as far as possible, in an adapted form, for example, by sufficiently frequent visits to the home and family.

Elimination of discrimination or social prejudice

Whether or not the disabled are able to integrate into society depends to a large extent on the attitudes and behaviour of the non-disabled. Activities in connection with the International Year of Disabled Persons successfully increased people's awareness, and helped to break down their prejudices against the disabled and to foster their understanding and readiness to meet the needs of their disabled fellow citizens. Carefully planned publicity campaigns, including information on the types, causes and effects of different disabilities, must continue. This task is essentially one for the media, although the Federal Government will also continue by all possible means, such as the issue of suitable pamphlets and brochures, to inform and educate public opinion. The Government believes, however, that the integration of the disabled into society can only be achieved if the circulation of such information is supplemented by direct contacts between the disabled and the non-disabled. The prospects for the full participation of the disabled in the life of the community will be greatly improved if, as far as possible, no distinction is made between the disabled and the non-disabled in education, training and subsequent professional activity.

Social reintegration and full participation

The Federal Government regards the complete integration into society of the disabled and the potentially disabled as the aim of all rehabilitation measures and other forms of assistance. Assistance towards integration into society consists of various forms of benefit and assistance, institutions and services. It is important to bear in mind, however, that integration is not only a matter of social payments.

Care, medical rehabilitation, technical aids

Effective medical rehabilitation is only possible if an adequate number of suitable institutions is available. Special treatment centres

118

have adequate to excess capacity, but the capacity is limited in rehabilitation wards in seriously overloaded hospitals, in rehabilitation clinics associated with large hospitals (such as university hospitals) and in rehabilitation centres for special groups of disability. The principle of outpatient treatment where possible, hospitalization where necessary, applies to the field of medical rehabilitation also. This principle can only be implemented, however, if more special rehabilitation centres are made available in the vicinity of residential areas.

The stringent financial situation has meant, however, that in recent years savings have had to be made in the field of medical rehabilitation also. Nevertheless, any disabled person can still call on the medical assistance required to eliminate or mitigate his or her physical handicap. The principle of rehabilitation before pension has at the same time continued to be applied to approved medical rehabilitation measures.

Restrictions on benefits for medical rehabilitation came into force with effect from 1982, relating mainly to the frequency with which rehabilitation measures may be carried out. These restrictions were intended to enable the rehabilitation authorities to continue providing rehabilitation benefits in the future by restricting their expenditure in the present. In fact, the number of applications for medical rehabilitation measures fell unexpectedly too. The main reason for this reduction — apart from the changes in the regulations — has been the deterioration in the economy and in the labour situation. As in the case of previous recessions, it has to be assumed that many disabled persons in need of rehabilitation have failed to submit justified applications for treatment as a result of anxiety that such treatment would involve the loss of their job.

The effective implementation of medical rehabilitation measures is not solely a matter of the entitlement to benefit and the availability of suitable institutions; a proper procedure is also required. The obligation laid on the individual services responsible for rehabilitation in Article 5 of the Rehabilitation–Adaptation Act to cooperate closely in the interests of the rapid and lasting integration of the disabled has been accepted by all the rehabilitation authorities in principle, although there is room in practice for considerable improvement, especially in regard to feeding back the results of rehabilitation measures to other services. The Federal Government fully supports the efforts of those concerned — sickness insurance offices, associations of health insurance medical offices, and hospitals — to devise a practical notification procedure to ensure that rehabilitation measures can be initiated in all cases in good time.

The range of appliances paid for by the particular rehabilitation institutions depends on their terms of reference. The most comprehensive benefits are available from the social assistance service, which is prepared to recognize appliances that promote social integration by compensating for the deficiencies of disabled persons. A comprehensive list of medicines and appliances is available to disabled persons under the statutory sickness insurance system. The advisory services of the rehabilitation institutions, in particular the sickness insurance offices, are available to assist in the choice of appliance suitable for the individual. Under social compensation legislation (relating to the war victims insurance and pensions insurance institutions), appliances are provided by orthopaedic supply centres, staffed by qualified personnel with medical officers in attendance.

Clothing can be a particular problem for the disabled. To meet the widespread practical demand for a general picture of what clothing is available, many years of research and testing have been summarized in a book subsidized by the Federal Ministry for Youth, Family Affairs and Health. Information on the choice of material, means of clothing, and other topics is provided, together with illustrations, section drawings and easily understandable explanatory notes. The book also contains instructions and patterns for the disabled to make and alter their own clothes, and easy ways to put on and take off clothing in the case of different forms of disability.

Housing and physical environment
Within its restricted competence in this field, the Federal Government is concerned to improve the accommodation conditions of the disabled. After 10 years' experience with the planning standard *Dwellings for wheelchair users* (DIN 18025, Part I), a start has been made on its revision, to dispense with unnecessary regulations. Depending on the revision of other planning standards, this should simplify and render more concise the content of the standard, thus leaving more room for the building authority and the future owner to exercise their discretion.

Article 26 of the Second Housing Construction Act provides as a matter of urgency for assistance to be given to particularly disadvantaged groups of persons in the housing market, including the severely disabled. The *Land* administrations, which are responsible for the implementation of social housing construction, have agreed to spend federal funds exclusively on these groups of persons and to give them priority in the use of *Land* resources. This procedure has enabled about 23 000 dwellings and about 8000 vacancies in homes

120

to be provided for severely disabled persons between 1973 and 1982, using federal and *Land* resources.

When determining their income for the purposes of a housing allowance, the severely disabled with a reduction in their earning capacity of at least 80% are allowed a free basic amount of DM 2400 (US $1297). This concession is also available to severely disabled persons included in the family household, if they are in need of domestic care in the sense of Article 679, paragraph 3, sentence 1 of the Federal Social Assistance Act. This results in a monthly increase in the housing allowance of about DM 50 (US $27) in comparison with persons eligible for housing allowance without this free basic amount.

Certain other concessions were discontinued with effect from 1 March 1983 under the Supplementary Budget Act 1983: these concessions included the entitlement for severely disabled persons, with a loss of earning capacity of at least 80%, to be counted twice in respect of the maximum amounts for rent and charges, and the free basic amount of DM 1500 (US $811) yearly for severely disabled persons with a loss of earning capacity of 50–80%. Neither the general assumption that households, including a disabled person with a loss of earning capacity of at least 80%, incurred higher accommodation costs on average than other households as a result of the disability, nor the assumption that severely disabled persons with a loss of earning capacity of 50–80% had a particular demand for accommodation, had been confirmed.

Housing construction for the disabled was the subject of a competition organized in 1982 by the Minister of Planning, Building and Town Construction for the design of model dwellings for the disabled to promote their rehabilitation and integration. The results of this competition revealed some practical efforts to achieve service-built, well laid out and properly fitted buildings for the disabled. They have been included in a series of publications by the Federal Ministry and are used as a practical stimulus and an indication of the lines for future buildings.

A prerequisite for the integration of the disabled in society is the elimination of obstacles to mobility, particularly by improving access to public and other generally used buildings and installations. There appears to be increasing readiness on the part of the responsible authorities, in particular in many districts, to undertake the necessary structural alterations. The requirements of the disabled are also increasingly taken into account in the building design of technical colleges. In some cases older buildings have been modified, for example, by the incorporation of ramps and lifts capable of taking wheelchairs.

121

Communications and transport
Travelling involves certain difficulties for the disabled and the elderly. The German Federal Railways have adopted guidelines for the construction of rolling stock that facilitates the use of the railways by the disabled. These guidelines make particular reference to planning standards DIN 18024 and 18025. The needs of the disabled have also been taken into account as far as possible in the construction or modification of railway stations, in particular by improving entrances and exits, by the construction of ramps, lifts and escalators, and by the installation of information centres. Toilet facilities for the disabled have been opened on many large stations and more are planned. At stations regularly used by severely disabled persons, such as at spa resorts, the Federal Railways intend to provide assistance for entering trains in the form of mobile steps, ramps and hoisting equipment. Measures to assist the disabled are easier to incorporate in new projects than in existing installations, some of which date from the establishment of the *Land* railway system. Problems arise in particular as a result of the different platform heights and for this reason the Federal Railways have begun to standardize them.

Travelling by railway is a particular problem for wheelchair users as many commercially available wheelchairs do not fit in the entrances and corridors of railway carriages. The Federal Railways are therefore installing wider entry doors in new railway carriages as well as a modified entrance with a fourth folding step, in which the step heights are lower and the angle of the steps less steep. These modifications will also be introduced in some existing carriages requiring substantial improvements. The Federal Railways, in conjunction with the Rehabilitation Foundation in Heidelberg, have developed as an intermediate solution the Offenburg model of wheelchair, which is suitable for use on the railways. The Federal Railways pamphlet *Travel guide for disabled passengers* provides elderly and disabled passengers with comprehensive information on the use of this wheelchair model and with general information on how to plan and undertake journeys.

The severely disabled, in particular wheelchair users, should be able to travel on intercity trains, which now have larger carriages suitable for wheelchairs. These carriages have storage space for two wheelchairs, two rotating seats and a toilet that will admit normal wheelchairs. Each intercity train should have one carriage of this type.

Similar modifications are being made to local forms of public transport such as trams and metropolitan and underground railways, as well as to intercity buses and trolley buses. All these vehicles have seats reserved for the disabled. Some taxis are modified to enable them to carry disabled passengers.

Amendments to the rules governing the free transport of the severely disabled in local public transport were made in the Supplementary Budget Act 1984. These changes were made to take better account of the original purpose of the regulations, namely to compensate for the fact that the severely disabled were obliged to make use of local transport resources where others were able to walk. The free transport concession for the severely disabled was therefore discontinued with effect from 1 January 1984 on railway transport, with certain exceptions. In addition, with effect from 1 April 1984 the entitlement to free transport was limited to severely disabled persons whose ability to move in road transport was actually severely restricted. Those who were still entitled were required to pay an annual contribution of DM 120 (US $65) in the form of an annual stamp. These annual stamps are provided free to the blind, the completely disabled and severely disabled persons drawing unemployment assistance or living assistance allowances under the Federal Social Assistance Act or corresponding payments from the federal war victims pensions institution. Severely disabled persons who enjoyed the right to free public transport irrespective of their income prior to 1 October 1979 (in general those injured in the war and victims of Nazi persecution) are covered by a personal exemption clause. The new Order also means that the reduced resources available are concentrated where they can be used more effectively on behalf of the disabled and where they are most urgently needed. The free transport concession for a permanent attendant of a disabled person remains valid, both on the railway and in other forms of public transport, irrespective of whether the severely disabled person him/herself is required to obtain an annual stamp.

Since 1977, the Association of German Civil Air Fields has been implementing the *Guidelines on the construction of installations for the disabled on air fields,* based on planning standards DIN 18024 and 18025. Airports and airlines provide their passengers with information sheets on routes and installations suitable for the disabled and provide individual assistance. Boats on inland waterways can be officially recognized as specially suitable for the transport of the disabled, if the vessels comply with the special conditions laid down in a service instruction from the shipping supervisory authorities. Passenger ships for maritime transport are now designed to meet the needs of the disabled.

Disabled persons are permitted to drive vehicles provided that they are capable of handling these vehicles safely. They are therefore issued with a driving licence, if necessary under certain specified conditions. Driving licences for and the licensing of mechanically operated invalid vehicles are covered on a comprehensive basis in the Road Traffic Licensing Order.

The Federal Postal Service has taken various measures to mitigate the difficulties of disabled persons. The telephone service introduced special public telephone booths for wheelchair users in 1976, and has provided specially developed Vitaphon telephones for disabled persons since 1983. Persons suffering from particular serious physical disabilities or those in low income groups are charged concessionary fees and persons who are particularly dependent on the telephone receive additional free metered units. The Postal Service also provides special assistance and facilities for the blind and those with defective vision.

Professional rehabilitation

The main aim of any policy for the disabled is to enable each individual to achieve long-term reintegration into working life. In this way, he or she can contribute to the welfare of the community, and gain personal satisfaction and a more optimistic attitude to life, while at the same time earning enough to live as independently as possible. The integration of the disabled into working life is therefore a prerequisite for social integration as a whole. The cost of their professional rehabilitation is also thus covered by their contribution to economic productivity.

In view of the importance of achieving this aim, a comprehensive general policy has been developed and implemented in recent years jointly by the rehabilitation services, the federal authority and the *Land* administrations, to assist the integration of the disabled and persons exposed to the threat of a disability. Despite the economy measures necessary to balance the national budget, this general policy has achieved a high standard in professional rehabilitation.

The services responsible for professional rehabilitation are required to render all necessary assistance, under Article 11 of the Rehabilitation–Adaptation Act and the corresponding regulations, to retain, improve, achieve or restore the earning capacity of the disabled and to effect their long-term professional integration as far as possible. The assistance provided under these regulations is intended specifically to enable a disabled or potentially disabled person to obtain or retain employment, and may come in the form of technical aids for use at the workplace, the payment of benefits to assist in obtaining work, or the payment of an integration benefit to the employer.

The nature or severity of the handicap may in many cases necessitate more far-reaching rehabilitation measures, that is, not only

124

advice on the form of activity and trial working periods but also professional training. This is in fact the central element in professional rehabilitation. Priority should be given to measures that reintegrate the disabled into their previous work and social environment, not only on grounds of cost but also in view of the positive repercussions on reintegration into society. Reintegration measures within firms should therefore be given preference, wherever possible. Rehabilitation in special institutions, especially where the disabled person has to be admitted, is only advisable where the nature or severity of the handicap prevents training in a firm even with special assistance. The Federal Institute of Labour alone has enabled about 5000 disabled persons annually to undertake rehabilitation training in a firm, by means of training grants to employers.

Restrictive changes have been made in the statutory regulations governing professional rehabilitation since the Rehabilitation– Adaptation Act of 1974, cutting rehabilitation benefits and transitional allowances among other things. These changes in the legislation, in conjunction with the increased demand for and the increased number of vacancies available in rehabilitation institutions have involved a substantial increase in the activities of the Federal Institute of Labour in the field of professional rehabilitation. The fraction of the cost of professional rehabilitation training measures met by the Federal Institute rose from 35% in 1970 to 77% in 1980. The various other institutions responsible for professional rehabilitation are the pensions insurance, accident insurance and war victims pensions institutions. The sickness insurance institutions are concerned mainly with medical rehabilitation, but are also playing an increasing role in reintegrating disabled people into the work environment.

It has become clear that disabled people welcome the possibility of attending training courses to acquire a professional qualification, irrespective of the deterioration in the labour market and even to some extent of the problems of finding employment in spite of their disability. The number of persons undergoing rehabilitation who were unemployed before starting a professional training course increased from 69 564 in 1981 to 77 047 in 1982. In spite of the reduced level of transitional allowances, rehabilitation courses are particularly important for the unemployed as a means — often the only one — of securing (re)integration into the wage-earning world. Other measures to promote professional integration, especially if they are likely to assist in the search for employment, are equally important and may include allowances for travel, examinations, accommodation, education and to compensate for loss of earnings.

A countrywide network of firms operating as professional promotion centres, professional training centres and workshops for the disabled has been established in recent years, on the basis of plans agreed between the federal authority, the *Land* administrations and the insurance institutions responsible for rehabilitation. About 12 000 training vacancies are available on courses for adults in the 21 professional promotion centres and about 10 000 vacancies for the initial training of disabled young persons in the 33 professional training centres. When the most recent establishments have been completed, the requirement for such establishments will have been met; no further construction is planned.

In view of the virtual completion of the professional rehabilitation system in recent years, the picture in the foreseeable future will be mainly one of consolidation accompanied by qualitative improvement. Many of the insurance institutions responsible for professional rehabilitation have undertaken to ensure that the principles of economy and saving are applied in the professional rehabilitation establishments. By application of these costing principles, it should be possible in coming years to restrict the increases in the costs of rehabilitation measures to an acceptable level for the next budget, without prejudicing the quality of the rehabilitation measures or endangering the continued existence of individual rehabilitation establishments.

Progress has been made in the gradual reintegration of long-term patients by the official sickness insurance offices. Company sickness insurance offices, in particular, have been more successful in recent years in implementing integration measures, as a result of which insured persons after completing their intensive medical treatment have been able by stages to resume their employment. The weekly working period beings in such cases with a few hours — depending on the particular condition and the need for treatment — and is then gradually increased to the standard working period. This adaptation phase may take several months. Several integration models of this type already exist. Preference should be given in reintegration models to those that involve no pension disadvantages to the disabled person and as far as possible distribute the costs equally between the responsible services. The Federal Government has prepared a bill that provides a satisfactory solution to such cases as partial fitness for work.

Expert vocational counselling is particularly important at present in view of the difficult situation on the labour market and the need to take into account the individual capabilities and problems of each disabled or potentially disabled person. The Federal Institute of Labour therefore provides professional counselling for

126

about 100 000 disabled persons every year, about half of whom have educational problems, 17% are physically disabled and 10% are mentally retarded.

The efficient use of the measures available for professional rehabilitation has to be kept under constant review. The procedure for initiating the necessary rehabilitation measures could possibly be improved, as could compliance with the requirement for an overall plan. The early initiation and resulting effectiveness of rehabilitation measures could benefit in particular from:

— an increase in the number of notifications on disabled persons in accordance with Articles 368s and 372 of the State Insurance Order;

— greater efforts to improve cooperation among the different insurance institutions responsible for rehabilitation;

— a reduction in the waiting periods, for example, in the services responsible for medical and psychological expert examinations in the Federal Institute of Labour.

Greater cooperation among the rehabilitation establishments themselves could likewise result in a shortening of the waiting times before rehabilitation begins. It could also ensure that the rehabilitation establishments are made use of more continually and therefore more economically. In addition the training programmes at rehabilitation establishments must continually keep up with changing requirements, by means of greater cooperation with training centres in factories. For instance, the training available for professional rehabilitation must be adapted to changes in the labour market and in the demands of industry. At the same time, the accommodation, care and training structures of the rehabilitation establishments must always take into account existing requirements, such as the increasing demand for rehabilitation opportunities for the psychologically disabled.

The relatively high drop-out rate from retraining courses (a mean of 25–30%) is a matter of particular concern. This may underline the need for a more stringent selection procedure to consider the chances of "problem cases" successfully completing their professional rehabilitation. These difficult cases have a greater chance of success if their profession is chosen with care, their motivation is maintained and intensified, and full use is made of all means to achieve a successful outcome. More far-reaching studies are required and some have already begun to cast more light on the problems associated with dropping out of courses and to find possible ways of remedying the situation.

127

The final question is how to improve on the present procedure for easing the transition from professional training measures to professional activity. Some professional training courses do have a practical orientation, along the lines of the training link between rehabilitation establishments and factories, and some additional help is given during and after the professional training course. Although the success rate of previous years will be hard to maintain in view of the current difficulties on the labour market, the employment rate on completion of rehabilitation courses remains relatively high. According to Federal Institute of Labour statistics, about two thirds of those who have completed retraining courses are in permanent employment, 15–18 months later. As in the case of the initiation of rehabilitation measures, greater attention will have to be paid to the transition from rehabilitation courses to professional activity, since professional rehabilitation can only be regarded as successfully completed once the individual has been permanently integrated into the work environment.

Working life

The integration of the disabled and of the potentially disabled into a profession and into society is a complicated task, particularly in times of industrial and financial difficulty. The unemployment rate of the severely disabled very nearly doubled between 1980 and 1983, although this increase is reasonable given the rise in overall unemployment.

Apart from the Rehabilitation–Adaptation Act, the principal instrument for improving the opportunities of disabled persons on the labour market is the Severely Disabled Act. As a means of ensuring the employment of disabled persons covered by the Act, and of improving their individual opportunities to exercise their profession, the Act specifies that:

— all public and private employers must fill 6% of their vacancies with severely disabled persons, or make penalty payments for the unfilled vacancies;

— all severely disabled persons are protected against termination of employment on completion of their probation period;

— a representative is appointed to protect the interests of the severely disabled in the firm, particularly through special follow-up assistance measures and the creation of additional employment opportunities.

Although employers do fulfil their obligatory employment quota on average, compliance with this rule varies widely. Thus in 1983,

128

some DM 230 million (US $124 million) was paid as a penalty by three quarters of the employers who are bound by the employment quota. The other quarter employed far more than the minimum required. The penalty payments are used to fund special assistance measures in the workplace, as well as programmes that provide special assistance benefits during the recruitment and employment of the disabled.

The obligation to employ severely disabled persons applies also to the civil service. Article 47 of the Severely Disabled Act lays down special provisions and principles for the filling of civil service posts. This is intended to promote the recruitment and employment of the severely disabled and to ensure that a reasonable proportion of severely disabled persons occupy civil service posts. This statutory obligation is taken into account in the Civil Service Act by the provision that only a minimum standard of physical fitness may be required for the recruitment, appointment and promotion of severely disabled persons. Similar provisions are contained in the civil service legislation of the *Land* administrations.

A wide range of different forms of incentive and compensation is available to employers to encourage them to provide employment and training vacancies for the severely disabled. This includes assistance in establishing new work and training vacancies for the severely disabled, including part-time vacancies, in fitting out existing workplaces and training sites for the severely disabled, and in meeting any exceptional expenses that may arise as a result of the employment of a severely disabled person, (for example, providing a reader for a blind worker). One of the most obvious impediments to the recruitment of the severely disabled is the prejudice in the minds of employers about their capacity and willingness to work. Employers are also ignorant about the financial and technical assistance available and the legal consequences of taking them on. The main plans to reduce unemployment among the disabled are therefore a publicity campaign, detailed discussion of the improved assistance measures for the severely disabled in the labour market by officials of the labour offices, and intensification of the campaign to obtain employment for the severely disabled, especially during factory visits to small- and medium-size establishments; employers who have not yet fulfilled their obligatory employment quotas should be approached directly.

It has not always been entirely clear which persons are to be regarded as severely disabled under the Act. As a result of a thorough revision of existing criteria, the Federal Ministry for Labour and Social Order issued in November 1983 *Guidelines for medical expert examinations under the Social Compensation Act and the Severely Disabled Act.* These guidelines now provide all medical officers with clear and easily comprehensible guidelines for expert assessments.

Certain groups of disabled persons require special assistance in gaining employment: young persons without a professional qualification, women with little or no practical experience, and the mentally handicapped. Special measures will be introduced under the Severely Disabled Act for problem groups of this type.

People who are unable to enter the open labour market can find work in sheltered workshops. These establishments fulfil a double purpose. First, they permit the disabled to work within their capabilities and in general to achieve a certain measure of productive output. At the same time, these workshops provide the disabled with more assistance and care than is available in the normal professional environment and enable them to experience life in a community. In many cases, workshops are the only alternative to full-time residence in an institution. In recent years, a comprehensive network of workshops for the disabled has gradually been built up, but future years may see even larger intakes and the necessity for further expansion. The acceptance of the mentally handicapped is a particular problem in the workshops as well as in the open labour market. Since the workshops are intended in principle to accept all those whose employment in the open labour market cannot be envisaged, one of their tasks will be to ensure that they cater adequately for the mentally handicapped.

Further clarification is needed of the legal status of disabled persons employed in sheltered workshops, especially with regard to the application of the provisions of general labour legislation, for example, with regard to holidays, maternity protection, sick pay and rights of co-determination. Another problem is the remuneration of disabled persons employed in the workshops, the costs of which are borne by the social assistance institutions. The output of a workshop is governed by a large number of factors, such as the nature and severity of the disabilities and the working capacity of the employees, although it is also influenced by demand and the regional industrial structure. Furthermore, workshops cannot use all the profit earned to pay the disabled workers, but are often obliged to devote some of the profit to cover the costs of their additional care. The monthly pay of disabled workers in the workshops does not therefore enable them to support themselves without outside help. The social insurance of disabled persons employed in sheltered workshops has been clearly laid down since 1975 in the Social Insurance of the Handicapped Act. The basis for assessment of the pension contribution (70% of the mean insured remuneration during the previous year) should in normal cases provide a level of pension that will enable the disabled person on reaching pensionable age to be broadly independent of social assistance.

Education and vocational training

Every disabled person must have the opportunity to develop his or her individual learning capacity and indulge personal preferences. Even persons with serious mental disability should receive a reasonable measure of encouragement. One important task of education policy is therefore to contribute to providing the best possible preparation of disabled children and young persons for their professional and adult life and for a broadly independent mode of existence.

The social assistance budget makes available free of charge educational/therapeutic facilities in the preschool age, during schooling and in the form of practical and vocational training to disabled children and young persons, irrespective of their parents' income and ability to pay. It would be preferable, however, for these costs to be borne by the *Länder* as part of their educational programmes.

Since the 1960s, the Federal Republic of Germany has built up an efficient system of special schools for the disabled. Some 600 special kindergartens offer 17 000 places, while about 320 000 pupils attend about 2800 schools for the disabled. Almost 9000 disabled children have been specially prepared to attend school in about 500 special school kindergartens.

An increasingly critical attitude is being displayed towards special schools for the disabled. They are often regarded as a form of residual education with low chances of success, and as a cause of the isolation that reinforces the prejudices against the disabled. To implement the principle of as much special assistance as necessary and as much joint learning as possible, the federal authority and the *Länder* have supported projects on integrated schooling since the 1970s. The experience gained from these model experiments indicates that many disabled children and young persons can be very effectively educated in normal schools, provided that they receive additional special education from qualified staff, a reasonable amount of additional care, and suitable equipment for the disabled, and that the number of disabled children per class does not exceed a determined figure. Compensation for a disability through early individual care in the kindergarten and the primary school can often obviate the need for subsequent transfer to a special school. This requires however that all staff in normal schools should have a thorough grounding in special education practices and adequate motivation to deal effectively with the special problems of the disabled.

131

Integrated schooling and training are based on as much joint learning as possible, with only as much special assistance as is necessary right from the start. The other prerequisite for integrated education is that the equipment, space and staff provided must take into account the special situation and individual educational requirements of disabled and vulnerable children. The greatest progress in integration so far has been made with physically disabled pupils, while children with visual and hearing defects still present a number of unsolved problems, requiring a new approach. It remains to be seen how far the specific impediments of the disabled can be overcome by modifying curricula, learning and working techniques and instructional material, without lowering the standards required in normal schools. Social integration will require measures over and above the actual instruction given.

Where disabled children and young persons cannot receive the best possible assistance in existing normal schools, they will have to be catered for in special institutions, if necessary supplemented by special homes or day centres. The risk of social isolation can be overcome by cooperation with normal schools, if possible in the vicinity. The choice of a special institution must never be final; a return to a normal school or transfer to professional training can be facilitated by close cooperation between schools, the parental home and the different social and therapeutic services.

Model experiments have shown that a voluntary tenth school year for the disabled is of great help in the transfer from school education to professional training. It can help pupils obtain their school leaving certificate, and begin preparing for working life. The materials used must be appropriate to their particular disability, but also provide practice in overcoming their particular problems.

A professional qualification is vitally important for the disabled, not only for their professional but also for their personal development. A comprehensive, professional diagnosis of their suitability for a particular profession is indispensable, and should involve close cooperation between schools, teachers and parents, with vocational advice from the labour administration. With proper guidance, most pupils from special schools for the disabled are capable of successfully completing their training in recognized professional fields. When selecting the correct profession, it is important not only to arrive at a complete and differentiated assessment of the disabled person's present capacity, but also to estimate as thoroughly as possible the potential for development. On-the-job training in a firm often facilitates permanent employment in the same firm at the end of the training period. Unfortunately, the number of vacancies in firms is insufficient to guarantee all interested disabled persons an appropriate professional training course, but there are plans to expand this facility.

Special assistance is also provided for disabled persons in technical colleges. The General Act on Technical Colleges and the corresponding provisions of the *Land* regulations on technical colleges oblige such institutions to take into account the special requirements of disabled students. No disabled applicant or student should therefore be excluded from the technical college of his or her choice as a result of disability. This will necessitate both individual assistance measures, and an improvement in the counselling service and the technical college environment as a whole. The national Advisory Centre for Disabled University Applicants and Students has set up a comprehensive and up-to-date information system for disabled students. By sharing their experiences, disabled students have helped solve many of their own problems, such as difficulties with accommodation, taking advantage of the services available for the care of the disabled, problems over the central allocation of student places, examination regulations for disabled students, problems over students' grants, sign-language interpreters for those with hearing defects and reading services for those with visual defects, the support of student self-help groups, and improving the cooperation between student and professional advisory services.

Correspondence courses provide a further opportunity of education for those who are unable to attend educational centres in person. The disabled student can determine to a large extent the time spent on study, the place of study and the learning rate. Study counsellors in student centres can also deal more effectively with the special problems of disabled students and their integration into student activities and provide the necessary advice or care.

The need for education continues throughout life for the disabled in the same way as for the non-disabled. A wide range of further education opportunities are available for the disabled, often integrated with classes for the non-disabled. The general aim is not only to provide additional opportunities to acquire a professional qualification but also to prepare the disabled to cope with the prejudices of the non-disabled; and to develop joint further education opportunities for the disabled and the non-disabled, so as to familiarize each group with the problems of the other and stimulate their learning processes.

Sport and leisure
Sport for disabled persons is an effective means of helping them to live a full life. It is both a means of treatment and therapy and also in

the wider sense a form of recreation. The main aim of re-habilitation sport is to restore the health of the disabled, while recreational sport serves predominantly their reintegration into society. The Rehabilitation–Adaptation Act enables all institutions responsible for medical rehabilitation (sickness insurance, accident insurance, pensions insurance and war victims' insurance) to count sport for the disabled, in groups and under medical supervision, as a rehabilitation benefit. Under the Federal War Victims Act, injured persons are entitled to participate in gymnastics and other physical activities in order to restore and retain their physical fitness, irrespective of whether the particular type of sport is directly related to their rehabilitation. They may continue to participate for as long as they wish. In the field of sickness, accident and pensions insurance, on the other hand, participation is permitted under medical supervision and only for a limited period, usually six months. Under the Social Assistance Act, sport for the disabled, if prescribed by a doctor and carried out in groups under medical supervision, is a medical measure for the promotion of integration and is without any time limitation.

A very substantial increase has occurred during the past 50 years in sport for the disabled but the type of people participating has changed steadily. War victims, predominantly men, are giving way to more children and young people, whose participation tends to be covered for only a limited period of time. These changes are causing financial and organizational problems that have still to be solved.

Leisure hours and holidays are particularly important for the disabled in order to compensate for the absence of social contact in other fields of life. In 1981, the Federal Ministry for Youth, Family and Health published a pamphlet entitled *We are all part of one big family — spend your leisure with the disabled*. This pamphlet informs the disabled of facilities available for their leisure time, and includes accounts of how disabled people have taken advantage of them and mixed with non-disabled people at the same time. Family holiday centres have been designed, modified and improved in recent years to suit the needs of the disabled, and families with disabled members are given priority in them. Holiday guides are produced, containing information about hotels, inns, and other facilities with particular reference to the needs of the disabled.

In spite of these improvements problems still remain. Many travel agents fail to provide information on travel facilities or types of accommodation that meet the needs of the disabled; and the description of a hotel as "suitable for the disabled" is not based on uniform criteria. The Federal Government has asked all those concerned to make travel brochures clear and intelligible, to provide

134

rooms suitable for the disabled at as many holiday resorts as possible, and to make hotels and other forms of accommodation inside and outside the country more accessible to disabled persons. Serious problems arise with disabled persons who, as a result of the severity of their disability, are not capable of looking after themselves adequately. An insufficient range of holidays is available where they can find someone to look after them or the costs are not too high. Greater efforts will have to be made to get over these difficulties.

Information

A pivotal factor in the integration of disabled persons into society is to improve their knowledge of the possible forms of assistance available. Great emphasis is placed on this in the activities of disabled self-help organizations. The rehabilitation institutions have made substantial progress in providing information and advice and also in cooperating with each other. In addition to providing expert advice on rehabilitation, they have concentrated on the provision of psychosocial assistance. The rehabilitation institutions have to an increasing extent called on the assistance of the social services to overcome resistance to medical rehabilitation in the personal environment of the disabled and to support their complete reintegration. Advisory services will hold interviews in rehabilitation centres or discuss the problems in the disabled person's own home.

Local information centres staffed with qualified persons have an important part to play. This approach will be developed further in the future, in conjunction with further changes in the legislation on the disabled. The standard of information available will also be improved not only on the social payments to which the disabled are entitled but also on the relevant forms of technical assistance and practical facilities for the disabled. The production, sale and dissemination of material on the integration of the disabled will be supported by funds from the competent federal ministries. Grants will also be provided — mainly to self-help organizations — for the provision of literature to the disabled and their families, largely free of charge. It is particularly important that foreign parents with disabled children should receive full information and the existing series of guides will be continued.

Promotion of self-help groups

To promote the social integration of the disabled, grants are provided by the Federal Ministry for Youth, Family Affairs and Health to national associations for the disabled which are active at the federal level (the German Association for the Rehabilitation of the Disabled, the federal association Help for the Disabled and organizations for the

blind throughout the Federal Republic). A number of functions —
mainly seminars, conferences and courses, in general organized
by self-help organizations of the disabled — are also subsidized by
grants. Planned measures in this field cover a wide spectrum of
different types of disability. Particular emphasis is placed on training
with multipliers.

The social services, organizations for the disabled and self-help
groups play a particularly important role in medical rehabilitation,
part of it voluntary. Fruitful cooperation has been achieved over wide
areas between the rehabilitation authorities (in particular the sickness
insurance offices) and these organizations, which have made important contributions to the professional health care system particularly in overcoming chronic degenerative diseases. The involvement
of these groups should not be misunderstood as a shift of the burden
from the rehabilitation services to the individuals concerned and to
voluntary organizations; it rather constitutes a further development
of the rehabilitation concept.

Independent living
Two thirds of all disabled people are cared for by their families,
usually by their mothers, who are generally without adequate social
insurance and forced to give up their paid employment. Material
disadvantages include the need to pay for a dwelling suitable for a
disabled person or for special equipment. In addition, the demands
made on helpers frequently leave them little free time for social life
or attending public functions. Furthermore, the physical and psychological burden of nursing and care tends to increase with the age of the
disabled family member. Finally, families with a disabled member
are often exposed to an uncomprehending or indifferent environment.

These burdens are in sharp contrast to the important function of
the family not only to care for the disabled but also to promote their
integration into society. The family is vital for the development of
most disabled persons and it is thus preferable for them to be able to
live with their family, provided that the family is relieved of as many
of these burdens as possible. Efficient outpatient institutions and
services must be available, including social centres staffed with
district nurses, attendants for the care of the elderly, home helps,
municipal services and trained voluntary helpers. Financial assistance is vital and substantial nursing allowances are already made.
The insurance institutions have found places for the temporary accommodation of disabled persons, to enable their families to take
short holidays. This procedure benefits the disabled as well, since
they are trained in social behaviour and encouraged to move towards
greater self-sufficiency. The availability of such facilities should

136

therefore be extended. Part-time work is often the only possible form of professional activity for many parents of disabled children. The Federal Government supports the development of part-time work as a fully valid form of work under labour legislation.

Youth work with the disabled is another activity aimed at relieving families with disabled members. The Federal Youth Plan is a means of promoting the work of central and interregional institutions concerned with the education and care of disabled children and young persons. In cooperation with the services responsible for helping the young, the Federal Government intends, by means of a special form of assistance, to assist disabled young persons to develop their personalities freely, recognize their rights and fulfil their obligations to society and the State. Over DM 2 million (US $1.08 million) is paid out annually by the Federal Youth Plan to 16 different institutions to cover staff training courses; personnel costs, in particular for youth training consultants and practical advisers; conferences; and individual measures such as those aimed at establishing contact between disabled and non-disabled young persons.

Permanent residence in institutions is today mainly envisaged for disabled persons requiring intensive therapeutic and nursing care. Special therapeutic and organizational measures are necessary to prevent or treat secondary mental handicaps in these people, caused by living in an institution. These measures may include the establishment of living groups under supervision and the allocation of a private living area, with suitable co-determination regulations. For all other disabled persons the priority is to arrange a pattern of accommodation, living conditions and care so as to develop their existing capabilities and encourage their independence, thus enabling them to live a life that befits their human dignity. This would entail, for instance, giving the disabled the opportunity of moving out of their parental homes at an age when they still have the learning capacity to meet the demands of everyday life. Many fairly young disabled adults have to live in old people's homes since more suitable accommodation for the disabled is not available. This should be remedied by setting up suitable living groups in appropriate institutions and promoting residential associations with outpatient care.

The accommodation in which they live has a great influence on the contentment and wellbeing of the disabled, especially those with restricted mobility. Most disabled persons do not want different accommodation than other people; like their non-disabled fellows, they are merely looking for a suitable, sound and affordable individual dwelling. Those who walk with difficulty are often best served by a ground floor flat, accessible without steps, with an immediate

137

environment suited to a disabled person and with optimal opportunities for contact with the non-disabled. Even when they are living with their families, disabled persons should have sufficient space to withdraw and develop their own individuality.

Public assistance is provided for accommodation for disabled persons living alone or with their families, who may be temporarily or permanently in need of care. One satisfactory solution is the combination of a small number of dwellings for the disabled with a larger old people's home, in which the disabled can live independently if they wish, but make use of commercial installations and if necessary nursing services. Disabled persons who can live independently, provided that advice and care is available, are best suited by dwellings or groups of dwellings with mobile care available over a restricted period. Disabled persons who have lived for a fairly long time in an institution often require attendant help to cope with the change-over from institutional to independent life. To avoid admitting some severely disabled persons in need of continuous care into institutions, the municipal services have provided full-time care in the home. This type of care, however, makes particularly high demands on the person responsible for providing it.

The prevention of disability

Preventive measures are most effective in the sphere of health and environmental policy, as well as in labour safety and accident prevention. The Federal Government also gives high priority to research on the disabled and on possible ways of averting disability. Another important task is to encourage people to adopt a healthy lifestyle, to reduce the risks liable to lead to disability, and to take full note of the results of the wide range of preventive care studies available. The Federal Government fully supports the current efforts in many fields to enlighten, advise and educate the population so as to increase their understanding of accident risks on the road, in school, at the workplace, at home and during leisure pursuits and thus avoid the danger of injury to health and disability during their working life.

Special emphasis is placed in social assistance policies on preventive care and early recognition measures. Preventive care measures include genetic counselling, regular examinations during pregnancy and in the first years of life, measures to prevent rickets, and vaccinations either prenatally or postnatally. Despite this, about 40 000 children are born disabled or with a potential disability every year. Many newborn infants are vulnerable as a result of risks during pregnancy or more particularly as a result of premature birth. An early recognition programme has been set up within the framework of the statutory sickness insurance system for children up to the age of

138

four, in order to forestall the occurrence of particular diseases that may give rise to lifelong disability. Early recognition programmes are of practical use if they result in successful early treatment and medical care. Disabled and potentially disabled children are now served by a widespread though uneven system of medical care, comprising about 3000 practising paediatricians employed in about 50 social paediatric institutions, and about 300 early medical care centres, supplemented by self-help measures on the part of parents. Super-regional social paediatric centres have facilities for the complex diagnosis and treatment of children suffering from serious multiple diseases (combining relevant specialist disciplines such as paediatrics, orthopaedic surgery, child and youth psychiatry, ophthalmology or ear, nose and throat); therapeutic plans are drawn up to coordinate the various forms of medical treatment and the pertinent psychosocial measures. The outlook for disabled and potentially disabled children has been greatly improved overall by the establishment of highly specialized diagnostic and treatment centres and the increasing number of advisory and assistance institutions.

As elsewhere in the world, early assistance embraces more than just medical care and therapy. Parents are essential "partners in therapy" and their participation is vital. Hence the particular importance of establishing regional early assistance centres with local and mobile services. These services have teams charged with care of the family, including where necessary doctors, psychologists, educational workers and different types of therapist. A particularly important aspect of this assistance is that to extend the responsibility of families for educating and assisting their children, they must be given explanations, counselling and education, and exchange their experience with others who are similarly affected.

Although the establishment of social paediatric centres and regional early assistance centres is largely complete, problems continue over their financing. The reason for this is that these centres provide not only medical services, the cost of which is borne by the sickness insurance system, but also nonmedical services, particularly educational assistance and various forms of psychological aid. Existing resources will have to be used even more effectively and if necessary supplemented, if the early assistance institutions are to cover requirements at the federal level.

Research
In spite of the serious financial situation, the Federal Government supports research and development aimed at improving the lot of the disabled. Federal research programmes include research and development in the service of health 1983–1986, research on the

humanization of the work environment and research in transport and communications. The aim of research and development in the service of health 1983–1986 is to use research and development resources to obtain information on the occurrence, avoidance and control of diseases (and disabilities resulting from them) and on the organization required for their treatment. The programme on the humanization of the work environment is concerned with examining and improving the situation of disabled workers. Programmes on transport and communications include research on the telebus service for the disabled in Berlin (West) and on the development of a special private car for the disabled. Other projects are looking at the development of technical aids for the blind and deaf and wheelchairs for the physically disabled, and at the problems of professional rehabilitation and training, and of reintegration into social and professional life.

Evaluation of Progress in National Legislation

The need for further changes in legislation
The main feature of future development in disabled legislation, based on the resolutions repeatedly adopted by the *Bundestag,* will be the updating of the Severely Disabled Act. This Act has now been in force for over 10 years. The increase in the number of recognized severely disabled persons to about 4.6 million has given rise to animated public discussion, covering both the actual concept of severe disability, the recognition procedure and the so-called concessions, and also the procedure adopted for the obligatory employment of the disabled, the level of compensation payments, the scope of the special protection against termination of employment and the eligibility of the severely disabled for additional holidays. The increase in the unemployment rate among the severely disabled has given rise to concern in all quarters.

A lack of knowledge and a number of misunderstandings have often marked the discussion of the subject in recent years. It has been incorrectly assumed, for example, that about 4.6 million persons are currently benefiting from the protection and assistance afforded to all recognized severely disabled persons under the Severely Disabled Act. This assumption overlooks the fact that the Severely Disabled Act — apart from travel concessions on public transport, incorporated in the Act in 1979 M only provides assistance for the integration of the severely disabled into the working environment, that is,

140

it only benefits about 1.2 million recognized severely disabled persons who are in work. The remaining 3.4 million persons recognized as severely disabled persons are not, not yet or no longer in work. This group benefits only from the so-called concessions, the legal basis of which (except for the free travel concession referred to above) is found outside the Severely Disabled Act in a wide range of federal, *Land,* communal and other regulations. In addition, not all severely disabled persons are eligible for all the concessions. Severe disability is only one of several grounds of entitlement. Other restrictive conditions affecting the severely disabled have to be taken into account, such as exceptional difficulty in walking, the fact that they are continuously housebound or that their disability has reached a particularly serious level.

There is broad agreement that as a special instrument for creating and maintaining working and training vacancies, the Severely Disabled Act has done a great deal to ensure that today over 1 million severely disabled persons are in work. The number of severely disabled persons unemployed would no doubt have been greater without this legislative assistance. The change-over from the causal to the absolute principle in rehabilitation, thus incorporating also severely disabled civilians, has however necessarily resulted in a substantial extension of the category of persons protected. The underlying reason for this change was the conviction that help to integrate into the work environment and society — as opposed to compensation payments — should depend not on the cause of the disability but merely on its nature, severity and repercussions.

The Federal Government believes that the Severely Disabled Act is now due for adaptation to changing conditions. The practical experience gained must be incorporated, unexpected developments that have appeared during the implementation of the Act corrected and real or reputed impediments to recruitment eliminated. The general aim is to increase the prospects of recruitment and employment of the severely disabled on the labour and training markets.

Intended legislative amendments
The following legislative amendments will be considered in the updating of the Severely Disabled Act:

- the purpose of the Act and the categories covered by it should be made clear; in this connection the misleading concept that has been held to stand in the way of recruitment, reduction of earning capacity, should be replaced by degree of disability;

- the legal principles underlying the recognition procedure should be made clear and the recognition procedure itself rendered more concise; provision will also have to be made for the possibility of checking other recognition documents;

— real or reputed impediments to recruitment must be eliminated; to facilitate the recruitment of the severely disabled, the special protection of the severely disabled against termination of employment should, on a trial basis, apply only after six months, in the same way as the protection afforded to the population as a whole; the question of the duration of the additional holiday entitlement of the severely disabled should be examined and the time spent on courses of treatment set off against it;

— the allowance for training vacancies when calculating the number of obligatory employment vacancies should be discontinued, since it has been held on occasion to inhibit training; at the same time the availability of training vacancies for the severely disabled should be increased by the possibility of a multiple setting-off procedure and the financial incentives for the training of the severely disabled fixed by law;

— the compensation payment, which has remained unchanged since 1974 at DM 100 (US $54) monthly per unfilled obligatory vacancy, needs to be modified in relation to its function as compensation and incentive, taking into account the development in the general situation that has occurred in the mean time;

— further consideration will be given to financial incentives for employers to recruit and employ severely disabled persons in particular;

— the legal status of the confidential representatives of the severely disabled and their deputy should be strengthened and greater emphasis placed on their cooperative function during the recruitment of the severely disabled.

Further legislative amendments may be found necessary in the final updated version of the Act.

Future development of the legislation on the integration of the disabled

The Rehabilitation–Adaptation Act will be updated at a later stage. In accordance with the relevant decisions of the *Bundestag,* the most recent dating from 25 June 1982, and the recommendations of the National Commission on the International Year of Disabled Persons, 1981, this Act will be combined with the Severely Disabled Act and other rehabilitation regulations to form a single, lucidly arranged act on the integration of the disabled. This will be a logical continuation of the procedure adopted for the Rehabilitation–Adaptation Act, so that the problems with the harmonization of the work of and cooperation between the rehabilitation insurance institutions, inevitable in a graduated system of benefits, do not have an adverse effect on disabled or potentially disabled beneficiaries. Medical, professional and social rehabilitation measures must be even better coordinated. Information and counselling on integration opportunities and cooperation between the rehabilitation institutions also need to be improved. Particular emphasis will have to be placed, moreover, on the harmonization of benefits in order to take better account of the basic aim of the Rehabilitation–Adaptation Act, namely that all persons of equivalent disability should receive equivalent rehabilitation benefits. Particular problems will arise here over the requirement, frequently emphasized by the *Bundestag,* that social assistance be incorporated into the rehabilitation system. The more far-reaching scope and characteristics of the social assistance legislation, in particular the criterion of need and the individual-case principle, conflicts with the principles governing payments in other fields of social insurance. In the Federal Government's view, the critical criterion in the revision of the relevant legislation must be to ensure optimal conditions for the integration of disabled and potentially disabled fellow citizens into society.

Hungary

General Principles

The Constitution of the Hungarian People's Republic ensures the equality of its citizens as a fundamental principle. It acknowledges and protects the right of citizens to life, physical safety and soundness as well as upholding their health. These rights are promoted by the state-organized labour-safety measures, health institutions and medical care, which protect the human environment. The Hungarian People's Republic ensures the right to work as well as to recompense according to the quantity and quality of the work performed. Citizens have the right to financial allocations in old age, and in the case of disease or inability to work. This support is provided by the State in the framework of social security and through the network of social institutions. Every citizen has the right to participate in the management of public affairs. The Constitution also guarantees citizens the right to public meetings.

Coordination mechanisms

In Hungary, activities in connection with the disabled are multisectoral, so that various organizations are involved. The central coordinator of the participation of all these organizations is the Ministry of Health. The Ministry of Health is also mainly responsible for the direction of medical and professional rehabilitation. As a part of this responsibility, the professional programmes, the priorities, and the aims of the five-year plans deal as appropriate with the improvement of the status of the disabled. When implementing these tasks, the Ministry cooperates with other leading state bodies, such as the Finance Ministry, the National Planning Office, the Ministry of Agriculture and Food, as well as with several national political and

145

interest-safeguarding organizations, such as the National Council of Trade Unions and the National Council of Agricultural Cooperatives.

The directive work of the Ministry of Health is supported by various institutions, several of which also collaborate with success at the international level. The main professional centres are:

— the National Institute for Medical Rehabilitation, dealing with the rehabilitation of patients with locomotor diseases;

— the National Institute for Forensic Medicine, concerned with assessing decreases in working capacity;

— the National Institute for Labour Hygiene, coordinating the activity of the physicians who work in factories and other enterprises;

— the Centre for Social Institutes, organizing the care and education of the severely disabled in special institutes;

— the National Institute for Health Education, fulfilling coordination tasks in prevention and health information;

— the Institute for Medical Extension Training, directing the training of health workers dealing with rehabilitation;

— the Works for Medical Appliances, supplying appliances for disabled persons.

The retraining and vocational rehabilitation of adult disabled persons is the responsibility of the National Office for Wage and Labour. The financial and social care of invalids and their family members is the task of the National Administration of Social Security, as well as the local administration or councils. The health departments of the local councils coordinate the work of rehabilitation in their given area. In each of the 19 counties, an area committee of rehabilitation effects coordination between the employers and the health organizations.

In this regard, it should be emphasized that Hungary is undergoing a remarkable decentralization that will mean an increase in the scope of authority and responsibility of the local administrations (towns, villages).

In the search for new cooperative methods of management, allocations to local authorities have been increased for improving services for the disabled.

The whole of society needs to collaborate to advance the productive life of the disabled and to ensure successful and lasting rehabilitation. Different social organizations (such as the Red Cross and the Patriotic People's Front) are undertaking an increasing role in the integration of the disabled into society. Their growing success can be traced mainly to the initiation of the process of rehabilitation and its social supervision, to the way workers are informed and educated, and to control of the labour-safety regulations. One further important task is to widen the social base of the disabled.

Other scientific societies of international fame play a role in advancing up-to-date rehabilitation, developing rehabilitation practice and disseminating scientific and professional knowledge.

The Ministry of Health maintains favourable connections with organizations safeguarding the special interests of the disabled, such as the National Association for the Blind and People with Visual Defects, the National Association for People with Hearing Defects, and the National Organization of Parents of Mentally Retarded Children; the last was inaugurated in response to the United Nations' proclamation of 1981 as the International Year of Disabled Persons, and the Organization has flourishing contacts with more than 600 enterprises.

Humanitarian features characterize the useful cooperation with the churches in this field; the correct relation of the State and the churches is advantageous in this regard.

One possible outlet for private initiative lies in small and medium-size enterprises that provide services to meet people's everyday needs at a reasonable price. The policy of the State is one of tolerance towards such initiatives and in some areas the State gives them preferential conditions.

National Involvement in International Action

Hungary has acceded to international agreements and treaties, and has accepted invitations to cooperate in projects aimed at improving the situation of the disabled population.

For example, Hungary supported the United Nations decision to proclaim the year 1981 the International Year of Disabled Persons, and the decade 1983–1992 as the Decade of Disabled Persons. In the experience of Hungary, this announcement was a step in the right direction, and in Hungary implementation has been successful.

Hungary has recently signed Convention 159 of the International Labour Conference on the Vocational Rehabilitation and Employment of the Disabled. In conformity with this agreement, Hungary has undertaken to set up a policy at the national level for the rehabilitation and employment of the disabled, in close harmony with national conditions, practices and possibilities, to apply this policy and from time to time to supervise it. This policy improves the chances of the disabled of finding jobs.

147

Hungary is participating in the WHO programme on community-based rehabilitation and one of its national health institutes takes part in this work. Hungary has worked out a method of applying this programme in the medium-developed countries. It offers a promising approach for the integration of the disabled into society through primary health care and education.

Methodology — Types of Legislative Approach to the Equality Concept

The constitutional fundamental principles are realized through the provisions of law. The situation of the disabled is regulated by the Health Law, the Law for Social Security, the Lawbook of Labour as well as the Educational Law. Further comprehensive provisions exist with respect to disabled persons, generally ensuring special rights and advantages for the disabled or their families. In addition, special provisions are made for certain categories of disabled, including the blind, and people with locomotor disorders.

Clearly, Hungary is not short of legislative provisions; the task is to adapt the regulations continuously to changing conditions.

Review of the Present State of National Legislation

Elimination of discrimination or social prejudice

According to the Constitution all citizens have equal rights. This fundamental principle ensures the protection of the disabled from discrimination, prohibits disadvantageous distinction and encourages equal opportunity.

Social reintegration and full participation

Working life and professional rehabilitation

The Council of Ministers frequently reviews the situation regarding professional rehabilitation and sets targets for its modernization. Fundamental decisions were taken in 1980, for example, to set up central and local networks for the direction and coordination of professional rehabilitation, and to elaborate plans for their functioning. The rehabilitation system was organized on the basis of those decisions. It is expected that the Government will soon review the whole matter, to determine the tasks ahead.

One possible approach would be to use the initiative of the participating organizations. The contradictions that can be seen in some fields must be eliminated. This can be done *inter alia* by providing adequate information systems and modernizing the statistical and administrative systems concerned with rehabilitation. It is the intention more accurately to specify the tasks and responsibilities of employers and to promote rehabilitation further, given its importance as an economic factor.

In recent years, legal provisions have been introduced to promote the re-employment of workers whose working capacity has been affected. Most deal with financial aspects, that is, they provide considerable state subsidies for workplaces that create new jobs for the rehabilitation and employment of workers with impaired working capacity (in 1983, 40% of the cost of wages for the disabled was provided by the State; by 1986 the proportion was nearer 70%).

No tax is payable on the wages of the disabled worker. In addition, on the occasion of the International Year of Disabled Persons, a new, separate foundation was established to support the creation of new jobs, partly using credits and partly a non-refundable state loan.

One of the provisions lays down that a company that has a telephone switchboard with several main lines and subsidiary lines must employ blind persons or persons with visual disorders as operators. This is the only job that in Hungary is controlled by provision of law.

Regulations exist that promote the employment of groups of disabled or handicapped persons in protected workplaces. The regulations lay down that a company and a local council may come to an agreement about the employment of disabled and handicapped persons. The council undertakes to ensure a continuous workforce as well as to supply a specialist for the treatment and care of the mentally retarded. The company undertakes to ensure continuous work for the mentally retarded as well as to provide the same preferential conditions as other workers get. If the company can establish protected workplaces only by making new investments or reorganization, it may get financial support or a credit from the contracting council.

Hungary has recently reorganized and regulated the functioning of the social employment office under the control of the councils. The social employment office provides work at home for the elderly in financial difficulties and for families with a disabled person at home, or for families where a parent cannot work fixed hours because a child has to have special care. In this way, work can be ensured for people with locomotor disorders or for mentally retarded persons who suffer a disadvantage on the open labour market.

Education and vocational training

The main principles of education are to provide equal chances and to overcome disadvantages. In Hungary, children between 6 and 16 years are of school age. This also applies to disabled children. If mentally retarded children are able to attend school, they have the right and the opportunity to do so, but in such cases various preferential conditions have to be provided. For instance, children with locomotor diseases are given six hours of extra teaching a week, and they may take private examinations, even in secondary schools. The institutional network for the education of the mentally retarded is well established.

Final diplomas issued by special education centres for children with locomotor or sensory diseases are considered equal to those from standard primary schools. The final diplomas for mentally retarded children in the eighth form correspond to the diploma for the sixth form of standard primary schools.

The continuation of studies following a special school education is possible. Young people with locomotor or sensory diseases may continue their studies in secondary, technical or even high schools.

Special institutes for vocational guidance help mentally retarded children to choose a specialization. Even when invalidity occurs later in life, it is possible to learn a new job or retrain. Disabled persons are encouraged to take high school studies by a special system of scholarships.

Hungary has a special academy that educates teachers for work with disabled children and provides special training for each type of invalidity.

Promoting participation in society

To illustrate the promotion of participation in society, the importance of the following measures should be stressed.

The proper mobility of people with locomotor disorders is as difficult as it is important. Special conditions encourage their use of public transport: they receive free local and railway transport, vouchers for taxis and reductions for other forms of transport. They may purchase special Hycomat personal cars under preferential conditions. People with locomotor disorders obtain 360 litres of fuel per annum for their car free of charge.

Other measures have been taken to improve the mobility of disabled persons. For example, in busy streets, traffic lights are equipped with special acoustic devices for the blind and persons with visual defects; for people with hearing defects, light signals in public vehicles show the closure of doors; and people with locomotor disorders have special parking licences. In the design of subways or footbridges, special attention is paid to the problems of people with locomotor diseases, and special ramps and slopes are built.

With state/government support, guide dogs are trained for the blind and people with visual defects, and every person with a hearing defect is provided with a hearing aid.

Special transport tariffs are provided to family members of patients cared for in institutions.

Special forms of telecommunication help the disabled to participate in the life of the community. For example the Hungarian television programme entitled *Companions in distress* gives regular information on the situation and problems of the disabled. Particular associations publish their own papers and have their own libraries.

Sports activities are also popular among disabled persons and are organized through sports associations, which also take part successfully in international competitions. Transport for participants is supported by the State. In addition to organized sport, swimming facilities are available to all free of charge and there is an extensive remedial exercise system in all hospitals.

Such activities need to be improved and extended in the future.

The prevention of disability
The importance and main fields of prevention set out in the WHO regional health for all strategy reflect those of Hungary and only the major steps taken for the implementation of the national strategy will therefore be summarized.

Within the system of Hungarian health care, the following institutions and activities ensure the protection of the health of the population and the prevention of invalidity. Medical care and health information, which are part of a system of therapeutic and preventive care, are provided to citizens free of charge as a right of citizenship. Primary health care is provided by the panel doctor service (together with special paediatric services), by specialized district polyclinics and by hospitals.

Within the unified institutional network, there are special institutes for family planning, genetic counselling, maternity services, nervous disorders, tuberculosis and the assessment of the degree of invalidity.

The rehabilitation of patients is also provided for in rest houses and sanatoria.

There are health care services in every mine, foundry, and chemical or food company employing more than 300 workers, metal works with more than 400 workers and all other companies with more than 500. Suitability tests are taken when candidates apply for a job and then on a regular basis. The health service provides treatment for smaller problems, participates in perfecting special screening tasks, and organizes and trains first-aid helpers.

The health service ensures adherence to the regulations in hazardous workplaces in order to prevent professional or occupational diseases. Hungarian law provides strict regulations for the prevention of industrial injuries.

In addition to the activities of the health system, the National Institute for Labour Safety coordinates activities in the field of labour safety. A worker may only start a given job when fully conversant with all the relevant labour-safety regulations. Only machinery and equipment corresponding to the relevant labour-safety regulations may be installed. Licences are issued by the inspector of labour safety. The employer must provide every worker with all the relevant safety appliances, otherwise the employee has the right to refuse to work. The inspector of labour safety is authorized to prevent the operation of a plant or a piece of machinery that does not meet with the regulations. The trade unions also ensure adherence to the labour-safety regulations. In addition, several research institutes work on the development and modernization of labour-safety devices and appliances.

Hungary intends to enforce these regulations more intensively and consistently in the future, for the sake of prevention.

Systems of income support

Social support and social security promote the integration of the disabled into society and provide the necessary financial support. The system of social security covers the whole population. About one third of the adult population receives wage substitution benefits. The main constituents of the social security system are: pension (allowances), sick pay in case of inability to work, maternity pay, free health care, the supply of medical appliances and medicaments, and other forms of support to families with several children.

One fifth of the population is over retirement age. A pension is allocated to all elderly persons who are not able to work actively any more owing to their age.

There are also a great number of people, however, who require state support, because of disability or poor health. Persons who have lost two thirds of their ability to work are classed as disabled and those suffering lesser impairments are classed as persons with changed ability to work. The disabled get a disability pension and those with changed ability to work receive other benefits. Persons working under hazardous working conditions have the so-called "exemption by age" facility.

152

Patients are entitled to sick pay for up to a maximum of one year in the case of temporary inability to work and up to a maximum of two years in the case of professional injuries or tuberculosis. Sick pay for inability to work caused by accidents is 100% and in other cases the amount paid is in proportion to the inability: 70–90%.

Families with disabled or handicapped children also receive special benefits, in addition to the basic state support due. Every mother can receive maternity pay until her child is three years old and in the case of a handicapped child until the age of six. In 1984, some 1 367 560 families were receiving children's allowances in Hungary. The amount of this allowance is higher in the case of sick or disabled children.

People with locomotor diseases may apply for regular social aid. This comes together with the so-called "public medical supply", the free supply of necessary medical appliances and medicaments. It is also possible to apply for extraordinary allowances (four times a year).

Disabled ex-servicemen obtain financial support according to their social status and rate of disability. A severely disabled person can be looked after at home through the network of social caregivers. Special personal allowances are secured for all citizens with visual defects.

Disabled people have priority in the allocation of accommodation. When purchasing a flat, a disabled person can obtain credits at favourable rates as well as other forms of support. Nevertheless, Hungary still has a long way to go in improving the housing situation for the disabled.

Evaluation of Progress in National Legislation

Among the targets of national social policy, the achievement of the social equality of the disabled takes a significant place. In harmony with Hungary's socioeconomic progress, efforts are continuing to mitigate the problems of the disabled and their family members. The main aim is to find solutions to the various difficulties and disadvantages faced by the individual disabled person and family, as well as to help them to integrate more readily into society.

Although the physical, economic and other problems restricting the integration of the disabled have not all been overcome, the following four factors show that some results have been achieved and that the prospects for further improvement are good:

— there is no legislative discrimination hindering progress;

153

- the social and economic conditions of the disabled are satisfactory and gradually improving;

- the political authorities keep problems concerning the disabled under constant review, and contribute to their solution;

- social policy, including that concerning the solution of the
problems of the disabled, is characterized by an open approach that encourages new initiatives.

Hungary intends to pursue legislative and health policies that will
build on the successes achieved so far and continue to improve the
care and integration into society of the disabled.

Iceland

General Principles

National policy concerning the disabled is outlined in Law No. 41 of 23 March 1983. The purpose of the Law is to ensure that disabled persons enjoy equal rights and have comparable living conditions to those of other members of the community, and to create conditions by which such persons can lead a normal life and find the most suitable place in the community.

There is no specific reference or allusion in the Icelandic Constitution to disability as such.

The national plans and programmes of action in favour of the disabled are set forth in Article 3 of Law No. 41/1983. The affairs of the disabled come under three ministries: the Ministry for Health and Social Security, the Ministry of Culture and Education and the Ministry of Social Affairs. Article 3 further stipulates the setting up of a national executive committee of seven members appointed by the three ministries, as well as some nongovernmental organizations for the disabled.

National Involvement in International Action for the Disabled

Iceland is a party to various agreements and resolutions on the disabled and handicapped in the Nordic countries, as well as in WHO and the Council of Europe.

Methodology — Types of Legislative Approach to the Equality Concept

In addition to Law No. 41 of 23 March 1983, there are various statutes concerning the disabled in Icelandic legislation, for instance:

(*a*) Law No. 67/1971, the Social Security Act, provides for free pension insurance, employment accident insurance and health insurance for anyone domiciled in Iceland, regardless of nationality or citizenship;

(*b*) Law No. 35/1980 concerns the Medical and Social Centre for those that are deaf or hard of hearing and/or have a speech impediment;

(*c*) Law No. 18/1984 concerns the Medical and Social Centre for the blind or partially sighted.

Review of the Present State of National Legislation

The main differences between Law No. 41 of 23 March 1983 and the Law it replaced, Law No. 47 of 30 May 1979, can be summarized as follows.

(*a*) The 1983 law was inspired by the aim of the United Nations International Year of Disabled Persons, 1981, that is, the principle of the full participation and equality of disabled persons in society, a principle that has in fact opened authorities' eyes and given a new dimension to the concept of rehabilitation.

(*b*) It therefore emphasizes all means to give the disabled the greatest possible independence.

(*c*) It furthermore recognizes the duty of society to adapt itself to the particular needs of the disabled.

(*d*) It places still more emphasis on prevention, and early intervention in the case of impairments, disabilities and handicaps, in order to eliminate risks or limit the effect of an impairment or disability.

(*e*) It stresses the valuable role of the family in caring for a disabled person at home.

(*f*) Furthermore, it stipulates moving from a system of institutional life and rehabilitation towards more community care.

(*g*) To that end, it emphasizes the setting up of half-way houses and small open-care houses where four to six disabled persons live and work with a foster family.

156

Law No. 41 of 23 March 1983 on Disabled Persons[a]

Chapter I
Purpose and Administration

Article 1. The purpose of this Law is to ensure that disabled persons enjoy equal rights and have comparable living conditions to those of other members of society, in order to enable them to lead a normal life and find the most suitable place in the community. Further, to enable the National Organization for the Disabled and its federation to implement measures and decisions in conjunction with matters of concern to them, e.g. by seeking the views of the National Organization for the Disabled or any of its subsidiary institutions or supporting unions on particular issues in the drafting and presentation of parliamentary bills, laws or regulations concerning them.

Article 2. The word "disabled" within the meaning of this Law shall signify "affected by a physical or mental handicap".

Article 3. Matters relating to the disabled come under three departments: health services, including medical rehabilitation, under the Health and Social Security Department; educational and paedagogical matters under the Education Department; social welfare and reintegration, labour matters, etc. under the Department of Social Affairs. The Department of Social Affairs shall be the administrator in matters relating to the disabled under the present Law.

A special committee shall be responsible for the central administration of matters relating to the disabled and shall be called the Executive Committee. This Committee shall ensure that the arrangements made in relation to all services provided by the public authorities are consistent. The membership of the Executive Committee shall consist of seven persons each serving for a four-year term of office. Each department shall nominate one member. The National Association of Communes shall appoint one representative; the Association for the Disabled, the National Development Aid Association and the Icelandic Invalids' Association shall appoint three representatives in accordance with more detailed regulations. The representative of the Department of Social Affairs shall be the chairman of the Committee. Alternates shall be appointed in the same way.

---

[a] *Stjóruartidindi, 1983, Part B,* 14 April 1983, No. 4, pp. 55–65. This text is based on a working translation provided by the author of the contribution.

The Committee shall settle any matters of dispute that may arise in connection with the implementation of this Law, but its decisions may be referred to the appropriate minister.

In matters relating to the employment of disabled persons, the Committee may call upon representatives of the labour market as and when appropriate.

Article 4. The country shall be divided into eight administrative districts in respect of the disabled, namely:

— Reykjavik;

— the district of Reykjanes, including Gullbringusysla and Kjósarsysla and the townships of Grindavík, Keflavík, Njardvík, Hafnarfjördur, Gardabaer, Kópavogur and Selt-jarnarnes;

— Vesturland, including Borgarfjardarsysla, Myrasysla, Snaefellsnessysla and Hnappadalssysla, Dalasysla and Akranes;

— the Vestfiràir district, including Austur and Vestur Bardastrandarsysla, Vestur Isafjardarsysla, Nordur Isafjardarsysla, Strandasysla, Bolungarvík and Isafjördur;

— Nordurland vestra, including Vestur Húnavatnssysla, Austur Húnavatnssysla, Skagafjardarsysla, Saudárkrókur and Siglufjördur;

— Nordurland eystra, including Eyjafjardarsysla, Sudur-Thingeyjarsysla, Nordur Thingeyjarsysla, and the townships of Olafsfjördur, Dalvík, Akureyri and Húsavík;

— Austurland, including Nordur Múdllasysla, Sudur Múdllasysla, Austur-Skaftafellssysla and the townships of Seydisfjördur, Neskaupstadur and Eskifjördur;

— Sudurland, including Vestur Skaftafellssysla, Rangárvallasysla, Arnessysla, Vestmannaeyjar and Selfoss.

Article 5. Each district shall have a district committee consisting of seven persons whose task will be to make suggestions for offers of service or to coordinate schemes in conjunction with those re sponsible for such matters in the district, e.g. directors of education, district medical officers, communes and associations for the disabled.

Each district committee shall include among its members a director of education, a district medical officer and five persons appointed by the minister. Two of these shall be appointed on the nomination of the district association in the commune, and one of them shall sit as their representative. The Association for the Disabled, the National Development Aid Association and the Icelandic

Invalids' Association shall appoint three persons in accordance with more detailed regulations, which will be drafted and codified in accordance with Article 3, second paragraph.

In Reykjavik, the local committee shall appoint two representatives, one from the committee itself and the other from the Reykjavik Social Welfare Board. The committee shall choose its own chairman. The term of office shall be four years. Persons sitting on the district committee shall be domiciled in the district. Alternates shall be appointed in the same manner as for the Executive Committee in accordance with Article 3.

Chapter II
Services and Institutions

Article 6. All districts shall endeavour to provide the following services:

— initial analysis and examination of newborn babies and preliminary checks on suspicion of disability of any kind;
— health care and recreation service;
— special education and educational counselling;
— appliances and transport service;
— physiotherapy;
— psychology;
— rehabilitation and training;
— occupational training and experimentation;
— ergotherapy;
— job-seeking;
— social advisory services.

Efforts shall be made to provide temporary or permanent stay in foster homes.

Disabled persons shall receive treatment in public institutions wherever possible. This shall be organized and managed in such a way that facilities are available for the disabled on the same footing as for other members of the community.

The competent minister may, after consultation with the Executive Committee, add to or reduce the services. The minister may also issue regulations giving details of this service by district or for the whole of the national territory, following proposals by the district committee and the Executive Committee.

Article 7. The institutions for the disabled are:
— day centres for children and associated facilities

— outpatient departments where aftercare is also available
— temporary foster homes
— a network of games collections
— treatment centres
— summer camps
— community housing
— day centres for the disabled
— nursing homes
— sheltered workshops
— labour exchanges
— training and rehabilitation institutions
— residential homes
— day school centres.

The appropriate minister may add to institutions or close them down on the proposal of the Executive Committee.

The appropriate minister or department may authorize new activities or services on the suggestion of the Executive Committee.

Article 8. Requests for services or custody in institutions under Article 7, sections 5, 7, 8 and 13, should be sent to the relevant district committee, which may recommend custody in consultation with the institution's director and the relevant representative of the diagnostic and advisory services. If the institutions in question are not run by public bodies, the directors and/or board must approve.

If a request for custody is rejected, it may be referred to the Executive Committee, which shall seek a solution.

On the proposal of the Executive Committee, the minister may decide that more institutions referred to in Article 7 shall come under the provisions of Section 1.

Article 9. Disabled persons who, in the view of the district committee, are unable because of local circumstances to obtain education or training outside their homes shall be provided with suitable education or training free of charge.

The district committees shall make suggestions in conjunction with those concerned about the use to be made of such services.

Article 10. A disabled child between birth and 18 years of age living at home, or receiving partial care, and requiring special care, or regarded by the district committee as qualifying therefor, shall have the right to such help as can be given.

The appropriate district committee shall ensure that the help is given. If the person in charge wishes to take a hand in it, and the district committee and the appropriate diagnosis and advisory service representative regards him or her as competent to provide such treatment and assistance, remuneration for 20–175 hours per month shall be made at the discretion of the district committee at tariff 8 of the *Verkamannafelagid Dagsbrun* (union for nonskilled workers). This payment can be increased if an imperative need calls for it in the opinion of the district committee.

The pensions division of the National Social Insurance System shall be responsible for payment of such help in accordance with the article in question.

Article 11. Authorization for the communes and associations of disabled persons to set up and manage institutions for the disabled in accordance with Article 7 shall be granted by the appropriate departments in consultation with the relevant district committee.

The district committee shall be responsible for supervising institutions for the disabled. The district committee's representatives shall have access to institutions with a view to supervision and information concerning all matters relating to their management and finances. The district committees may indicate improvements and reforms for the institutions.

Where the district committee itself is in charge of the institutions, the Department of Social Affairs shall be the supervisory body. At the suggestion of the Executive Committee, the minister responsible shall be empowered to withdraw the authorization to operate from any institution not considered necessary by the district chairman and/or the Department of Social Affairs because of alleged shortcomings in management, within a reasonable time limit.

Article 12. The minister shall draw up regulations governing this service, either for the district or for the entire country, in accordance with Articles 6 and 7, on the proposal of the district committee or committees and the Executive Committee.

The district committee shall make suggestions on the planning and establishment of such institutions.

Chapter III
Obligation to Report Cases

Article 13. If a suspicion of a child's disability arises while the child is in its mother's care, the relevant supervisory body must so inform the parents and in connection therewith arrange for further tests and preventive measures where appropriate.

Article 14. If symptoms should appear following birth which point to development disorders in a child, the appropriate health officer, in conjunction with the parents, shall arrange for a preliminary diagnosis to be made. If the medical diagnosis indicates the need for further diagnoses or treatment, a report to this effect shall be sent to the diagnostic and advisory centre, which shall try to find suitable solutions in consultation with the parents, the district committees and other parties concerned as appropriate.

Article 15. In regular health check-ups on children, special attention shall be paid to psychological and physical skills. The same duty is incumbent on the school psychological service. If symptoms of disability appear, they shall be brought to the notice of the district committees and duly handled in accordance with Article 14.

Chapter IV
The State Diagnosis and Advice Centre

Article 16. In addition to the diagnosis made in the districts in accordance with Article 6, the State shall maintain a central diagnosis and advice centre (State Diagnosis and Advice Centre) attached to the Department of Social Affairs. The aims and activities of the Centre are mainly as follows:

— registration, examination and diagnosis of disabled persons referred to the Centre or attending it on their own initiative;

— implementation, review and operation of a suitable treatment and training scheme, and advice and guidance for parents and guardians or other interested parties;

— long-term treatment for individuals in need thereof if this is not available in other institutions or elsewhere;

— referral to other treatment facilities or institutions able to provide the client with the service and training needed at any given moment; the Diagnosis and Advice Centre shall be responsible for providing those concerned in the treatment with information and guidance when so requested;

— management of games collections; the loan of toys to parents or guardians and provision of advice and guidance; in addition, technical assistance and advice regarding the establishment and management of other games collections throughout the country;

— training of personnel to look after services for the disabled in accordance with Articles 6 and 7, in conjunction with the district chairman and the schools that handle the training of personnel in these matters;

— registration and keeping of records on disabled persons in conjunction with the social, school and health authorities;

— providing the district committees with technical assistance and expressing opinions on services and institutionalization;

— occupying a leading role in technical investigation in the disability area and giving technical guidance on research into the status of the disabled, in conjunction with the Department of Social Affairs and the district chairman;

— supporting the Department of Social Affairs by publishing information sheets on the subject in accordance with Article 25;

— therapeutic equipment service.

The director of the State Diagnosis and Advice Centre shall be specially qualified in matters concerning disabled persons and shall be responsible for the technical activities of the institution and cooperation with other institutions.

A manager shall be in charge of the institution's finances and shall be responsible for day-to-day management. The Minister of Social Affairs shall appoint the director and manager on the proposal of the board of the institution.

The Executive Committee handling matters relating to disabled persons is also the Executive Committee of the State Diagnosis and Advice Centre.

The Minister shall issue regulations detailing the activities of the State Diagnosis and Advice Centre at the request of the Executive Committee.

Chapter V
Training and Rehabilitation

Article 17. The aim of training and rehabilitation is to reduce the effects of disability and to prevent them as far as possible. The Executive Committee and the district chairman shall in conjunction with the appropriate department ensure that disabled persons can receive suitable training to enable them to look after themselves in the best possible way, including by independent work.

They shall also ensure that those requiring such services can voice their demands and they shall make plans to meet them.

Article 18. The institutions concerned with training and rehabilitation shall be given support as further prescribed under the present

Law. The Executive Committee shall try to achieve the most appropriate apportionment of jobs and practical coordination of labour matters.

In conjunction with these institutions, the Executive Committee shall be responsible for the implementation of investigations and schemes. The aim of the investigations is to ensure that at all times clear information is available on the status of these matters and that the arrangements cope with current needs to the greatest possible extent. The object of the schemes is to provide for the training and rehabilitation needs of the disabled, and they must be reviewed at least once every five years.

Article 19. On the proposal of the district committees, help may be given to persons covered by the present Law as follows:

— financial assistance if their financial position is such that they are unable to take care of themselves and their family during the period of rehabilitation;

— allowances or loans for the purchase of apparatus and equipment in conjunction with work in the home or independent activity following rehabilitation;

— allowances or loans to help to pay for outlay in conjunction with training not otherwise payable in accordance with the provisions of other legislation;

— the pensions division of the National Social Insurance System provides assistance in accordance with sections 1 and 2, and the Department of Social Affairs makes loans under section 3.

The Minister shall issue regulations concerning the implementation of these provisions and the conditions required to qualify for allowances in accordance with this Article, and the amounts concerned.

Article 20. The district committee shall at all times stress the optimum relationship between training and rehabilitation on the one side, and the search for work on the other.

Chapter VI
Housing and Employment

Article 21. The district committees shall take up and deal with the question of improvements in the housing situation of the disabled in respect both of institutions and of private persons and shall make concrete proposals in such matters to the State Housing Institute.

Article 22. The district committees shall support the search for employment for the disabled each in their own district with a view to finding suitable employment opportunities for disabled persons.

The search for employment shall be closely linked with the Department of Social Affairs, the relevant local labour exchanges, labour market agencies and other interested bodies.

The district committees shall bear in mind that the best possible approach for disabled persons is to make new jobs available and shall make proposals for the adaptation of existing work sites in that respect. The district committees shall also, in conjunction with entrepreneurs and shop stewards in the trade unions concerned, take the lead in finding work opportunities for the disabled at work sites.

Emphasis should be laid on the planning of part-time work where appropriate for persons who cannot sustain full-time work.

Where the labour exchange in a particular commune has a separate section for the disabled in accordance with Law No. 52/1956, the district committee shall entrust the search for work referred to under section 1 to the labour exchange.

Article 23. The Department of Social Affairs in conjunction with associations of the disabled, labour market agencies and the National Social Insurance Centre shall take the initiative in investigating the position of the disabled in the labour market and shall make suggestions for its improvement accordingly. Such investigation shall be reviewed at least every five years.

Article 24. Persons who have undergone rehabilitation shall be given preference in State or commune employment where their qualifications are greater than or as great as those of others seeking a post. If the district committee feels that a disabled person is being passed over in the competition for a post, it may request those responsible for the hiring for a written report for its consideration in conjunction with the appointment.

Chapter VII
Guidance in Matters concerning the Disabled

Article 25. The Department of Social Affairs shall be responsible for guidance on matters relating to disabled persons in conjunction with the other bodies concerned. Disabled persons should regularly learn about their rights through the publication of brochures, etc. Guidance on matters concerning disabled persons should be included in the sociological instruction given in primary schools. Pupils at the primary level shall be entitled to education in sign language for the deaf in accordance with detailed regulations issued by the Department of Education. In accordance with regulations issued by the Department of Education, one day in each year shall be set aside for information on the situation of the disabled in the basic and more advanced schools throughout the country.

Chapter VIII
Management and Expenditure

Article 26. The State shall set up institutions in accordance with Article 7, sections 2–14. The communes shall find places for disabled persons in day centres for children in accordance with Article 7, section 1 and set up special departments. The expenditure involved comes within the provision of Law No. 112/1976.

The State shall pay all establishment costs in connection with Article 7, sections 5, 6, 7, 8, 12 and 13.

The State Exchequer shall pay 85% of the establishment costs and the communes 15% in connection with Article 7, sections 2, 3, 4, 9, 10, 11 and 14.

Disabled persons shall be housed free of charge in the institutions referred to in Article 7 (see also Article 28). The State Exchequer shall bear the costs under Articles 9 and 10.

Article 27. If associations should set up institutions in accordance with Article 7, sections 3–10 and 12–14, financial help may be granted through the Investment Fund for the Disabled. The Executive Committee may authorize support from the Investment Fund for the purpose of protecting jobs or improving equipment and technical apparatus making operations more practicable. Financial help can also be obtained from the Investment Fund for adapting the general manning tables and improving technical equipment so as to provide work for disabled persons in the general labour market; but the district committee and the job centre authorities must recommend such changes.

Article 28. Operational costs under Article 7, section 1, shall be paid in accordance with Law No. 112/1976. The Exchequer shall also pay any additional expenditure incurred over and above the general costs in the institutions concerned, but the child's right to other allowances shall not be reduced accordingly.

Of the operational costs of institutions not paid out of the institution's own capital under Article 7, sections 3, 4, 11 and 14, the Exchequer shall pay 85% and the commune 15%.

Operational expenditure in accordance with Article 7, sections 2 and 12, is governed by Law No. 57/1978, on the management of health care centres, but such institutions must also be set up and managed in accordance with this legislation.

The Exchequer shall pay the whole of the operational costs for other institutions in accordance with Article 7 except in cases where special expenditure items arise. In the case of special transport services for disabled persons who cannot use public transport to and from institutions, this shall be paid by the institution concerned out of its operational budget.

Article 29. If an independent business which has received financial help in conjunction with the installation costs is liquidated, the nominal value of the support given can be claimed back together with interest at any time.

Article 30. The Exchequer shall pay the operational costs of the State Diagnosis and Advice Centre.

Rules shall be drawn up for payment of the cost of individual travel to and from the State Diagnosis and Advice Centre in conjunction with the Social Security Act.

Article 31. The Exchequer shall pay the running costs of the Executive Committee.

Article 32. The Exchequer shall pay the running costs of representatives on the district committees.

Article 33. Regular custodial costs for disabled persons in private institutions shall be paid in accordance with Article 7. Daily custodial costs, not under licence, shall be payable for all institutions not publicly owned, by the Executive Committee, in consultation with the committee for statutory daily custodial costs under the social security legislation of the National Social Security Centre, and with a representative of the institution concerned.

Chapter IX
Investment Fund for the Disabled

Article 34. An Investment Fund for the Disabled shall be set up and administered by the Department of Social Affairs. The Fund shall take over the Investment Fund for Disabled Persons and Invalids set up in conjunction with Law No. 47/1979, and its liabilities. The purpose of the Fund shall be to finance schemes governed by Article 26, first paragraph, and Article 27, and other special education schemes. Investment schemes are governed by the provisions of Law No. 60/1976, concerning public investment, except for investment in accordance with Article 27. It is also provided that up to 10% of the

167

Fund's liquid resources may be used for joint special education and rehabilitation schemes and certain other items where neither the State nor the commune clearly has any obligation to pay, including subsidies based on the productivity of the disabled at home, in accordance with Article 19, section 2.

Loans and subsidies may be authorized from the Investment Fund in accordance with Article 27.

Article 35. The Fund shall be financed as follows:

— the Exchequer shall in the next five years provide the Fund each year with a sum equivalent to not less than ISK 5 million (US $99 500) as at 1 January 1983; this sum shall rise with the cost of living index at the time of entry into force of the Law; after that time, the State's contribution shall be reviewed;

— income from the inheritance fund;

— voluntary contributions and other casual income;

— income interest.

Article 36. An Executive Committee as referred to in Article 3, second paragraph, shall administer the Fund. The task of this Committee is to use the resources of the Fund in connection with schemes as laid down in Article 34 following proposals by the district chairman and discussions with the department concerned. The district committees shall send their suggestions to the department concerned, which shall in due course pass them on to the Executive Committee together with its views.

The Executive Committee shall seek confirmation from the relevant minister of its suggestion for the outlay of the Fund's resources.

Applications for grants under the Fund must reach the Executive Committee not later than September of each year.

In apportioning the Fund, special attention shall be paid to the number of persons requiring assistance in each district and each commune.

Article 37. The Department of Social Affairs shall be in charge of the day-to-day management of the Fund.

Chapter X
Special Provisions

Article 38. The district chairman shall compile information on service needs for disabled persons within his or her own particular district under this legislation. The district committees shall transmit this information to the department concerned together with investment schemes covering three-year periods. A copy of the schemes shall be sent to the Executive Committee.

The health, education and social departments shall on the basis of these suggestions forward their schemes and comments to the Executive Committee.

The Executive Committee in conjunction with the Department of Social Affairs shall coordinate the schemes and prepare the definitive investment scheme relating to the service requirements in conjunction with the needs as justified in each instance.

The investment programme shall likewise be placed before the Finance and Budget Department and the finance committee of the *Althing*.

Article 39. The district chairman shall observe the implementation of the Law in his or her own district, and shall make suggestions for improvement to the appropriate department if it should transpire that the service provided for by the Law is not being used as it should be.

Information on this shall be forwarded to the Executive Committee along with genuine plans for improvement. The Executive Committee shall check the suggestions made to ensure that they are being followed up and carried out.

Article 40. The district chairman shall put forward each year suggestions on finance and investment projects for use in preparing the budget estimates, which shall be forwarded to the appropriate department before 1 April of each year.

Article 41. The district chairman and institutions in accordance with Article 7 shall submit management accounts to the appropriate department each year not later than the end of March.

An itemized estimate of the expenditure on schemes granted financial support shall be sent by the end of the year to the Executive Committee.

Article 42. All persons working in connection with this Law must observe the greatest discretion in matters with which they become acquainted in the course of their work.

Article 43. The Minister of Social Affairs shall issue regulations giving detailed provisions about the implementation of the Law, including the Executive Committee's tasks under Article 3, the district committees' activities under Article 5 and the provisions of Chapter IX concerning the Investment Fund for the Disabled (*cf.* Articles 34, 35 and 36).

Regulations governing the implementation of Articles 10–16 and 19 of this Law shall be transmitted to the social committee of the *Althing* for comment.

Chapter XI
Entry into Force

Article 44. This Law shall enter into force on 1 January 1984. Simultaneously, Law No. 47/1979, on aid to the disabled, along with subsequent amendments, Law No. 27/1970, on rehabilitation, and Articles 2 and 3 of Law No. 12/1952, on the disposal of inheritance taxes and State legacies shall be repealed.

The transitional provisions under Section II below shall come into force immediately.

Transitional Provisions

Section I

The institutions for the disabled already functioning when the Law entered into force shall within a year of its entry into force make application for authorization to operate in conjunction with Article 11, and the application shall include a precise description of the activity planned. Such authorization shall be granted within a year of the date of the application.

Section II

1. The Minister of Social Affairs shall immediately appoint a five-man committee with instructions to submit suggestions on future planning for the State Diagnosis and Advice Centre in conjunction with the provisions of Article 16. The Minister of Education shall appoint a representative from the Observation and Diagnosis Division, Kjarvalshus; the Minister of Health, a representative from the Maternity Division of the National Hospital; the Minister of Social Affairs, a representative suggested by the district committees; and the National Development Aid Association and the Icelandic Invalids' Association shall each appoint one representative.

The committee's suggestions shall be placed before the *Althing* for its approval.

2. The Department of Education shall immediately make arrangements to hire or purchase suitable temporary premises for the Observation and Diagnosis Division at Kjarvalshus.

The cost of temporary premises shall be financed by the Investment Fund for Disabled Persons and Invalids.

If premises should be purchased which are not suitable for long-term planning by the State Diagnosis and Advice Centre (*cf.* Article 16), the cost of such premises when resold shall be paid into the Investment Fund for Disabled Persons and Invalids which financed the facilities in accordance with transitional provisions, Section II–2.

Ireland

General Principles

As part of its follow-up programme to the International Year of Disabled Persons, the Irish Government published a Government Green Paper on services for disabled people, on 19 April 1984. This was a statement of Government policy on the development of services and facilities that will enable disabled people to achieve full participation and equality in society.

The aim of the Green Paper is to provide a clear indication of Government policy in some of the main areas of concern to disabled people, and to initiate a constructive public debate on the areas requiring further attention and on the strategy to be adopted in meeting these objectives. The various services provided by statutory and voluntary bodies are selectively reviewed and proposals made for change and development. Areas of policy that require clarification or reappraisal are identified and various options discussed. Some of the areas dealt with, such as maternity and child development services, are not directly related to disability, but improvements in them should have a significant influence on the extent of handicapping conditions.

Subject to available resources, the Government is committed to carry through, in an orderly and planned way, the various proposals outlined in the Paper. The amount being spent on services for the disabled is very significant. In 1983 over £IR 400 million (US $569 million) was spent by the Exchequer. It is important to ensure that this money is reaching the right people and is providing effectively for their needs. The Green Paper allows an opportunity for views to be given on whether value is being obtained for the money being spent and whether the present extent of state involvement in services for the disabled is appropriate.

173

In introducing the Green Paper, the Minister for Health made the following statement:

I am conscious of the need for the greatest possible involvement of disabled people themselves in these discussions. For too long now the services for disabled people have resulted from an interpretation of their needs by non-disabled people. Rarely have they been consulted in any meaningful way. We have, to a great extent, been fostering their dependence while at the same time engendering attitudes of compassion among the general public.

We must now actively pursue a policy of independence for disabled people. They don't need others to dream dreams for them. Disabled people are well capable of dreaming their own dreams and must be given every facility and assistance to express their own desires and aspirations. It is the right of each individual, disabled and non-disabled, to contribute actively and positively to decisions affecting his development. That is the philosophy we must support and encourage.

The publication of the Green Paper has been warmly received by the various bodies providing services for disabled people. To date, the Minister for Health has received 33 written submissions about the Green Paper. A number of seminars have been held dealing with specific areas of the services reviewed in the Green Paper. Arising out of those seminars certain initiatives have been taken to improve residential care facilities for the physically disabled and to develop some new independent living units. In addition, expert committees are being set up to report on (a) the introduction of uniform training allowances for people in special training centres and for those undergoing training for open employment in community workshops, and an examination of the wages of people in sheltered employment; and (b) all aspects of transport for disabled people.

The Minister for Health, who has overall responsibility for the disabled, relies on a number of bodies for advice on the development of services, in particular the National Health Council (general matters in relation to health) and the National Rehabilitation Board. The Minister also meets representatives of the various nongovernmental bodies and voluntary organizations for the disabled on a regular basis to discuss matters of mutual interest.

National Health Council

The National Health Council is a statutory advisory body that was first established in 1948. The legal provisions for its establishment were contained in the 1947 Health Act, though these were later altered in the 1953 Health Act.

174

The functions of the Council are solely advisory, and the advice it furnishes to the Minister for Health may be rejected or accepted at the Minister's discretion. It can advise the Minister for Health on any matter relevant to the health of the people, with the exception of matters relating to the conditions of employment of staff and the payment of grants or allowances.

In addition, the Minister may refer any matter to the Council for advice but must seek the advice of the Council on any regulations that are proposed under the Health Acts and the Mental Treatment Acts.

The number of members on the Council is not fixed by statute and is therefore at the discretion of the Minister who appoints all its members. Not less than half of the members who are appointed, however, must be nominated by bodies that, in the opinion of the Minister, are representative of the medical and ancillary professions and of the management of voluntary hospitals. In practice, the Council has a large membership (usually more than 30) and is very broadly based. It cannot therefore be regarded as a specialist advisory body.

The term of office of members of the Council is limited to two years, but they may be reappointed and there is no statutory limit on the number of terms they may serve.

The Council may if it so wishes prepare and submit to the Minister an annual report. The Minister must publish this report, together with any comments he or she may wish to add about any specific item in the report.

The Minister for Health provides the day-to-day funds that the Council requires to carry out its functions.

National Rehabilitation Board
The National Rehabilitation Board was established in 1967 as the central coordinating authority in the field of rehabilitation. The Board was charged with supervising, providing or arranging for the provision of services for the welfare of persons who are disabled as a result of physical defect or injury, mental handicap or mental illness. Its functions include:

— the coordination of voluntary bodies engaged in rehabilitation and training services;

— the assessment of disability;

— the provision of specialist medical treatment, prosthetic appliances, artificial limbs and hearing aids;

— vocational guidance and the placement of disabled persons in employment;

— the arrangement of training for persons engaged in the rehabilitation services.

The Board is funded by the Minister of Health.

The role and organization of the Board have recently been reviewed by a team of management consultants, and their recommendations have been accepted in principle by the Minister for Health. In future the Board will play a more active part in overseeing the orderly development of rehabilitation services and will have a greater input into all policy decisions affecting disabled people. The Board has been reorganized to enable it to discharge its new responsibilities and to establish itself as the authoritative voice of disabled people. A new Board of Directors, designed to be more managerial in character, has been appointed.

It is also proposed to establish a consultative council under the National Rehabilitation Board to advise and assist the Board in discharging its role in matters relating to disabled people. The council will include representatives of relevant voluntary and statutory agencies together with other organizations whose activities impinge on disabled people. A number of disabled people will be appointed to this council.

National Involvement in International Action

Ireland was a co-sponsor of the United Nations General Assembly resolution on the Rights of Disabled Persons (Resolution 3447) and fully supported the resolution on the Rights of Mentally Retarded Persons (Resolution 2856). Ireland also supported the adoption by the General Conference of the International Labour Organisation of Convention 159 on the Vocational Rehabilitation and Employment of the Disabled.

In Ireland there is a long tradition of involvement by voluntary and nongovernmental bodies in the provision of services for disabled people. Indeed many of the present statutory services were originally initiated by voluntary organizations. The Department of Health and the regional health boards work in close cooperation with the voluntary and nongovernmental sector. Many of these bodies are fully funded by the State, and all are supported in some way. For example, the regional health boards are charged under the 1970 Health Act to provide vocational rehabilitation services for the disabled. In practice, most training centres and community workshops for disabled people are operated by voluntary and non-statutory bodies. All these bodies are funded, however, by the health boards. Various other services for disabled people are provided in a similar manner.

Ireland has also taken part in the European Community social integration programme for the disabled, in particular through a district project in the Midland Counties (for further information on this programme, see the details already mentioned under the Belgian contribution, pp. 33–37).

Methodology — Types of Legislative Approach to the Equality Concept

All sections of the population, including the disabled, are covered by the 1947–1970 Health Acts. There are special acts, the 1945–1961 Mental Treatment Acts, covering the mentally ill.

Section 68 of the 1970 Health Act gives the regional health boards the responsibility of providing disabled persons with vocational rehabilitation and placement services. This section of the Act allows the health boards to provide these services themselves or to designate another body to provide the services on their behalf. In practice, the services are provided by a combination of both methods.

Section 69 of the 1970 Act obliges a health board to pay a maintenance allowance to a disabled person aged 16 years or over, where neither the disabled person nor the disabled person's spouse (if any) is able to provide the disabled person's maintenance.

Review of the Present State of National Legislation

Elimination of discrimination or social prejudice
The rights of all citizens are guaranteed under the Irish Constitution. People, including the disabled, who feel they are being discriminated against, whether by private or statutory bodies, have recourse to the ombudsman and may request him or her to intervene on their behalf.

Social integration and full participation
As indicated earlier, Section 68 of the 1970 Health Act obliges the health boards to make available a service for the training of disabled people for employment suitable to their condition of health, and for making arrangements with employers for placing disabled persons in suitable employment.

All sections of the community whose income is below a certain level are entitled to free medical services. In addition, disabled people who do not qualify for free medical services on income grounds, may be entitled to free medical services if they suffer from certain specified disabilities.

The Department of the Environment provides grants to disabled people to help meet the costs of making any necessary modifications or extensions to their homes to make them more accessible. Grants are also available for house purchase. Persons in receipt of certain disability allowances are also entitled to free public transport and free telephone services.

The National Rehabilitation Board and some health boards operate an information service on the following items: bathroom and toilet equipment; beds, chairs and dressing aids; children's aids; eating, drinking and household equipment; incontinence aids; wheelchairs and walking aids; communication aids and home adaptations; and lifting equipment and leisure aids.

A person in receipt of a maintenance allowance from a health board may also be entitled to the following benefits: free travel on public transport, free electricity, free television service, free telephone rental, free fuel, and footwear for children.

There is a well developed system of educational provision for disabled children in Ireland. As far as is practicable, the approach is to enable disabled children to receive their education in ordinary schools, but where this is not feasible, special educational arrangements are made.

Special provision is made for disabled children in special classes attached to ordinary schools, in special schools, and in centres operated by voluntary organizations. Among the categories specially catered for are the visually and hearing impaired, the physically and mentally handicapped, the emotionally disturbed, and those with multiple handicaps. In each case a programme suited to the needs of the particular disability is provided, and school buildings are planned to cater for the special educational requirements of disabled children.

The Department of Education and various voluntary and non-governmental bodies cater for the cultural, sporting and other leisure activities of the disabled. The special Olympics for the Disabled were held in Ireland in 1985. The Wheelchair Games are held on an annual basis. The aim of the rehabilitation services in Ireland is to integrate as many disabled people as possible into community life. Self-help groups are encouraged, and it is the policy of the Department of Health to promote the establishment of independent living units for disabled persons.

The Health Education Bureau
Largely as a result of the recommendations of the Committee on Drug Education made in April 1974, the Government established the Health Education Bureau in 1975, to supply the needs of health education and to coordinate the existing work. Although established

in 1975, the Bureau was limited in its field of action by financial restrictions until a full staff was appointed in January 1978. The functions of the Bureau are as follows:

— to advise the Minister on the aspects of health education that should have priority at the national level;

— to draw up, in accordance with the agreed national priorities, programmes of health education for promotion at the national and local level;

— to carry out such programmes with the cooperation of the statutory and voluntary bodies engaged in health education;

— to maintain contact with voluntary bodies engaged in particular aspects of health education and, in accordance with the agreed national priorities, to give financial assistance to such bodies as appropriate and to the extent that the resources of the Bureau will permit;

— to provide statutory and voluntary bodies engaged in health education with help in carrying out their local programmes, including the production and distribution of educational material;

— to promote and conduct research and to evaluate health education activities;

— to act as a national centre of expertise and knowledge in all aspects of health education; and

— to promote greater concern for health education generally in the community.

In 1982, the Health Education Bureau adopted a life-cycle model of health education as a framework for the future development of the programmes. This model identifies the key issues, phases and needs in health and illness throughout the life cycle from birth to death, and reflects the general aim of the Bureau, which is to provide the means and opportunities for all vulnerable people to protect, maintain and improve their health as far as educational methods permit. This general aim is further elaborated in more detailed subsidiary aims, as follows:

— to increase the level of information among the entire population concerning factors that affect their health;

— to increase the value that people put upon health in their everyday lifestyle;

— to reduce significantly unhealthy behaviour and other factors that precede illness;

— to reduce the actual incidence and prevalence of preventable diseases;

— to increase the general level of health and wellbeing in the community/society.

The programmes that are currently being undertaken by the Bureau represent areas of special and immediate importance and may be amended or added to in future years. Each programme is drawn up to state its aims, audience, origin and content and can be generally categorized under the following headings: voluntary organizations; community health education; pregnancy education and education for parenthood; infant welfare; childhood, adolescence and young adulthood; mid-life; later life; essential services; positive health promotion and public visibility.

The prevention of disability
A continuous programme is needed to inform and stimulate people to pursue a healthier way of life and to avoid situations likely to result in illness, stress or disability. The Health Education Bureau has a central part to play in programmes that provide encouragement and advice about healthy living and in the organization of campaigns directed towards preventing or ameliorating specific disabilities. A number of projects sponsored by the Bureau may be mentioned as examples of its part in the campaign to raise public consciousness about different types of health hazard. The Bureau has produced a health education pack for schools entitled *Survival kit,* which is designed to create an awareness of safety in children from 4 to 12 years of age. This programme deals with safety in the home, road safety, water safety and safety in the environment. A short film for television has been produced entitled *Think child ... Think safe,* dealing with home accidents, including burns, scalds, electric shocks, poisoning and falls. The Bureau has contributed to the production of a 15-minute film highlighting the need for immunization against rubella. There is a continuing campaign against smoking, and the Bureau is also involved in efforts to promote a moderate approach to the consumption of alcohol, and to encourage participation in sport.

Ireland has a comprehensive health care programme for mothers and infants. The Minister for Health accepts that if the basic aims of ensuring safe delivery and giving the infant the best chance of optimal health and normal development are to be achieved, every expectant mother should have ready access to care at a consultant-staffed obstetric/neonatal unit.

The National Drugs Advisory Board issues advice to general practitioners on the teratogenic effects of drugs and on the prescribing of drugs and medicines to nursing mothers.

Immunization programmes have been the most important factor influencing changes in patterns of morbidity and mortality during this century and this is reflected in patterns of disability. The eradication of smallpox represents the ideal result of an immunization programme, but this is a unique experience; control rather than eradication is generally a more realistic objective. The objective of the national programme is to ensure that all infants receive immunization against diphtheria, pertussis, poliomyelitis and tuberculosis.

The Department of Labour has overall responsibility for the safety, health and welfare of persons employed in factories, offices, mines and quarries. This responsibility is solely related to the prevention of occupational accidents and diseases. The principal measures undertaken to ensure that occupational safety is promoted are:

— adopting statutory standards (acts and regulations)

— enforcing these through inspection, advice and prosecution

— stimulating awareness of the need for safe and healthy workplaces.

The Department of Labour's functions in these areas are exercised primarily by the Industrial Inspectorate. The Inspectorate includes engineers, architects, chemists and physicists and has offices in Dublin, Cork, Limerick, Waterford, Galway, Sligo, Athlone and Drogheda.

The National Industrial Safety Organisation (NISO) is a voluntary body whose aim is the promotion of safety awareness in industry. It receives a grant from the Department of Labour, which also supplies the full-time staff and office accommodation. NISO organizes training courses and lectures for managers, supervisors, safety officers, general operatives and other personnel concerned with safety. It has also produced a wide range of safety literature and posters and maintains a film library service for its members.

Source and Cost of Services for Disabled People

Various services, benefits, allowances and pensions are specifically available to disabled persons. The cost of these was over £IR 400 million (US $569 million) in 1983. Disabled people are also entitled to avail themselves of the whole range of benefits and services, such as the general medical services scheme, hospital services, the public health nursing service, social services, welfare services and educational services, but there are no separate figures available to show the extent to which these services are taken up by disabled people.

The Department of Health provides 11 000 places in psychiatric hospitals with services for the diagnosis, care and prevention of psychiatric ailments; 7000 residential places for the mentally handicapped, about 2000 of which are in psychiatric hospitals; 2400 places in day-care centres for the mentally handicapped; 1200 places for persons with hearing impairments, visual impairments and other physical disabilities; grants to voluntary agencies; and training fees for rehabilitation services. The National Rehabilitation Board is responsible for such matters as the assessment and placement of disabled people and hearing aid services.

The health boards provide various allowances. The disabled persons' maintenance allowance is payable to disabled persons between 16 and 66 years of age who are substantially handicapped. The allowance is subject to a means test. A person who qualifies for this allowance may also qualify for additional benefits from the Department of Social Welfare: free travel, free electricity, free bottled gas, free television licence, free telephone rental, free fuel and footwear for children. The disabled persons' rehabilitation allowance is payable to disabled persons undergoing training who are living away from home. The domiciliary care allowance is payable for the domiciliary care of handicapped children who need constant care and attention, substantially greater than would normally be required by a child of the same age and sex. The allowance may be paid for children between the ages of 2 and 16. The supplementary blind welfare allowance is payable to blind persons over the age of 16 years who are regarded as unemployable; the mobility allowance is payable to severely handicapped persons over the age of 16 years who are unable to walk; and the infectious diseases maintenance allowance is payable to persons undergoing treatment for certain specified diseases. These three allowances are subject to a means test. The health boards refund the cost of drugs and medicines for specified long-term ailments. They also make grants up to a maximum of £IR 1500 (US $2133) for the conversion of an existing motor vehicle or for the purchase of an adapted new motor vehicle for use by a disabled person. This grant is subject to a means test.

The Department of Social Welfare pays various pensions, benefits and allowances. The invalidity pension is payable to insured persons who are permanently incapable of work. The disability benefit is payable to an insured person who as a result of an occupational accident or disease is suffering from loss of physical or mental faculty. The blind pension is payable to a blind person who is over 18 years of age, is ordinarily resident in the State and satisfies a means test. Free travel is available to persons receiving the blind pension, invalidity pension, disabled persons' maintenance allowance or invalidity pension benefit from the Department of Health and Social Security in Great Britain or Northern Ireland. Subject to certain conditions, recipients of the invalidity pension and disabled persons' maintenance allowance may qualify for free electricity or bottled gas, and a free televison licence. Subject to certain conditions, recipients of the invalidity pension, blind pension and disabled persons' maintenance allowance qualify for free telephone rental. The Department of the Environment makes grants available for structural alterations and extensions to houses which improve the living conditions of disabled people. Loans are also available towards the balance of the costs of adaptation work for low-income applicants. Invalid carriages not exceeding 6 cwt (about 300 kg) unladen weight and vehicles specially constructed or adapted for use by persons wholly or almost wholly without the use of their legs are exempt from parking restrictions and fees. Such persons may also be entitled to the following benefits: repayment of value added tax and excise duty on new cars, and repayment of excise duty on petrol up to 600 gallons (about 2700 litres) per person per annum.

The Revenue Commissioners make similar concessions. The full amount of the excise duty and value added tax charged for a new motor vehicle specially built or converted for a disabled driver is refundable provided it qualifies for the road tax relief. Excise duty on petrol up to 600 gallons (about 2700 litres) per person per annum is repayable. This concession applies to vehicles extensively adapted (30% or more) to carry disabled passengers. The Revenue Commissioners also make certain income tax allowances. A single blind person is entitled to an extra £IR 500 (US $710) on top of his or her single allowance. For a married couple the extra allowance is £IR 1200 (US $1706). The incapacitated child allowance of £IR 500 (US $710) is for children permanently incapacitated before the age of 21 or while in full-time education. The dependent relative allowance of £IR 110 (US $156) is given to a taxpayer who maintains an incapacitated relative aged 65 or over, or who has a son or daughter living with him/her and on whom the taxpayer is dependent. An incapacitated person who employs a housekeeper to take care of him/her may claim a tax allowance of £IR 700 (US $995). If the person employed is a relative, the taxpayer may not claim the dependent relative allowance in addition to the housekeeper allowance.

The Department of Education provides a wide range of teaching services for disabled children including special schools, special classes in ordinary schools, remedial teachers, preschools, vocational training centres and home tuition. The Department also provides child care assistants in special schools for the mentally handicapped, physically disabled, hearing impaired and visually impaired. Free school transport is provided for children attending special centres. The cost of these services is included in the overall allocation of the Department and separate costings are not available.

Luxembourg

General Principles

In the Grand Duchy of Luxembourg no single ministry is solely and exclusively responsible for disabled persons, nor is there any single piece of legislation covering all aspects of this problem. Various ministries (in particular the Ministry of Health, the Ministry of the Family and Social Solidarity and the Ministry of Social Security) are responsible for particular aspects of the question, their actions being governed by legislation specific to the disabled or by the general framework of national legislation. Similarly, financial assistance to the disabled is funded from the budgets of different ministries.

The Constitution of the Grand Duchy, which dates back many years and has not been revised recently, makes no reference to disabled persons. It sets out in general terms, however, the rights of all citizens, the right to work, the right to social security and the right to health protection, principles which have been applied in practice in the legislation in favour of the disabled.

A government policy statement, made by the Prime Minister on behalf of the Government after the 1984 elections, gave notice of a number of measures in support of the disabled, namely a revised structure for the recruitment and professional retraining service for disabled workers, modernization of the infrastructure of psychiatric care, and increased financial support to sporting activities for the disabled. It also announced a draft bill on the education of children and adolescents suffering from mental handicaps.

Reference should be made in connection with the coordination of such activities to the decision by the Government in 1985 to create a National Council for the Disabled. It coordinates, for instance, the various private but state-subsidized associations representing the interests of particular groups of disabled persons. These associations have set up various homes for the disabled with state support, covering in particular the fields of drug addiction, physical re-education, mental disease and gerontology.

National Involvement in International Action

Luxembourg authorities have supported the movement in favour of the Charter for the 80s, drawn up by Rehabilitation International. The Grand Duchy is participating in the European network of rehabilitation centres under the auspices of the European Community. It also supports the Community's social integration programme for the disabled through the participation of the Capellen Rehabilitation Centre in a four-year pilot project. This is sponsored by the European Social Fund and aims at linking rehabilitation with the demands of the labour market, and providing assistance in educational, psychological and social fields to disabled persons leaving rehabilitation centres, in order to reduce the risk of "professional de-adaptation" and to encourage the recruitment of the disabled. The team responsible for this project is also assessing the concrete results of the probationary employment of the disabled. A consultative committee has been set up in connection with this project, with representatives from the competent departments of the ministries concerned, private organizations dealing with the disabled, trade unions and employers' associations. (For further information on the European Community programme, see the details already mentioned under the Belgian contribution, pp. 33–37.)

Methodology —Types of Legislative Approach to the Equality Concept

Legislation has been introduced in Luxembourg at different times, dealing in each case with a specific aspect of the situation of the disabled; in consequence there is no specific act or code that incorporates all measures to protect their interests.

In some cases a law of general scope will be found to include a specific provision in favour of disabled persons. For example, under the legislation on children's allowances, the age limit of 18 years does not apply for the parents of a disabled child who is incapable of earning his or her living. Legislative regulations for the disabled are in most cases derived from other laws that deal expressly with this category of person. No distinction is made in general between different categories of disability, although there is, of course, a threshold below which a disability is not recognized as such.

Review of the Present State of National Legislation

Elimination of discrimination or social prejudice
Some of the measures adopted to eliminate prejudice against the disabled are mentioned under other headings; special reference should be made to the compulsory schooling of disabled children and the measures taken to find employment for the disabled.

In regard to education, a pilot project is at present under way on the integration of children with serious physical disabilities into normal school courses. Children suffering from dyslexia at nursery school age, who receive special treatment during the week at logopaedic centres, attend their local town or village schools on Saturdays.

The social legislation of the Grand Duchy does not guarantee disabled workers the minimum social salary when their output is clearly reduced, but it prohibits the employer from fixing the wage rate unilaterally. In the event of a dispute, the Disabled Workers Office has the last word.

The service that provides training for work in the open labour market is privately run but subsidized by the State, and is also responsible for placing the disabled in normal firms, assisted only by a guardian.

Social reintegration and full participation

Working life and vocational rehabilitation
The Office for Recruitment and Vocational Retraining of Disabled Workers, which operates within the Department of Employment, was established by the Act of 28 April 1959. As its name suggests, this Office sponsors the professional recruitment of disabled persons, where necessary after special training or professional retraining, financed under the budget of the Office. Irrespective of whether the handicap is physical or mental, congenital or acquired, the working capacity must have been reduced by at least 30%. These services are available not only to Luxembourg citizens but also to nationals of other countries in the European Community who have suffered an accident at work in the Grand Duchy, and also to nationals of countries with which Luxembourg has concluded a reciprocal agreement on the subject.

The 1959 Act requires the national civil service and the local authorities, the national railway administration and other public

187

establishments to reserve at least 2% of their staff vacancies for disabled workers. This obligation applies equally to firms in the private sector employing more than 50 staff.

Victims of work accidents are given priority for recruitment in their own firm to a position suited to their capacity.

In addition, the Office for Recruitment and Vocational Retraining of Disabled Workers makes a financial contribution to the wage paid by the employer to disabled workers, so as to ensure that they receive a normal salary, even if their output fails to reach the norms achieved by healthy workers.

Education and vocational training

The Act of 14 March 1973, relating to the establishment of special educational institutions and services, requires the State to ensure that children who, by reason of their mental, behavioural or sensory characteristics, cannot attend normal schools, receive the specialist education their condition requires. These children are subject in the normal way to compulsory schooling. Special schools or vocational training centres have in the mean time been set up by the State to meet this requirement. Teaching in these establishments, together with teaching materials, medical treatment, transport and, where necessary, boarding facilities, is provided free of charge.

The Act of 16 August 1968, relating to audiometric and orthophonic services, established a logopaedic centre in which children suffering from deafness, hearing defects or dyslexia are able to receive special schooling.

Communications and transport

A distinguishing symbol for the physically disabled was authorized under a Ministerial Order of 12 December 1977 allowing vehicles driven by or transporting disabled persons to use special parking facilities. In particular, specific parking spaces are reserved for disabled persons. A Ministerial Order of 2 June 1981 granted recognition of the validity on Luxembourg territory of similar symbols or cards issued by other European countries.

Disabled persons enjoy the privilege of free transport on the railway system of the Grand Duchy, priority seats being reserved for them. They are also exempted from paying 50% of the motor vehicle tax. Further exemptions below 50% are granted on an optional basis and according to the financial situation of the disabled person.

Leisure and sport

The Luxembourg Disabled Sport Federation is approved by the Ministry of Sport in accordance with the Act of 26 March 1976 relating to physical training and sports and in consequence enjoys the advantages set out therein, in particular eligibility for Government grants.

Workers with a certain degree of disability are entitled under the law to an additional six days' leave per year.

Independent living

The Government is firmly in favour of disabled persons remaining at home when, although they require the assistance of another person, transfer to a specialized institution is not absolutely necessary. In line with this approach, an Act passed on 16 April 1979 authorized payment of a special allowance to disabled persons requiring the assistance of another person in the performance of everyday activities in the home. This allowance is intended to encourage families wherever possible to keep disabled relatives at home. In the same way, disabled persons without a family are able to pay for the services of another person to provide them with regular care. This allowance also is payable in cases where the visual acuity of the better eye is less than one tenth of the normal.

Further encouragement to keep the disabled in the home is provided by the establishment, for disabled and elderly persons, of home-help services and meals-on-wheels.

Housing and physical environment

A Grand Duchy regulation of 25 February 1979 enables the Government to cover part of the costs of equipping a home according to the needs of a disabled person. This subsidy can represent up to 50% of the total cost.

An Act passed on 11 April 1983 authorizes the Government to build and equip a home for children and young persons in the north of the country and to plan the layout of its immediate surroundings. Similar homes have been established by private associations with support from the national budget. The State also contributes to the running costs of many homes established by private associations with which an agreement has been concluded.

Social services

No special social services for the disabled have been established by legislation. Disabled perons may, however, call on the social services at the local and national levels, or on those provided by private organizations such as the Luxembourg League for Preventive Medicine and Medico-Social Action and the Luxembourg Red Cross, the staff of which consist mainly of social workers, all paid by the State.

The Act of 1 March 1974 relating to the organization of the National Neuropsychiatric Hospital requires it, as the only psychiatric hospital in the country, to provide a social assistance service for its patients.

Care, medical rehabilitation, technical aids
Under current legislation, the social security services assume responsibility for expenses incurred in the medical care and medical rehabilitation of the disabled, who are also eligible for 100% reimbursement of the cost of prostheses. Although the current reimbursement rate applicable to invalid chairs is far from adequate, the rate is being revised and a fairly substantial grant is available for this purpose from national funds.

The prevention of disability

Public information
The Act of 21 November 1980, relating to the organization of the Directorate of Health, established within this Directorate a division of preventive and social medicine responsible *inter alia* for all matters relating to the prevention of disease and the medicosocial supervision of the disabled. This division undertakes periodical campaigns for the dissemination of information among the population, placing particular emphasis on the importance of care and preventive measures, such as poliomyelitis vaccination. Brochures have been distributed in the series *Letter to parents* dealing with the subject of child safety in the home.

Sécurité routière, a Luxembourg association for the prevention of accidents on the roads, undertakes poster and press campaigns to reduce traffic accidents.

Health education
The division of preventive and social medicine referred to above periodically distributes free brochures and pamphlets to schools emphasizing the benefits of a healthy life. This division is also responsible for campaigns against drug addiction and alcoholism. The main elements in such campaigns are the circulation of information on the subject, lectures to target groups, and the provision of advisory centres.

Health promotion and disease prevention services
The Act of 21 November 1980, relating to the organization of the Directorate of Health, established the necessary services in the fields of orthoptics, pleoptics and audiophonology, to cater for the

detection and rehabilitation of persons suffering from visual or auditory disorders, or defects affecting vocalization, speech and language.

Public advisory centres are run throughout the country by the Red Cross Society and the Luxembourg League for Preventive Medicine and Medico-Social Action. Consultations on infant disorders are free of charge.

Safety measures at work, on the roads and in other public places
The use of seat belts in the front seats of vehicles and the wearing of helmets by motorcyclists are obligatory under the Highway Code.

Health protection and workplace safety are governed by the Act of 28 August 1924 and its implementing regulations. The Act covers in particular female labour (including the prohibition of nightwork, apart from rare exceptions), the employment of pregnant women and women after childbirth (the prohibition of certain forms of heavy or insalubrious work, the authorization of maternity leave and a break from work during the lactation period) and child and adolescent labour (prohibition of employment before the fifteenth birthday and of certain types of employment, and the need for a medical suitability examination).

Preventive medical examinations
A prenuptial medical examination is obligatory under an Act passed on 19 December 1972. Other preventive medical examinations, for children in schools, for licensed members of accredited sport federations and for blood donors, are also undertaken.

With the aim of the prevention or early detection of handicaps in young children, the provisions of an Act of 20 June 1977 make payment of the various instalments of the childbirth allowance dependent on a specific number of medical examinations to be undergone by the mother during pregnancy and after delivery, and by the child up to the age of two years. These obligatory examinations of children were extended to the age of four years by an Act passed on 15 May 1984.

Miscellaneous
To prevent iatrogenic drug addiction, some drugs that are liable to induce dependence in the patient may only be prescribed by a doctor in a prescription book with stub counterfoils, so as to enable the health authorities to detect prescription abuses.

Systems of income support
At present a disabled person who has never worked is not personally covered under the social security system. A draft bill to alter this state of affairs, however, is at present before Parliament.

Disabled persons who are employed enjoy all the normal benefits guaranteed by social legislation. Any reduction in the remuneration to a disabled person owing to reduced work output in no way affects the pension to which he or she will eventually be entitled.

If an employed person falls victim to an occupational disability, he or she continues to enjoy the benefits of sickness insurance and receives a disability pension. This pension is increased if the disability has been caused by an accident at work or an occupational disease.

By virtue of the provisions of an Act of 29 April 1954 and its subsequent amendments, payment of the family allowance, which is due in principle until the child completes his or her eighteenth year, may be continued without any age limit for persons who are suffering from a chronic condition or disease whereby they are unable to support themselves. The family allowance for minors is increased if the child is suffering from a permanent reduction of at least 50% in physical or mental capacity.

All Luxembourg citizens and persons resident in the country for at least 15 years, who have been in regular work, are guaranteed a minimum income under the provisions of the Act of 30 July 1960, which established the National Solidarity Fund. Persons who are incapable of working are exempt from the condition relating to regular work, so that any disabled person having no other source of income will still receive a pension from the National Solidarity Fund. Persons entitled to such pensions are automatically included in the sickness insurance system. The allowance applicable to the seriously disabled is again paid from this Fund.

The Income Tax Act grants persons with a physical handicap a rebate, the amount of which depends on the degree of disability.

Various ministerial departments also have funds available from which grants can be made to the disabled for various purposes, such as the modification of a vehicle for a disabled driver.

Evaluation of Progress in National Legislation

The International Year of Disabled Persons, 1981, brought home to the public authorities and to the population of the Grand Duchy as a whole the problems faced by disabled persons. This has been reflected at the national level not so much in the promulgation of new legislation as in the provision of specific aid to the disabled, in particular the establishment of new forms of residential accommodation and rehabilitation centres. Even the most carefully drafted legislation will be ineffective if the political will is lacking to translate it into action, in particular by the provision of adequate financial resources. On the other hand, the public authorities have almost boundless opportunities to improve the situation of the disabled without the need for legislation, by setting up an appropriate infrastructure and providing generous subsidies for private initiative. It is generally felt that existing legislation meets current needs, apart from the gaps referred to in the following section and in the projected legislation described on pp. 33N37. The Government therefore intends in the main to concentrate on administrative rather than legislative measures.

Gaps in the legislation

The main gaps in the legislation relate to accommodation and the living environment. Although most recently constructed public buildings are designed to provide access for the disabled, there is no actual legislation imposing this requirement. This applies also to flats in residential buildings.

In the same way there are no regulations in force covering the design of areas open to the public, such as pavements or underground parking areas.

Associations of disabled persons would like to be able to benefit from the setting up of a public service that could provide information and advice to disabled persons wishing to equip their home (for example, to install a bathroom or a lift). They would also like to have a special home opened to accommodate disabled persons temporarily during any unexpected absence of the person who usually takes care of them at home (for example, while on holiday or for health reasons).

It is reasonable to suppose that Government action in favour of the disabled would be more effective if centralized under a single ministerial department or at least under a body given competence for all problems relating to the disabled.

Recent concrete achievements

Two new vocational training centres were set up in 1984 by Grand-Ducal Decree, within the framework of the Act of 1973 on special educational institutes and services. These centres, which are intended for persons suffering from mental and sensory handicaps, provide both theoretical instruction and practical training covering, in particular, woodwork, metalwork, packing and bookbinding operations, gardening and forestry. The centres try to obtain professional employment for their trainees and provide follow-up support in their subsequent career.

A third centre has recently been established for disabled adolescents completing orthopaedic classes and courses at graded education centres, which operate in conjunction with the Higher Institute of Teaching Studies and Research.

A new home to accommodate disabled children and adolescents has been built in the north of the country in accordance with an Act of 1983. At the same time the Government is continuing to subsidize other homes and medical/vocational training institutes run by private associations.

One successful example of activities in this field is a pilot project to stimulate the creativity of seriously disabled persons, carried out in the Capellen Rehabilitation Centre. Working in conjunction with artists from Luxembourg and Austria, disabled persons have successfully designed a public garden and park. Their creative ability was found to exhibit an astonishing degree of spontaneity and originality.

The general conclusion may be drawn that the International Year of Disabled Persons has made not only the public but also the authorities much more conscious of and sensitive to the problems facing disabled persons, which has resulted in a far greater willingness to release funds for various forms of assistance to them.

Constraints and difficulties encountered

The situation of the disabled of Luxembourg can be considered fully satisfactory in regard to their income, accommodation in a protected environment, education and professional training. Difficulties begin to arise, however, as regards integrating or reintegrating the disabled into professional life. Here again the situation is satisfactory in protected workshops, but integration into normal professional life is complicated by the requirements of the labour market for higher qualifications and/or increased output. There is no need to stress the point that the disabled are competing on the labour market with people already unemployed. Furthermore, the new technologies that now dominate the market necessitate qualifications that most disabled persons are unable to obtain. At the same time the traditional sectors based on handicrafts are in decline in industrialized societies, giving place all the time to these new technologies. In other words, there is a great gap between the professional training provided for the disabled to suit their capabilities and the demand for their services on the labour market.

It has already been pointed out that the Office for Recruitment and Vocational Retraining of Disabled Workers is prepared to contribute part of the salary paid by the employer to disabled persons. This has helped greatly in finding employment for the disabled, but the total number of vacancies available is still clearly less than the demand.

Legislative programme for the future

Two bills have been drafted by the Ministry of Health that, although they do not relate directly to the situation of the disabled, will nevertheless contribute to the prevention or at least the early detection of a disability. One of these will centralize school medical services under the control of the Ministry of Health, while the other will establish industrial medicine on a systematic basis.

Another bill before Parliament is aimed at coordinating and extending the medical, social and therapeutic services in Luxembourg, so as to cover persons suffering from mental disease, drug addiction, age-related illnesses and disability generally. The need for this has been made amply clear by the regrettable lack of coordination and cooperation between the different spheres of public and private activity. Its principal aims are:

— to provide a legal basis for existing centres, homes and services;

— to establish a coordinating and planning body, so as to avoid duplication of effort;

— to clarify the relationship between the public authorities and private organizations, in particular by the conclusion of agreements on proportional responsibility for operating costs;

— to make available to centres, homes and services multi-disciplinary assistance from the wide range of scientific sectors concerned;

— to arrange, in agreement with parents, for the care of disabled children to be taken over at an early stage by the competent service.

Another facet of government policy, being implemented in conjunction with various private organizations, is to extend the availability of care in the home, so as to enable disabled persons to remain as far as possible in their home environment.

The suitability of accommodation and the urban environment is to be covered by regulations guaranteeing access and possibility of use by the disabled.

The Government is sponsoring a special drive to encourage the employment of disabled persons. Although this does not form part of a short-term government programme, it is reasonable to suppose that any measure to relieve the congestion of the normal labour market, in particular a reduction of the working week, will at the same time effectively promote the employment of the disabled.

195

Monaco

General Principles

The Principality of Monaco is a small town of 27 000 inhabitants, so that the problems facing the public authorities differ greatly from those of larger states. At the same time, the number of disabled persons resident in Monaco, adults and children, is very low (about 30 overall).

Under Article 26 of the Constitution, Monegasque citizens are entitled to state aid in the case of destitution, unemployment, sickness, disability, old age and maternity.

Foreign nationals in the Principality enjoy all rights that are not expressly reserved to Monegasque citizens.

All social measures in favour of the disabled are in practice provided by the State or under its supervision. An example of this is the subsidization by the State of private associations that include disabled persons or represent their interests.

National Involvement in International Action

Where its resources permit, the Principality participates in international action.

Methodology — Types of Legislative Approach to the Equality Concept

The promulgation of legislation relating to particular categories of disabled persons has not proved necessary in view of their very small numbers. The rights of disabled persons are guaranteed by general legal texts that are of sufficiently wide scope to be adapted to particular cases.

197

Review of the Present State of Legislation

Elimination of discrimination or social prejudice
Legislation has not been found necessary, since there is no discrimination against disabled persons and they are spontaneously accepted in the national community.

Two associations look after the interests of the disabled, specifically those with motor and mental disabilities, apart from associations of more general scope such as the Red Cross Society and the Friends of the Children (AMADE).

Social reintegration and full participation
No legislation has yet been passed that is solely concerned with disabled persons. In practice, a great deal has been done by the public authorities to promote the reintegration of the disabled into society. This includes special lifts, parking facilities, the modification of pavements and the holding of special classes.

Where young disabled persons have to attend an establishment providing both education and medical treatment, either on a boarding or half-boarding basis, accommodation and travel expenses are met *in toto* by the social security or social assistance services.

Financial assistance is also provided to meet the needs of disabled adults.

The prevention of disability
Preventive action consists mainly of supervision during pregnancy: prenatal examination (free of charge or reimbursed by social security) is obligatory.

Reference may also be made to an important regulation on work hygiene and safety, which it is the responsibility of inspectors of labour to enforce.

Systems of income support
In addition to the financial assistance mentioned above, a very comprehensive social security system exists in Monaco, providing sickness and disability insurance, protection against accidents at work and occupational diseases, and special allowances for disabled children.

Evaluation of Progress in National Legislation

The interests of the disabled are in practice looked after with particular care by the public authorities, special attention being paid to adults who have lost a measure of their working capacity by placing them in employment.

The Principality has contributed to the establishment of a Centre for Aid Through Work, situated in France. This establishment, which is to come into operation shortly, will further promote the social reintegration of disabled persons.

A bill, at present in draft form, will set the official seal on a wide range of measures that are at present being taken in favour of the disabled.

Netherlands

General Principles

In 1981 and 1982, the objective and starting points of a policy for the disabled were presented in Government documents to the Netherlands Parliament. Parliament responded with approval, but the objective and starting points never became law. While the Netherlands does not have a separate overall law on rehabilitation or the care of disabled persons, it does have various lesser laws that relate principally to them.

The broad objective of the policy for the disabled is to ensure that the disabled can function as well as possible in all contexts and in every sphere of life, in accordance with their age and in relation to their social and cultural setting, and can achieve full development within their limitations.

The words "in all contexts and in every sphere of life" indicate that the activities undertaken to achieve the objective cannot be limited to the disabled person alone. The family or environment, housing, education, work and leisure situation, and society at large must all be involved to an equal extent.

As the nature and severity of the handicap differ, the meaning of the words "function" and "full development" will vary. For all that, the objective remains applicable to such (mentally) handicapped people in whom a high degree of dependence is a permanent condition and who are not or barely able to perform any activity. The policy for the disabled will endeavour to create for these seriously handicapped people as much as for those with less serious handicaps, ways of achieving a measure of self-fulfilment, however small, and to make and keep life for them and for their immediate environment as bearable as possible.

The overall objective of the policy permits the derivation of more specific objectives for various categories.

The broad objective defined above can be analysed and interpreted to produce several starting points.

The first general starting point must be that the disabled are part of the community. The community will have to be structured so that disabled persons can live in it and be recognized and accepted as full members of that community. To the extent that, and for so long as, the development of the individual's potential requires that he or she should live under special conditions, these special conditions should be continually reviewed and properly adjusted to the personal development, phase of life and choice of the disabled person.

A second starting point, typical for the Netherlands situation, is that the assistance and treatment of, and the encounter with, the disabled and those close to them should offer them adequate scope to develop and experience their own conception of the world and of humanity, or their own personal ethos.

Preservation of the freedom and power of decision of the disabled person is the third starting point arising from the broad objective of the policy of the disabled. The words "can function" and "can achieve development" imply that the disabled person keeps the primary responsibility for deciding in what measure and at what rate to make use of opportunities for improvement. Such free choice and power of decision presuppose, of course, that disabled individuals are properly informed about the options and about the implications of their decisions. The recognition of the freedom and responsibility of the disabled person further implies that emancipation and participation in policy development should be encouraged. By coordinating their activities and ideas, the organizations of disabled persons in the Netherlands have enhanced the effectiveness of their participation.

A fourth starting point is that any facilities must be appropriate to the situation of the disabled person. The nature and extent of the facilities and rehabilitation aid provided should be a function of the goal they serve: the creation of conditions enabling the disabled person to be a full member of society. The extent and duration of rehabilitation, care or assistance should be restricted to the needs of the disabled person. As soon as he or she has found a place in society, the policy for the disabled will only be of indirect concern. Existing facilities, arrangements and aids will regularly be tested for their effectiveness; care will be taken to prevent the creation of fresh barriers to participation in society. As members of society, the disabled will primarily have to turn to the general facilities and arrangements open to the entire public. To complement these, special facilities and aids will continue to be necessary in meeting additional needs.

202

Various policy areas and the coordination and continuity of care and the provision of facilities for the disabled person are obviously interrelated. The disabled person is a whole person, whose life has a variety of aspects. Each of these aspects may be the object of several sectors of policy and care. The proper temporal sequence in the provision of facilities is also vital. It is therefore important that measures taken by the various policy sectors are mutually consistent and that coordination and continuity in social care are ensured by careful management.

The coordination of the policy for the disabled at the central level is a matter for the joint ministers who are significantly concerned with the policy and care for the disabled, under the direction of the minister in charge of coordination of policy for the disabled — either the Minister or the State Secretary for Welfare, Health and Cultural Affairs. The joint ministers are assisted by the Interministerial Steering Group on Policy for the Disabled, established in 1968.

The Interministerial Steering Group consults regularly with the umbrella organizations covering organizations for both the physically and mentally handicapped, in order to ensure that their ideas and proposals are taken into consideration in developing new policies. Finally, within the Lower House of the States General there is a Special Committee on Policy for the Disabled, which monitors the policies of the various ministries involved to ensure that they are properly coordinated and integrated.

National Involvement in International Action

Although the Netherlands has not always literally endorsed all international charters, declarations of rights, resolutions and the United Nations World Programme of Action, its policy for the disabled is according to the spirit of these documents.

For example, if the United Nations Declaration on the Rights of Mentally Retarded Persons (1971) is compared with the Netherlands parliamentary document *Principles for coordinated policy development on the mentally handicapped* (1981) and the later more elaborate policy document *The mentally retarded* (1983), it is clear that, disregarding differences of emphasis, they agree on all major points. Because of the considerable agreement between the United Nations Declaration and the policy documents, and as the two complement one another, it has been decided to adopt them jointly as a touchstone for the policy proposals elaborated in these documents.

During the International Year of Disabled Persons, the Netherlands Committee for the Year launched several international projects, such as a vaccination programme in Upper Volta.

The Netherlands participates in the Committee on the Rehabilitation and Resettlement of the Disabled of the Council of Europe.

Information on policy for the disabled is given regularly to international organizations such as the United Nations, the European Community, WHO (particularly in the context of the WHO strategy for health for all by the year 2000) and the Council of Europe.

The Netherlands is active in the European Community's action programme to promote the social integration of disabled people. In particular, two district projects have been set up in the Netherlands as part of the European Community network. The idea of the district projects is based on the fact that the most important services for disabled people are delivered locally, and that in all member states there exists a problem about the satisfactory coordination of all these services. It follows that a concerted effort to improve this coordination, while it cannot solve all the problems of disabled people, will make a significant contribution — one, moreover, that cannot be made in any other way. (For further information on the European Community programme, see the details already mentioned under the Belgian contribution, pp. 33–37.)

Methodology — Types of Legislative Approach to the Equality Concept

Three types of legislative approach are applied in the Netherlands:

(*a*) integration of the various disability issues in a number of different laws, for example, regulations about the accessibility of accommodation, in the conditions of subsidy and guidelines;

(*b*) adoption of a specific law to secure the rights of the disabled, for example, the Handicapped Workers Employment Act (see p. 208).

(*c*) provisions specific to a category of disabled persons, for example, the proposal for a law on guardianship that would deal with the property matters of mentally disabled persons.

Braille documents and recorded sound tapes are handled free of charge by the postal and telecommunications services.

Review of the Present State of National Legislation

Elimination of discrimination or social prejudice

There is no specific legislation against the elimination of discrimination or social prejudice against the disabled.

Article I, paragraph 1, of the Netherlands Constitution states that all persons in the Netherlands shall be treated equally in equal circumstances. Discrimination on the grounds of religion, belief, political opinion, race or sex, or on any other grounds whatsoever shall not be permitted.

Article I, paragraph 10a, states that everyone shall have the right to inviolability of his or her person, subject to limitations to be laid down by or by virtue of the law.

In December 1985, the Ministry of Housing, Physical Planning and Environmental Protection sent a circular letter to all municipalities, asking them to guard against discrimination when setting up small-scale living accommodation for the mentally retarded within the community.

Measures to remove general prejudice against the disabled by enabling them to participate in many aspects of life are described in the following section.

In 1980, a committee was set up to investigate alleged discrimination against mentally handicapped persons when travelling or on vacation.

Social reintegration and full participation

Care, medical rehabilitation, technical aids
The Health Insurance Act provides the right to medical, pharmaceutical and dental care, hospital nursing and numerous other forms of treatment and provisions (in some cases a contribution is due). It covers wage-earners and persons in a comparable position with an income not exceeding an annually fixed amount.

The Exceptional Medical Expenses Act provides for a national insurance scheme that, in principle, applies to all residents of the Netherlands. It also covers expenses for treatment and nursing in (recognized) institutions for the mentally retarded, institutions for people with sensory handicaps (the deaf and hard-of-hearing, the blind and the partially sighted), nursing homes, medical children's homes, medical day nurseries for the handicapped, family-substitute homes for the handicapped (with coverage of day treatment in a nursing institution from the first day onwards), hospitals, including sanatoria and mental hospitals (with coverage from the 366th day onwards). It also covers assistance from a home nursing association and (recognized) regional establishments for ambulatory assistance for mental health, in which the institutions for psychotherapeutics, sociopsychiatric services, medical pedagogical bureaux and bureaux dealing with questions on everyday life and the family all cooperate. A contribution of at most f. 1350 (US $637) per month is requested from the insured person who is staying in a hospital, an institution or a home under this law.

Under the General Disability Benefits Act all insured persons up to the age of 65 qualify for measures to maintain, restore or improve their ability to work, for medical services and for measures to improve their living conditions. Benefits that were awarded before a person turned 65 may continue to be granted beyond that age.

Measures taken under this law include special vocational training, adaptation of the workplace, refund of the cost of special diets, and transport facilities (such as an invalid carriage or car and the reimbursement of taxi fares). In brief, they amount to any item that does not form part of ordinary household equipment, is specifically required because of the handicap in question, and cannot be obtained under other statutory schemes. The measures taken are geared to the individual disabled person.

At the request of Parliament, the Government has taken steps to help those parents who want to care for their physically and/or mentally handicapped children at home rather than sending them to institutions. Home-training projects are subsidized for parents with a disabled child at home. There are opportunities for ambulatory teaching support. Furthermore, proposals have been made to engage the personnel, the knowledge and the provisions of health care institutions, to make more use of the existing services such as the Home Help Service and the national Red Cross, to support local and regional tending (baby-sitting) centres, and to intensify the information and advice to parents with a disabled child. In 1981, the Information and Documentation Centre for the Disabled Child and its Parents was founded. The development of regional terminals for the computerized data network of this centre has been given priority.

Housing and physical environment
A Decree on financial aid for housing the disabled instituted a scheme in 1978 whereby the cost of converting an individual house and/or moving to a converted house is reimbursed up to a maximum of f. 45 000 (US $21 240). A larger sum may be granted if the person concerned would otherwise be forced to live in an institution.

A combination of the above-mentioned scheme and the General Disability Benefits Act opens up the possibility for persons with severe physical handicaps to live independently in cluster compounds. The cost of the assistance required by the inhabitants to carry out the activities of daily life is reimbursed under a special order under the General Disability Benefits Act.

206

A model building regulation was drawn up by the Union of Netherlands Municipalities and concerns local building regulations. It contains some paragraphs regarding the accessibility of new dwellings and public buildings. The Central Coordination Agency for Promotion of Accessibility for the Disabled has been set up as a government committee in which representatives of local authorities and private organizations participate, with the aim of promoting accessibility, and coordinating and advising on measures regarding accessibility. Existing government buildings are being adapted and new buildings will be made easily accessible and easy to use.

Transport
A national invalid's parking card can be obtained by a person who is not able to walk more than 100 metres. The entitlements are, for example:

— parking during a limited period in places where other people are not allowed to park;

— unlimited parking in places where other people can park for a restricted period;

— parking in special parking places for invalids.

A local invalid's parking card is only valid in the municipality where it is issued. The criteria for obtaining this card are less stringent and the facilities often more extensive. Besides special general invalid parking places, there exist individual invalid parking places near the home address or working address of disabled people.

The position of wheelchairs on the public road is regulated by law within general legislation.

The Ministry of Transport has sent guidelines to all municipalities concerning the adaptation of traffic and road provisions for the disabled. An experiment using these adaptations is being carried out in Gouda.

Persons escorting all categories of disabled person can travel free of charge on all public transport. To this end a card is issued by the Netherlands Railway Association (*Nederlandse Spoorwegen*).

Most platforms on railway stations are accessible to the disabled, if necessary with the help of railway personnel. A number of platforms can be used independently by wheelchair users. On major stations collapsible ramps are available to get wheelchairs into the railway carriage, while wheelchairs can be provided for those who cannot walk long distances. A plan is in operation to make all intercity stations fully accessible to the disabled.

In several municipalities adapted transport services are available. This is not a government policy but has come about because quite a few commercial transport companies have adapted buses for wheelchair users, and because there are several volunteer organizations that provide transport for the elderly and the handicapped. In addition, many institutions provide adapted transport for disabled residents, employees, pupils and trainees.

Communication

The national postal and telecommunications services provide various ways of adapting telephone equipment for different categories of handicapped users. Personal services can be provided at home on request, while a number of institutions for the aged and the handicapped are visited weekly. Braille documents and sound tapes are handled free of charge.

Other assistance includes the marking of banknotes to help the blind, and the subtitling of a considerable number of television programmes (teletext).

Working life

The aim of the Sheltered Employment Act is to offer social security in the form of substitute employment suited to individual abilities and directed as far as possible at maintaining, restoring or improving the individual's capacity for work. The stimulation of the ability to work can lead to acceptance of work under normal conditions. The municipal authorities are largely subsidized by the Government for the running of the sheltered (or social) employment system.

The Disabled Persons Employment Act lays down that any firm with a staff of more than 20 must employ at least one disabled person and at least a further one disabled person for each additional 50 staff. This law has been superseded, however, by the Handicapped Workers Employment Act (*Wet Arbeid Gehandicapte Werknemers*) presented to Parliament in 1982. The social partners decide what measures have to be taken to integrate the people who are subject to this Act — the main group being those who are entitled to benefits under the Disability Insurance Act and/or the General Disability Benefits Act — into employment either in industrial firms, social institutions or governmental agencies. If, after a period of about three years, the measures taken are not up to standard, the Minister of Social Affairs can lay down a compulsory percentage (between 3% and 7%) for the staff that must be disabled. The Act introduces additional compulsory measures and better conditions for employers in order to create a better atmosphere from social, financial and technical points

208

of view, so that the improved integration of disabled workers into a normal social life may be guaranteed.

Vocational rehabilitation and training
Vocational training for the disabled is given in the training centres in Hoensbroek and Werkenrode. In Hoensbroek, two-year courses are given to those aged 18–40 years in the fields of fine metalwork, electronics, technical design and administration. Werkenrode has a one-year training course for those aged 16–25 in printing, trade and horticulture.

At the Sonneheerdt and Loo Erf rehabilitation centres for the visually impaired, training is provided for the jobs of bookbinder, administrator, piano tuner, electrical engineer, upholsterer, mechanical weaver and others.

Training is also given in industrial rehabilitation departments or sheltered workshops.

Education
Regulations for primary and secondary special education have been laid down since 1 August 1985, in the Interim Act on Special Education and Secondary Special Education. This law is only temporary and will be replaced after a period of 10 years by more permanent legislation. A law with an interim character was chosen so as to enable people in the sphere of special education to work systematically towards a system of special education and secondary special education that will have a completely new content.

What is remarkable in this field is the great diversity of schools for special education and secondary special education, there are 15 types, divided into education for: deaf children, children who are hard of hearing, children with serious speech troubles who do not belong to the previous two groups, blind children, children with poor eyesight, physically handicapped children, children who have been admitted to a hospital, children with prolonged diseases, children with learning deficiencies, children with serious learning deficiencies, children with severe pedagogic problems, children with both learning deficiencies and pedagogic problems, children in schools connected with pedagogic institutions, multihandicapped children, and toddlers who appear likely to be hindered in their development.

While the interim law is in force, attention will be paid, among other things, to the following developments within the fields of special and secondary special education.

1. Schematic work within the field of special and secondary special education. From 1 August 1987, all schools for special and

secondary special education are expected to have at their disposal a school-work scheme, giving an outline of the organization and content of the education. Apart from an enumeration of the aims set out for learning and development, attention will have to be paid within this scheme to subjects such as:

— the way in which pupils are being prepared for placement in elementary or secondary education;

— the way in which pupils are being prepared for their place in society;

— the relations of the school with other schools for special or normal education;

— the way in which the progress of pupils is assessed and reported;

— the way in which progress is being examined, and whether and how far the desired results are achieved by the organization with respect to the content of the educational learning process;

— the way in which non-teaching staff charged with diagnostic, therapeutic or other tasks in support of education are supervising their pupils;

— the way in which the commission that controls admission to the schools for special and secondary special education is functioning.

Schools for education and secondary special education will be supported in the development of innovative activities by means of an activation scheme for special education, within the framework of which specific personnel and material facilities will be granted.

2. In connection with this schematic work while the Interim Act is in force, further attention will be paid to:

— working with individual plans of action;

— broader admission to schools for children with learning deficiencies, children with severe pedagogic problems and children with both these types of problem, and for children in bad health, with the eventual aim of enabling admission of all kinds of children into one school type, instead of the four different types of school now taking care of them;

— readmission of children into normal elementary and secondary schools; in this connection, schools for special and

210

secondary special education are given the opportunity of offering supervision to their former pupils for a fixed period of time after they have entered normal education (so-called ambulatory supervision).

In order to increase the opportunities for education for pupils in secondary special education, the so-called symbiosis arrangement has been developed. This comprises facilities for cooperation between a school for secondary special education and a college for elementary vocational training. In this way, the school is given the opportunity of carrying out parts of the educational programme in colleges for elementary vocational training and by teachers of those colleges, in particular in a number of professional subjects.

Social services and work
No specialized branch of social work institutions has been created specifically for the physically handicapped. They receive help from the existing social services as a whole. Support and coordination in this area are provided by special rehabilitation advisers to the social services in each province. The Ministry of Welfare, Health and Cultural Affairs subsidizes the social workers attached to schools/institutions for people with auditory and visual handicaps, as well as the Social Service Association for Blind and Partially-Sighted Adults, which provides assistance and home teaching for people who lose all or some of their sight in later life.

Specialized social work for the mentally handicapped is provided by the social work services, with the aim of restoring or improving the social behaviour of the mentally retarded in order to promote social integration. The activities comprise, for example, family guidance for parents who take care of their disabled child at home and guidance for projects for independent living.

A scheme called Specialized Work with Young People and Adults is intended to provide constructive leisure pursuits (games, sports, holiday facilities, clubs) for mentally handicapped young people and adults. The scheme makes as much use as possible of existing facilities.

Special services
A number of special services have been set up to help the disabled (particularly the mentally handicapped) to live as socially integrated a life as possible, and to become self-sufficient. The main services specifically for the mentally handicapped are:

(*a*) day centres for children and adults — in 1984, there were 269 centres, accommodating some 11 500 people and offering

211

opportunities for various activities, companionship and social integration;

(b) short-stay homes — in 1982, there were seven of these, with room for 260 residents; by admitting mentally handicapped persons for limited periods, the homes offer support and assistance to their families;

(c) hostels — in 1984, there were 447 hostels with some 10 500 residents; the hostels aim to give the disabled a place in a community, and provide guidance and long-term accommodation for people who are at work or otherwise occupied elsewhere during the day;

(d) guided, independent living for mentally disabled persons, stimulated by the Government by means of innovative projects.

Special services available for the physically disabled include sheltered housing units, of which there were 20 in 1982, accommodating some 600 persons, and activity centres, of which there were 15 in 1982, catering for about 450 people. They provide opportunities for integration into the community, social contacts, and for training and personal development through constructive leisure pursuits. Financial contributions to enable someone to accompany the disabled on holiday are also available.

The provisions for the day centres and hostels come under the Temporary Social Provisions Act and financially under the Exceptional Medical Expenses Act.

Information
As previously mentioned, an Information and Documentation Centre for the Disabled Child and its Parents was established in 1981 and is operating in Utrecht. It has several decentralized information points. Preparations were made recently, in cooperation with this Information and Documentation Centre, for a national information system for the disabled. For this purpose an experiment with a computerized network for the supply and exchange of information is taking place in Rotterdam.

The prevention of disability
Parents are advised on health at the 5000 clinics for babies and preschool children. Over 90% of children born alive are registered at a baby clinic, and between two thirds and three quarters of preschool children at a preschool clinic. A very small proportion of babies and a small percentage of preschool children are cared for outside the clinics by general practitioners or paediatricians. Baby and preschool clinics are organized and run by the local Red Cross societies.

Health education is also given within the framework of school health care and youth health care. The school health service offers information to teachers as well as to parents and children when the children are medically examined. Furthermore, health education is part of the school programme in all primary schools.

In the last few decades the main objective of youth health care has been to promote the best possible health and development (including psychomotor and psychosocial development). The work of the youth health services is chiefly directed towards preventing somatic and psychological disorders and researching the effects of environmental factors on children's development. The youth health service is geared not only to the individual but also to young people as a group, systematically detecting the first signs of deviation and harmful environmental factors in groups of children.

Informing the public about disability is part of the responsibility of all kinds of professional worker and service in the health care system. Specialized information is also given by organizations to parents and patients. A small number of these organizations are financially supported by the Government.

Activities to improve knowledge about the importance of vaccination as a preventive measure take place within the framework of maternity care and the care of babies and preschool children, carried out by the Red Cross societies. Provisions are made under the Exceptional Medical Expenses Act for genetic counselling and information about the possibilities of genetic counselling; a national immunization scheme, which includes immunization against diphtheria, tetanus, pertussis, poliomyelitis, measles and rubella; and phenylketonuria screening.

The National Committee for the Early Detection of Developmental Disorders in Children has been asked by the Government to set up a system for the early detection of all developmental disorders in children up to the age of seven. The Committee's suggestion to set up a national network of multidisciplinary teams is currently being evaluated in experimental projects. These teams collect information on cases of abnormal development to facilitate a comprehensive coordinated multidisciplinary approach to all stages of detection, diagnosis, treatment and guidance. After completing the evaluation survey by 1987, the Government intended to take definite measures on the recommended network.

The Working Environment Act, in force since 1 January 1983, deals with safety and health at work. Measures are taken by mutual arrangement between employers and employees. The area of responsibility of the Labour Inspectorate is being increased.

The road safety plan for the Netherlands contains numerous measures to increase road safety on all fronts. Some of the measures relate specifically to people (education), some to vehicles (design and visibility) and some to roads and the environment (safe design of streets and roads). Emphasis has been placed on measures to give greater protection to those who are most at risk on the roads: children, old people and the disabled.

The Government subsidizes two research programmes on matters regarding disability and rehabilitation: a programme concerned with the innnovation of technical aids for disabled people and a programme on the quality and usefulness of technical aids for disabled people.

Research on the prevention of disability and on rehabilitation development is done in rehabilitation centres, in universities, in colleges of advanced technology and in specialized research institutions. Ministries finance research as far as it is relevant to their policy.

Systems of income support

The Sickness Benefits Act, 1913, is a social security law under which wage-earners and persons in a comparable position qualify for benefits to supplement loss of income due to illness, injury, or mental or physical disability for a maximum of one year. The Act also makes provision for rehabilitation benefits.

The Disablement Insurance Act, 1966, is a social security law that provides for the payment of benefits to wage-earners and persons in a comparable position up to the age of 65 who have been disabled for more than a year and therefore no longer qualify for a benefit under the Sickness Benefits Act.

Under the General Disability Benefits Act, 1976, Netherlands nationals between the ages of 18 and 65 who are disabled can qualify for benefits; for certain services persons under 18 are also eligible. (A state retirement pension is payable to every Netherlands national at the age of 65 under the General Old Age Pensions Act.)

There are separate laws with similar provisions to the General Disability Benefits Act for members of the armed forces and for civil servants, and schemes for special categories of the population such as the 1940N1945 victims of persecution.

The National Assistance Act provides for assistance or supplementary assistance in individual cases of disability where exceptional circumstances exist and the acts referred to before are not applicable.

A modification of the social insurance system was under consideration in 1986.

214

Evaluation of Progress in National Legislation

The changing position of the disabled

The first half of the 1970s saw the beginning of a process of growing awareness and emancipation among the disabled. Organizations of disabled people, the chronically sick and parents of disabled and chronically sick children combined forces. They made strong calls for a say in the development of policy and how it is implemented, and clear demands for better conditions for educating disabled children at home, for disabled people to be able to use normal facilities instead of only special ones, for special consideration within general policy, and for better conditions for participating in the life of the community. This process of emancipation, supported by Government and Parliament, has had its effect in various areas of official responsibility.

Shift of emphasis from inpatient to outpatient
welfare facilities

As regards the physically handicapped, the data on clinical and non-clinical rehabilitation reveal a distinct shift towards outpatient and daytime inpatient treatment (particularly in the case of children).

As regards the blind and severely visually handicapped, the shift has been reflected in a reorganization away from mainly inpatient care to a regionalized system of mainly outpatient care.

The restrictions on communications have so far made it essential to combine assistance, supervision and education for the deaf and very hard-of-hearing in a small number of special (inpatient) facilities. A "total communication" supervision system is currently on trial; this is designed to encourage the deaf to communicate with those with normal hearing in many different ways from a very early age, so as to equip them with better linguistic abilities and thus enable them to integrate.

The mentally handicapped are increasingly using less drastic forms of care: there has been a shift from large institutions to group housing in residential areas and individual housing with supervision. Mentally handicapped children are brought up and cared for in their own families wherever possible; a network of practical teaching assistance has been set up for this purpose.

Normal welfare services to the disabled at home

The primary health care services — family practitioners, voluntary organizations, home help services and social workers — provide help where necessary to disabled people living at home or on their own. These services are gradually becoming better equipped to help the disabled with 24-hour accessibility and availability.

Within the Netherlands health services there are countless facilities geared to caring for young children and detecting actual or potential developmental disorders at an early stage. Coordination and cooperation between these services is to be improved by creating a national network of regional associations and teams of experts.

Experimental schemes are currently being carried out in various parts of the Netherlands, the findings of which will form a basis for the Government's final decision on this matter.

Normal and special schools

On 1 August 1985, the Interim Act on Special Education and Secondary Special Education came into force. Special schools are designed for children who clearly require special help with learning and other difficulties; wherever possible they prepare children to attend normal schools. In addition, it is government policy to expand the range of normal schools, that is,they should be able to provide a good standard of education to as many children as possible, so as to reduce the numbers allocated to special schools.

The new law contains a number of measures to encourage disabled children to attend normal schools, such as ambulatory educational guidance from the special education system for disabled pupils at normal schools. Experience so far with ambulatory educational guidance for certain specific categories such as the blind and severely visually handicapped has been favourable.

Participation by disabled people in various types of adult education and training, the Open University and other post-secondary education is increasing considerably.

Improving access

The disabled cannot participate independently in the community unless they have access to buildings and other facilities. Progress is gradually being made with adaptations to existing public buildings, post offices, stations, transport and recreational facilities, the media, the postal services and the telephone system. As a rule, the cost of adaptation is borne by the owner or administrator. New buildings must satisfy certain requirements as to accessibility.

The legal status of the mentally handicapped

The existing guardianship system has undesirable associations for many people. A few years ago a new, separate system was introduced in the financial sphere, under which mentally handicapped persons who are of age and are unable to manage their financial affairs can

216

have them placed "under administration". The advisability of also introducing a mentor system is under consideration. The current idea is that mentors would be given powers over the care, nursing, treatment, education and employment of the mentally handicapped adults in their charge.

Discussion

Factors impeding the shift from inpatient to outpatient care, from special facilities to normal facilities, and the continuing emancipation process include: financial limitations; the employment situation, which is also unfavourable to the disabled; physical access to public transport and buildings; and social inaccessibility, misapprehensions and unease in relation to the disabled.

Thought should be given: to maintaining the quality of treatment and aid to smaller subcategories, and to those with severe or multiple handicaps, who have little if any real opportunity of living an independent life integrated in the community; to the improved chances of survival and longevity resulting from medical progress; to the fact that more children with a combination of disorders are now being kept alive; and to the fact that mentally handicapped people are living longer.

Poland

General Principles

Article 70 of the Constitution of the Polish People's Republic enacted by the Parliament (*Sejm*) states that the citizens of the Polish People's Republic have the right to health care and assistance in case of sickness or disability.

This right is supported by:

— the development of social insurance in the case of sickness, old age and work disability as well as the development of various forms of social welfare;

— the development of health care organized by the State and the improvement of the population's health, free medical care for all working people and their families, the continual improvement of labour protection and hygiene, the extensive prevention and control of diseases, and the care of the disabled;

— the development of hospitals, sanatoria, outpatient departments, health centres and sanitary appliances.

This law is implemented in Poland through an organized, integrated system of health care, social welfare and social insurance. With reference to the disabled, conditions have been created for their complex rehabilitation, that is, medical, vocational and social rehabilitation.

In September 1982, the Polish Parliament adopted a resolution concerning invalids and the disabled, recognizing the necessity of providing them with opportunities for full participation in professional and social life. It requested the Government to prepare appropriate laws and to undertake action in the field of State economy and administration, aimed at securing the full participation of invalids and the disabled in social and professional life and assisting in the fulfilment of their life, social and cultural needs. The Parliament recognized the purposefulness of establishing a consultative body to create a plan for the cooperation of all sectors for the benefit of the disabled.

As a result of the above resolution, a Council for the Elderly, Invalids and the Disabled was set up by the Council of Ministers on 28 October 1982. This Council has considered such important issues as:

— development trends in the medical, vocational and social rehabilitation of invalids and the disabled;

— the employment of invalids in normal establishments;

— the situation of handicapped children in the field of medical care and conditions for their education;

— the activities of the invalids' cooperatives, such as vocational rehabilitation employment in cooperative workshops, sheltered workshops and homework schemes for severely handicapped persons;

— the situation in the sphere of orthopaedic equipment and rehabilitation appliances for the disabled;

— problems with architectural and urban barriers.

Central government bodies and institutions, as well as provincial organs, have been committed by the Council's resolutions to implement tasks defined by its plan of procedure.

National Involvement in International Action

In 1983, on behalf of the Polish People's Republic, the Vice-Chairman of the Council of State signed the Charter for the 80s, declaring Poland's participation during the decade 1981–1990 in the activities for disabled persons until the attainment of the aim of full participation and equality for the disabled throughout the world. This Charter was drawn up by Rehabilitation International. Representatives of Poland work actively in Rehabilitation International, as members of different commissions and also as members of the Rehabilitation International Board.

Polish specialists participate in the work of numerous WHO committees and, in the field of vocational rehabilitation, in the work of the International Labour Organisation. Poland is also on the

Executive Committee of the World Confederation for Physical Therapy. Frequent contacts are also maintained with the International Blind Sports Association, the International Sports Organization for the Disabled, the World Federation of the Deaf and the World Council for the Welfare of the Blind.

Methodology — Types of Legislative Approach to the Equality Concept

Laws granting privileges to persons with defined health disorders are included in many acts, decrees, regulations, announcements, directions and instructions.

Legal regulations on rehabilitation should create a basis for activities aimed at giving the disabled a chance to participate actively in various forms of social life, and especially a chance to enjoy such constitutional civil rights as the right to education, the right to work, and the right to culture and the arts.

Review of the Present State of National Legislation

Social reintegration and full participation

As already mentioned, Article 70 of the Constitution of the Polish People's Republic and the Parliamentary resolution concerning invalids and the disabled are the basis for further, more detailed executive regulations. Yet, in considering the role of law in the process of rehabilitation of the disabled, it is important to realize that legal solutions and their practical implementation depend on the attitudes of healthy persons towards the disabled, as well as on the positive attitude of invalids.

In Poland, rehabilitation is a broad activity that is considered as one of the tasks of all ministries and heads of central offices. Regulations defining the tasks of the Minister of Health and Social Welfare make him/her responsible for creating a state policy in this field. The Minister is entrusted with a coordinating function in formulating programmes and plans in the field of rehabilitation, as well as with supervision of the realization of the plans and programmes in force. These tasks are reflected in legislative activity, namely in:

— determining the principles and procedures for working out plans for the employment of invalids and the basis for their rehabilitation;

221

- determining, together with the Central Union of Invalids' Cooperatives, directions for the annual and long-term plans of invalids' vocational rehabilitation in invalids' cooperatives and the principles carried out by these institutions;

- solving problems of orthopaedic supplies and determining the procedure for using the services of establishments for orthopaedic equipment and other relevant organizational units;

- determining programmes and forms of postgraduate education in rehabilitation for physicians and other professionals.

The Minister of Health and Social Welfare cooperates with the Minister of Labour, Wages and Social Affairs, as well as with the Minister of Education, in the performance of tasks concerning invalids.

Education
The Minister of Education provides a network of special schools for children and young people with some kind of congenital or acquired handicap, creating the opportunity for an adequate line of training and education. The opportunities for special education are provided by:

- Regulation of the Minister of Education of 30 September 1976 on the organization of the individual education of children unfit for school education;

- Regulation of the Minister of Education of 26 June 1962 giving young people with vision and hearing defects, dysfunction of locomotor organs and other diseases, access to education in technical schools;

- Regulation of the Minister of Health and Social Welfare of 18 December 1979 on the organization and principles of functioning of establishments for the vocational rehabilitation of the disabled;

- Regulation of the Minister of Health and Social Welfare of 29 December 1979 on the principles of procedure for referring disabled people to vocational rehabilitation workshops;

- Resolution of the Board of the Central Union of Invalids' Cooperatives on vocational training in the invalids' cooperative movement.

Working life
The social policy of Poland has adopted the principle that employment is one of the main forms of assistance given to the disabled. The

principle is fully put into effect by the Decree of the Council of Ministers, dated 5 May 1967, on the planned employment of the disabled. This Decree obliges the departments of the praesidia of People's Councils to render special assistance in finding proper jobs for the disabled. The recommendations and contraindications concerning their employment are issued by the relevant medical commissions for disability and employment, working according to the directions of 12 August 1980 of the President of the Social Insurance Institutions (with later modifications made in 1983) on the activity of the medical commissions for disability and employment:

— Decree of the Council of Ministers of 11 December 1981 on working time and additional leave on full pay for the disabled in the first and second group;

— Decree of the Council of Ministers of 19 July 1985 on assurance for the proper activity and development of the cooperatives for invalids and the blind;

— Regulation of the Minister of Health and Social Welfare on the employment of persons with limited proficiency in invalids' cooperatives.

Medical rehabilitation

Medical rehabilitation is developed according to the directions of the Minister of Health and Social Welfare of 9 August 1971 on the medical rehabilitation development programme. This long-term programme is implemented as part of the plans for each administrative area (*voivodship*). The programme concept for the organization of rehabilitation has created conditions for early rehabilitation, undertaken simultaneously with treatment of the patient's basic disease, and late rehabilitation, carried out in specialized rehabilitation centres.

The idea of introducing rehabilitation procedures into the primary activities of health service establishments was the starting point for the programme. Its further development in the following fields was recognized as a guarantee of proper progress: diseases of the locomotor system, the circulatory system, and the respiratory system, and psychological disorders.

The organizational structure of medical rehabilitation, besides the basic units of rehabilitation in health service establishments at all levels, also has complementary links with sanatoria, and with industrial rehabilitation centres whose task is to combine vocational rehabilitation with medical rehabilitation. This task is implemented with the assistance of the medical treatment and prevention dispensaries of the industrial health service. Rehabilitation activities carried out in invalids' cooperatives, with organized camps for rehabilitation and sport for the disabled, also complement the model.

The programme of medical rehabilitation development recognizes the significance of orthopaedic supplies, the provision of which has been subject to modification over the years, aiming at constant improvement. Depending on their type and designation, orthopaedic appliances either cure the disease, prevent its deterioration, mitigate its effect, enable the person concerned to move, or compensate for any loss of function. The ultimate objective of the supply of orthopaedic equipment is to create conditions that help a disabled person overcome the effects of disability, start or continue education or gainful employment, and attain independence in the activities of daily living. The citizen's right to be provided with orthopaedic appliances is laid down by the Regulation of the Minister of Health and Social Welfare of July 1974 on the procedures for obtaining orthopaedic appliances and auxiliary appliances.

In 1980–1985, the programme activities aimed at increasing the accessibility of rehabilitation services to the whole population. In 1983, the Minister of Health and Social Welfare issued a recommendation to the chief medical officers of each administrative area on the organization of units in hospitals for the dispensation and fitting of orthopaedic and accessory appliances.

Persons entitled to free medical care receive, free of charge, wheelchairs, prostheses, crutches, canes, orthopaedic shoes and other orthopaedic appliances that facilitate the independent daily living activities of the disabled.

Social rehabilitation
In the Polish system of rehabilitation, an important role is played by the associations of the disabled, such as the Polish Association of the Deaf, and the Polish Association of the Blind. They are mainly occupied with social rehabilitation aimed at the integration of the disabled into society, as well as with cultural, social and educational activities. Increasing public awareness of the problems of the disabled is an important aspect of their work. The associations of the disabled supplement the State's activity in the field of rehabilitation and are supported and financed through the Ministry of Health and Social Welfare.

An important role is also played by the Polish Society for Rehabilitation of the Disabled as a socio-scientific organization that concentrates its activity on shaping positive attitudes in society towards the disabled, on improving the quality of specialized

224

personnel for rehabilitation needs through various forms of seminar and symposium, as well as conducting and initiating research in this field.

The prevention of disability

Preventive activities are guided by the recommendations of the health sector, for example, with respect to acute infectious diseases by obligatory vaccinations, with respect to noncommunicable diseases by the prevention and early diagnosis of cancer and cardiovascular diseases, with special stress on ischaemic heart disease and arterial hypertension, and the prevention of traffic accidents, traumas and poisoning (especially among children and young persons).

Health education is widely conducted in the form of lectures, films and folders on health risks and methods of avoiding them.

The so-called active health care of communities with a high health risk, determined by increased exposure to noxious factors or by reduced physiologically conditioned immunity to them, as well as the care of persons with chronic diseases or with congenital defects, are significant preventive and curative activities. This mainly concerns the care of pregnant women, newborn babies and infants, and children, pupils and academic students.

Certain age groups and those exposed to health risks are expected to undergo medical examinations:

— comprehensive medical examinations at birth and at the ages of 2, 4, 6, 10 and 16 years;

— periodical medical examinations up to the age of 2 years;

— screening examinations up to 18 years;

— regular preventive medical examinations for workers.

Plans and instructions in the field of prevention at the central level are adapted to the tasks of individual primary health care establishments and are also recommended to the People's Council at the district and lower levels.

Besides the programme of medical rehabilitation development already mentioned, other programmes include the development of health care for women; the development of health care for workers; the prevention and control of circulatory system diseases; and the prevention and control of cancer. The harmonious development of health care in Poland is connected with the implementation of particular legal acts, including the following general provisions:

— the Statute of 28 October 1948 on social health service establishments, and many executory regulations to this Statute;

225

— the Parliamentary Resolution of 19 January 1974 on the health care of the population, and the Statute of 4 July 1984 on physical culture.

Systems of income support

The system of social insurance is characterized by constant development and the search for new legal, organizational and financial solutions, according to social and economic conditions. In the Polish People's Republic, social insurance is, along with the medical care service, the most important part of the social welfare scheme in which the State performs protective functions for its citizens. Nowadays, practically the whole of society is covered by social insurance. The social insurance schemes ensure benefits in the event of sickness and maternity, employment accidents and occupational diseases, and old age.

Allowances are granted on the basis of the provisions in the Act of 17 December 1974 on social insurance payments in the case of sickness and maternity, in the Decree of the Council of Ministers of 6 June 1983 on the principles of calculating social insurance and covering their costs, and in the Instruction of the Social Insurance Institutions of 6 July 1983 on social security payments in the case of sickness and maternity.

A nursing allowance is granted to employees for members of their families for whom they get family allowances, that is, children and spouses who satisfy the conditions stated in the Decree of the Minister of Labour, Wages and Social Affairs of 23 January 1984 on family and nursing allowances:

— for a child aged up to 16 years if, owing to the state of health, he or she requires permanent nursing care or systematic cooperation in medical and rehabilitative activities (congenital defects handicapping the locomotor system, cerebral palsy, mental deficiency, epilepsy, etc.);

— for members of the family who are aged over 75 years or who are invalids of the first group, and for children who are invalids of the second group and whose disability occurred at the age when they qualified for a family allowance.

The decision to grant a family allowance or nursing allowance, as well as the classification in a particular disability group (I, II or III), is made by a branch of the Social Security Institution on the basis of the opinion of a medical commission on disability and employment.

Apart from the above-mentioned allowances for the elderly and the disabled, there is a wide variety of social welfare services provided on the basis of information submitted by social workers.

The disabled and the parents of disabled children have the privilege of obtaining cars on very advantageous financial terms.

Portugal

General Principles

The Constitution of the Portuguese Republic, in its first democratic formulation in 1976, imposes responsibility on the State for the prevention of disability and for the care, rehabilitation and social integration of disabled persons.

The general principles governing national policy on rehabilitation are expressly laid down in the Portuguese Constitution of 1976 (Article 71). They are: to prevent disability, to undertake rehabilitation, and to ensure the rehabilitation and integration of disabled persons. With a view to carrying out these principles, a National Secretariat for Rehabilitation was set up in 1977 within the Office of the President of the Council of Ministers, to plan and coordinate action in the various fields of rehabilitation. In addition, government departments and private institutions carry out activities in such areas as health, education, labour and social security, in an effort to overcome the existing difficulties and shortcomings.

In a general way, the bodies involved in the process are gradually adopting an integrated approach to the treatment of disabled persons, with a view to giving them as easy access as possible to the services available to the population in general.

The current version of the Constitution dating from 1980 charges the State, in addition, with the task of making society aware of its responsibilities towards the disabled and instilling a feeling of solidarity with them (Articles 71–72).

A national plan comprising several coordinated programmes of action was drawn up and implemented to coincide with the International Year of Disabled Persons, 1981. Under this plan, submitted to Parliament on 6 March 1981, a number of committees were set up, with the following terms of reference:

— prevention (pre-, peri- and postnatal care, health education, the prevention of disabling diseases, safety at work and safety on the road);

— rehabilitation and early acceptance into care (integrated education, special education, medical rehabilitation, social and professional rehabilitation and integration into the family);

— integration (covering the rights of disabled persons, full participation in education, work, sport and other cultural activities, the elimination of attitudes of discrimination and of physical barriers, transport and the living environment, and social facilities for the disabled);

— research (in such fields as rehabilitation and the training of technical and professional staff);

— the study of people's attitudes to the severely disabled (in particular those with serious mental disorders and multiple disabilities);

— the study of screening systems and the guidance of the disabled, leading on to the demarcation of responsibilities in this field;

— the development of home aid services (public and voluntary services, in particular for the elderly).

The governing principles of the national plan of action follow closely the recommendations made by the United Nations, for example in the drawing up of medium- or long-term prevention and rehabilitation plans, campaigns to promote awareness and disseminate information among the public, intensified research, the development of public services for the disabled, the provision of information to the disabled population, and agreement on the recommendations to be made to associations of or for the disabled to encourage their participation in national programmes. Plans were also laid for action in the legal field, involving the drafting and amendment of legislation to meet the needs of the disabled. The programme as a whole was to be implemented by decentralized committees, down to and including local commissions.

The Standing Committee on Rehabilitation, established by Legal Decree No. 474 of 25 September 1973 and substantially amended by Legal Decree No. 425 of 29 May 1976, does not adequately meet the new requirements. Provision was therefore made in Legal

Decree No. 346 of 20 August 1977 for the establishment in the Prime Minister's Office of a National Secretariat for Rehabilitation, consisting of the National Secretary and the National Rehabilitation Council, together with an administrative board. The Council is multisectoral in nature and includes representatives from the ministries of national defence, internal administration, finance, labour, transport and communications, public works, housing, town planning and buildings, school administration and equipment, teacher training, social security and, of course, health, as well as the Secretariat of State for Population and Employment. Representatives of two nongovernmental organizations (the Portuguese Association of the Disabled and the Association of Disabled Servicemen) also sit on the Council.

At a later stage, Resolution No. 411/1980 of the Council of Ministers set up a National Committee for the International Year of Disabled Persons with an even wider participation of other governmental and nongovernmental organizations in accordance with the priorities recommended by the United Nations. No provision was made for participation at regional and local levels.

National Involvement in International Action

By various ways and means, Portuguese participation in international action on behalf of disabled persons is being stepped up, either through the adoption within the country, subject to appropriate adaptation to the situation obtaining in Portugal, of the priorities, programmes, directives and guidelines laid down by the United Nations, in particular the World Programme of Action concerning disabled persons, or through membership or participation in the activities of the various specialized commissions and groups belonging to various bodies such as Rehabilitation International, the Council of Europe, the International Social Security Association, or again through the development of joint projects such as that of the Centre for Educational Research and Innovation of the Organisation for Economic Co-operation and Development.

In another direction, it is important to mention the influential role played, particularly since 1974, by relevant nongovernmental organizations in the protection of the rights of disabled persons. Some of these organizations (for example, the Portuguese Association of the Disabled and the Association of Disabled Servicemen) are affiliated to kindred international bodies and some may be involved in collaboration in drafting legislation.

The celebration of the International Year of Disabled Persons, in which the National Secretariat for Rehabilitation played a leading role at all levels, has been an important landmark in the development of rehabilitation in Portugal during the 1980s. The International Year and the priorities, programmes of action and governing principles set out in the United Nations guidelines breathed new life into the national plan. The very close cooperation with WHO (especially in its programme for the disabled) has been even further intensified. Nongovernmental bodies (both national and international) have also played their part in measures to assist the disabled. Several national associations, dealing with handicapped children, mental disease, the elderly and disabled servicemen, have been cooperating closely with the public services in the achievement of the aims of the plan. A number of organizations of international origin or with international representation, such as the Rotary Club and the Lions Club, have collaborated in the implementation of the relevant programmes.

Methodology — Types of Legislative Approach to the Equality Concept

In the legislative field, two basic approaches have been used to draw up a series of measures: on the one hand are measures that affect the whole of the population, including the disabled, and on the other, measures designed to meet the specific needs of the disabled, according to the degree of severity and type, and following the principles of standardization and integration.

In the absence of any single specific law, which might indeed be a desirable development guaranteeing the rights of the disabled (although such a guarantee is in any case enshrined in the Constitution), the problems of disability are dealt with under different forms of general legislation. For example, Legislative Decree No. 167 of 20 May 1980, which introduced part-time work in the public service, restricts this work regime to particular groups of civil servants, including those suffering from at least a 75% disability. In the same way, Legislative Decree No. 538 of 31 December 1979 regarding compulsory registration for basic education provides that handicapped persons may on occasion be exempted. These two decrees give an indication of the type of legislation adopted.

Legislation has also been passed relating to particular disabled categories, primary attention being paid to the mentally handicapped in view of the serious problems involved. Legislation is at present being drafted to define the rights of patients suffering from mental disease, which follows closely the recommendations of the Council of Europe.

232

Review of the Present State of National Legislation

Elimination of discrimination or social prejudice

Article 71, paragraph 1 of the Constitution provides that Portuguese citizens suffering from a physical or mental handicap shall enjoy all the rights and be subject to all the obligations enshrined in the Constitution, except those rights and obligations that they are incapable of enjoying or performing.

All legislation must, of course, comply with the Constitution and a special court sits to ensure such compliance. One of the Constitutional Court's primary concerns is with the guarantee of non-discrimination — in respect of economic and social status, sex, or state of health (including physical or mental handicaps) — bearing in mind, of course, the exceptions in the final part of the aforesaid Article of the Constitution.

No special committee has been set up to ensure observance of the rights of the disabled, who are entitled, like all other citizens, to the protection of the courts or of the administrative or other authorities.

Social reintegration and full participation

The basic text on the rehabilitation and social integration of the disabled is Act No. 6 of 8 November 1971, although it has never been issued in the form of an implementing regulation. A special transport service for the disabled operates satisfactorily, although it is rather thin on the ground. Ministerial Order No. 878 of 1 October 1981 provides for the identification of the personal transport of disabled persons in conformity with the relevant recommendations of the European Conference of Ministers of Transport.

A working group is at present discussing the elimination of physical barriers (in the architectural field) and a wide range of specific measures have been taken in connection with building design, for example the replacement of staircases. A great deal remains to be done, but specific legislation hardly appears necessary. Nevertheless the General Regulation on Urban Building was revised in Legal Decree No. 43 of 8 February 1982 in a number of important aspects affecting the disabled.

Act No. 66 of 4 October 1979 is concerned with the special education of children and adolescents in need of special care. This law includes measures with a direct impact on the disabled as well as other indirect measures affecting their families, teaching staff and special education establishments. Over and above the general principles of education, the special education of the disabled must concentrate on the following aspects: strengthening the physical and

233

intellectual potential of disabled children, with particular emphasis on emotional stability, developing the ability to communicate, reducing the impact of the limitations induced by a handicap, providing support for integration into the family, school and society, developing independence at all levels, preparation by suitable vocational training and helping the young disabled to integrate into active life.

The progressive integration of pupils with a physical or mental handicap into the normal education system is governed by Order No. 59 of 8 August 1979, issued by the Secretariat of State for Primary and Secondary Education, in implementation of Legal Decree No. 174 of 2 May 1977, while Legal Decree No. 310 of 17 November 1981 makes provision, among different forms of instruction, for the special education and integration of the disabled (integration being interpreted to cover both the social and professional aspects).

Sporting and leisure activities for the disabled are actively encouraged, although without legislative support, apart from provisions dealing with the organizational aspects of offering incentives.

A number of legislative texts give priority to disabled persons in regard to employment in the public service, in banks and in other fields.

Various government services, including social services, have been set up to ensure coordinated action in favour of the disabled. These services are mainly responsible to the Secretary of State for Social Security, or included in the overall Family and Social Assistance Institute, which has particular responsibility for the disabled.

Special committees, set up as stated above in connection with the International Year of Disabled Persons, ensure a wide distribution of information on the subject of disability and on participation in the relevant programmes.

The prevention of disability

Legislation on prevention is needed, although accident prevention programmes and administrative measures have been implemented. Some legislative support does exist, however, once again mainly concerned with the organizational structures of the public service, in particular the health education services, and the needs of various age groups.

In the context of preparatory studies for compilation of the Health Code, special priority has been given to legislation on primary health care and mental health, both these sections of the Code being already in their final versions.

Research has been actively pursued in various spheres, for example on rehabilitation and reintegration, and also on the training of the disabled, although no significant legislation has been passed.

Systems of income support
Disabled persons are exempt from import duties on a number of items essential for their health, education, employment and social integration; the list of items, enumerated in Legal Decree No. 362 of 31 December 1981, includes, for example, television sets.

The disabled are entitled to special credit facilities for the purchase of a home (Legal Decrees No. 230 of 16 July 1980, No. 435 of 2 October 1980, No. 535 of 7 November 1980, No. 544 of 10 November 1980, No. 131 of 28 May 1981, No. 149 of 4 June 1981, No. 340 of 11 December 1981). In addition, Legal Decree No. 435 of 2 October 1980 and Ministerial Orders No. 969 of 12 November 1980 and No. 693 of 13 October 1981 contain specific incentives to encourage the disabled to acquire their own homes.

Provisions are made for specific social security benefits to be paid to the different categories of disabled person, and these have been continuously updated by successive amendments to the legislation. Grants are also paid for special education both to the parents and to the institutions providing the special education.

Social security and the prevention of accidents at work and occupational diseases are governed by a number of complex legal texts, which follow the general pattern of those of most western countries.

Evaluation of Progress in National Legislation

The impact on Portuguese legislation of the International Year of Disabled Persons in 1981 and the United Nations World Programme of Action concerning the Disabled has been considerable. The major items of legislation as well as the corresponding organizational structures have been derived virtually *in toto* from this source. Nevertheless, the Portuguese Constitution, which already existed at that time, resolutely proclaims the rights of the disabled and calls for the implementation of a policy that will protect their interests.

Although a number of constraints stand in the way of the relevant programmes of action, and even of the final drafting of the legislation and its implementation, the essential basis already exists. In any case there are valid arguments for keeping legislation to a minimum, since reliance on legal texts is only a final recourse in social action. Further legislation is now being drafted, however, especially in regard to the blind and various problems that have arisen in connection with the mentally handicapped.

New projects and appraisal of the existing legislation
In the light of the nature and functions of the National Secretariat for Rehabilitation and the conditions obtaining in Portugal, the plan of activities for 1986 in the technical area of rehabilitation comprised the following main objectives:

— coordination and planning of action in the various fields of rehabilitation;

— publicity and research;

— information and creation of awareness;

— implementation of the response to the needs of the disabled in the most underprivileged areas.

In this context, the development of the following main new projects may be singled out:

— a census of the disabled population;

— education of young disabled persons and transition to an active life (the second phase of the OECD Centre for Educational Research and Innovation project);

— ways and means of dealing with serious mental illness over the long term;

— the social and vocational rehabilitation of psychiatric patients;

— the establishment of the Maria Candida da Cunha Training and Research Centre.

Appraisal of existing legislation is one of the concerns of the National Secretariat for Rehabilitation. Whenever possible, in conjunction with the government departments involved and the associations of and for the disabled, and on the basis of the information collected from the disabled themselves and members of their families, the Secretariat tries to put the legislative provisions and regulations into operation. In the light of each situation, the Secretariat draws the attention of the departments concerned to the need to improve the legislation in force, or collaborates with them in drawing up new legislative measures and regulating those that already exist.

Romania

General Principles

In the Socialist Republic of Romania, everything possible is done at the state level for the reintegration into society of the disabled, so that they can take their place on an equal footing with the healthy. This is achieved mainly by medical, material, technical and financial measures, and the use of educational psychology and vocational and social guidance, supported by statutory provisions to ensure the efficient rehabilitation of the handicapped and their incorporation into the community.

The equality of rights of all citizens of the country, irrespective of nationality, race, sex or religion, is enshrined in the Constitution of the Socialist Republic of Romania. Equality of rights is guaranteed in all fields of economic, political, legal, social and cultural life, no discrimination whatsoever being permitted (Article 17). The Constitution also guarantees the right to material security in the case of disease or unfitness for work within the state social security system or with the assistance of the social services. Medical care is provided by the State through various medical health institutions (Article 20).

Equal opportunities for the disabled are ensured by the state social services at the central and local levels. These services are responsible for the prevention and treatment of disease and for medical/educational and social/vocational rehabilitation, depending on the nature and degree of disability, age, school and professional training, employment prior to the occurrence of disease or accident and family situation.

The authorities mainly concerned with the problems of the disabled are the Ministry of Health, the Ministry of Labour, the Ministry

237

of Education and Instruction, the Committee on Problems Arising in People's Councils, the Central Union of Trade Cooperatives, children's, youth, trade union and women's organizations, the Association of the Deaf, and the Association of the Blind.

As a fundamental principle of social policy in the context of health for all by the year 2000, and within the framework of the general economic and social development plan of the country, which is aimed at raising the level of civilization and culture, the Government guarantees all Romanian citizens progressively more favourable conditions for a continual improvement in their state of health, the creation of the best possible environment for healthy and balanced physical and psychological development, and the restoration of the working capacity of the disabled (Act No. 3/1978, Preambular Articles 5 and 8). Particular attention has been paid to preventive measures at the primary, secondary and tertiary levels (Article 5).

Measures to deal with the problems of the disabled have been included in programmes at the national and local level, the allocation of financial resources being made annually in accordance with the integral national economic and social development plan, approved in legislation adopted by the Grand National Assembly.

The rehabilitation of the disabled, which has been a matter of close concern in Romania for over a century, is being pursued in the context of a long-term programme in accordance with United Nations recommendations. This programme involves the cooperation of all organizations and services active in this field, since the protection and maintenance of the health of the population is a very important element in the social and cultural policy of the Romanian State.

Coordination mechanisms

The activities of the services responsible for assistance to the disabled are coordinated, as appropriate, by interdepartmental councils or commissions. They examine meticulously, check and analyse the activities of specialized institutions and take any necessary steps to increase their efficiency. The interdepartmental councils and commissions also analyse periodically the whole range of problems affecting the disabled and the changes occurring in the morbidity and disability rates, making recommendations or issuing instructions to upgrade preventive, therapeutic or rehabilitative measures, to mitigate a particular problem or to intensify rehabilitative measures as the circumstances require.

The main interdepartmental bodies responsible for assistance to the disabled are:

— the Higher Health Council;

238

— the Social Insurance Council;

— the Central Commission for the Protection of Minors;

— the Central Commission on Pensions;

— the Commission on Special Instruction of the Higher Council for Education and Instruction.

The activities of these coordinating bodies, their structure and method of operation are set out in Act No. 3/1970 relating to the protection of various categories of minor, Act No. 3/1977 relating to state social insurance pensions and social assistance, Act No. 3/1978 relating to protection of the health of the population, Act No. 28/1978 relating to education and instruction, and the orders issued in implementation of the provisions of these basic laws.

The councils and commissions set up at the national level are represented by equivalent bodies in the district services, the structure of which is determined by the executive committees of district people's councils. Implementation of the provisions of the legislation is continuously monitored by special staff in the central and local services responsible for dealing with the problems of the disabled, by deputies of the Grand National Assembly, and by deputies in people's councils as regards the situation in the constituencies they represent. Periodical analyses are carried out at the national level in the Standing Commission of the Grand National Assembly for Labour, Health, Social Insurance and Environmental Protection, on the basis of proposals by deputies and reports submitted by the central services responsible for dealing with the particular problems of the disabled. These analyses provide the basis for measures to be taken at the central or local levels, to render the legislative framework more flexible and to improve the performance of the specialist services primarily responsible for the disabled.

Review of the Present State of National Legislation

Under the provisions of the general legislation, disabled persons enjoy the right to free medical attention and training, the right to work, the right to social insurance and the right of association, without any discrimination whatsoever. The specific rights applicable to certain disabled categories are covered in special regulations. Children and young persons with sensory, physical or mental defects, for example, are entitled to education, training and professional qualification under special conditions in nursery schools, general state schools and special professional training establishments where normal instruction is given in smaller classes and pupils are assisted by an educational psychologist specializing in the problems of the disabled (Act No. 3/1970; Act No. 28/1978).

Social reintegration and full participation

Article 94(i) of Act No. 3/1978 contains the obligation to provide medical assistance to children suffering from defective physical and psychological development and to provide the necessary treatment to facilitate their rehabilitation and integration into society. The same regulation stipulates that training establishments and physical education teachers shall provide, if recommended by a doctor, special gymnastic training programmes for pupils or students whose physical development is inadequate.

In the case of diseases involving a temporary incapacity for work, medical staff are required to undertake the necessary measures to restore working capacity, according to the therapeutic indications. They must also monitor the implementation of the therapeutic regime, in conjunction with the enterprises and institutions where the patients work. Health services are also required to recommend the employment of persons suffering from such conditions in a form of activity suited to their working capacity.

Education, training and the technical qualification of the disabled are carried out in mainstream schools and centres, where the persons concerned receive medical rehabilitation and assistance from specialist educational psychologists. Those who cannot be adequately trained even under these conditions are sent to special training institutions run for persons with visual defects (blindness and amblyopia), auditory defects, mental defects and physical and behavioural disorders. The functioning of these special schools is governed by Acts No. 3/1970 and No. 28/1978.

The special establishment training system has the necessary material basis in the form of buildings, furniture and fittings appropriate to the specific type of handicap, that is, presenting no architectural barriers, and specialist staff working on a team basis (consisting of teachers, instructors, psychologists, social assistants, doctors and orthophonic specialists) who teach only small classes. The characteristic features of this training system are specially designed curricula and manuals, flexible working hours, alternating physiological activity with rest during the day and during the week, training in professions open to the disabled and in demand in the economy, recruitment for specialized employment in a normal or protected environment, and arrangements for the progressive follow-up of the professional and social integration of disabled people after completion of their training.

Qualification or requalification courses are run in related professions or in new fields of activity for disabled adults, depending on their residual functional skills and the possibility of achieving productive activity.

Social organizations with a cultural and educational bias, such as the Association of the Deaf and the Association of the Blind, coordinate assistance to the disabled. These associations are based on a membership of disabled persons and have a hierarchical organizational structure from the local up to the national level; the directing staff are drawn from among the members. These associations enjoy the support, in particular financial support, of the State.

Cultural and sporting activities, such as chess, football, table tennis, literary competitions and publications in various national journals and abroad, are organized with the support of associations for disabled persons with a view to their reintegration into social life. These associations are equipped with libraries and clubs where their members can increase their cultural and professional knowledge and undertake studies in civic behaviour. The aim is to promote these activities among the non-disabled also, so as to help the disabled towards social and professional reintegration.

These associations are also closely concerned with vocational training, and organize visits by members of different professions, in the home, at work and at schools attended by disabled children. All disabled persons are guaranteed employment on a par with the non-disabled, thus enabling them to become economically independent. Those who make the grade professionally can be promoted, and positions of responsibility (for example, as foremen) are not excluded.

The prevention of disability
All activities aimed at health protection (in accordance with Act No. 3/1978) have a preventive bias. Particular emphasis is placed in this connection on risk factors liable to give rise to disability. Campaigns in the information and educational fields are accompanied by, for example, mandatory labour safety measures (Act No. 5/1965) and road safety regulations (Decree No. 328/1966). Institutions are allocated funds by law, to promote labour safety, the effective dissemination of information and the provision of training (Act No. 5/1965).

Annual health education plans at the national and local levels include specific activities for different groups of the population. These plans are implemented by medical and educational staff, senior staff at institutions and social organizations. It is worth noting the obligatory nature of this activity and its systematic organization. All doctors, for example, are required to put in four hours per month on

241

different forms of health education and all auxiliary personnel seven hours per month.

To guard against the occurrence of sickness and a consequent deterioration in working capacity, the engagement of new staff or a change of workplace must be preceded by thorough medical examinations in accordance with the provisions of the law. Industrial medical officers are required to determine a person's aptitude for a particular workplace on the basis of his or her health status and professional aptitude charts, or to recommend a transfer to a more suitable post. Health legislation again requires that the health of newly recruited personnel shall be kept under observation during the initial period at a new workplace. Workers undergo periodical medical examinations, the periodicity and nature of these examinations being specified in the legislation as a function of the workplace conditions. The necessary preventive and/or rehabilitative measures are implemented on the basis of the results of these examinations (Act No. 3/1978, the Labour Code and Order No. 15 of 18 January 1982 issued by the Ministry of Health).

Systems of income support

In accordance with the principle enshrined in the Constitution that all Romanian citizens are entitled to the material benefits of insurance against old age, sickness or unfitness to work, and the further principle of the absolute equality of rights without any discrimination whatsoever, disabled persons are entitled to assistance in the case of temporary inability to work or accidents at work and guidance in the prevention of disease and the restoration and consolidation of their health (Decision No. 886 of 21 August 1965 of the Council of Ministers). Persons drawing group I and II disability pensions are also entitled to a monthly allowance in respect of care (Article 28, Act No. 5/1977). The wives of men doing military service are also entitled to monthly allowances if they are suffering from group I or II disabilities (Article 6, Decree No. 197 of 2 July 1977).

Disabled minors enjoy the right to a pension in succession to their deceased parent or parents even after the age of 16; if their handicap prevents them attending special training or obtaining employment, this pension will continue to be paid so long as they remain disabled (Act No. 3/1977). Disabled persons are entitled to a pension in case of the temporary or final loss of their ability to work, the scale of which will vary as a function of the degree of disability (groups I, II or III) (Act No. 3/1977).

The blind, group I disabled and persons accompanying them are entitled to two free return trips by rail annually and free travel on public transport in the locality where they live (Decisions of the

Council of Ministers No. 1060/1968 and No. 2466/1969). The blind are eligible to retire at the age of 50 (for men) and 45 (for women) (Act No. 3/1977). They are entitled to 18 days' annual holiday if they have worked for less than 5 years, and 24 days' annual holiday after 14 years in work (Act No. 26/1967).

Financial and social facilities are granted to groups I and II disabled persons, whereby they are exempted from national and local taxes, and from participation in various forms of social work (Act No. 2/1977, Article 18; Act No. 20/1971; Act No. 25/1981). Group I and II disabled persons are not required to purchase radio and television licences (Order No. 473/1977) and persons with visual defects are allowed a 50% reduction on their telephone bill (Presidential Decree of 1982 relating to Decision No. 719/1982 of the Council of Ministers).

Blind and group I disabled persons are entitled to receive both their pension and their salary when they are employed (Act No. 3/1977). A state allowance is paid up to the age of 18 to children with group I or II disabilities (Decree No. 246 of 28 July 1977). The law provides that disabled persons shall receive assistance in obtaining accommodation and reductions in the rate of rent charged (Act No. 5/1973). It also specifies the financial assistance to be provided for the acquisition of the necessary prostheses. This form of assistance, like that available for the acquisition of suitable means of transport, can be any amount up to the full price. The law again provides for financial assistance and price reductions to be granted up to the amount of the total price for therapeutic bath treatments and holidays spent in rehabilitation centres. Persons accompanying the disabled are also entitled to these privileges, where the state of the disabled persons necessitates their being continuously accompanied.

Evaluation of Progress in National Legislation

The International Year of Disabled Persons in 1981 imparted a sustained impetus to the organization of campaigns for the integration of disabled persons into society, and these campaigns have left their mark on the relevant legislation in a number of ways. For example, there has been an increase in the disability pension and in state children's allowances, including disabled children, in the active and early detection of disability and the introduction of rehabilitation measures as soon as possible, and in the staffing of medical and professional rehabilitation centres for the disabled. In addition, regulations have been issued on the specialist and advanced training of staff working in specialized institutions, and a prompt and uniform system has been set up to monitor the social and professional integration of disabled persons after completion of rehabilitation measures.

Two pilot studies

Again as a follow-up to the International Year of Disabled Persons, two pilot units for the rehabilitation of children with neural and psychomotor deficiencies have been set up with the assistance of the United Nations Development Programme and WHO in two major university centres, Bucharest and Iassy. These units combine two of the most important principles governing the social and professional integration of the disabled into society, namely work in an interdisciplinary team and the implementation of the concept of combining the medical/educational and social/professional aspects of rehabilitation.

The tasks of the pilot unit at Bucharest are as follows:

— to give assistance in this specialist field in the Bucharest zone (about 2 million inhabitants);

— to provide a methods study centre where courses of a practical nature are run for doctors, auxiliary staff, psychologists and other professional categories providing assistance to the disabled;

— to give specialist guidance to local units working in this field;

— to undertake scientific research.

The pilot unit also runs classes giving general instruction to autistic children. The unit has its own means of transport, covering any staff movements that may be required for the purposes of consultations, treatment or physiotherapy, or in the course of instruction. The unit also includes social assistance and employment staff and advisory services for members of the family. All these services are available free of charge in accordance with Acts No. 3/1978 and No. 28/1978 and with Decision No. 880/1965 of the Council of Ministers. The staff of the unit (doctors, nurses, psychologists, logopaedic specialists, teachers and social assistants) have the necessary specialist training (16 members of the staff were trained in the United Kingdom).

The Iassy pilot unit provides similar assistance to disabled persons in the eastern zone of the country (about 1.5 million inhabitants).

Other developments

Again during the International Year of Disabled Persons, provision was made for disabled persons to receive state financial assistance in finding accommodation as close as possible to their place of work; this is arranged by the Committee on Problems Arising in People's Councils and the local authorities.

Specialists at the Orthopaedic Prosthesis Centre have designed and introduced into mass production some equipment of the Hycomat type that adapts vehicle controls to meet the needs of persons with locomotor defects. Persons in this disability category are visited at home by teams established by the Red Cross Society and the National Council of Women, to provide guidance in solving their social and economic problems.

In addition, the General Association of Trade Unions, the Ministry of Labour, the Central Union of Trade Cooperatives and the Institute of Medical Assessment and the Recovery of Working Capacity have stepped up their activities in regard to the adaptation of workplaces for the disabled in various industrial enterprises and the establishment of routes of access to these workplaces. They have also increased the capacity of a number of cooperative protected workshops for the disabled and of some home workshops.

San Marino

General Principles

Article 4 of the Declaration on the rights of citizens and on the fundamental principles governing San Marino legislation (Law No. 59 of 8 July 1974) states that all are equal before the law, without distinction as to their personal, economic, social, political and religious state. Further, all citizens have the right of access to public office and to elective positions in accordance with the procedures laid down by the law.

The Social Health Service was established in accordance with Law No. 21 of 3 May 1977 to provide care for the individual at various ages: from the health standpoint by carrying out preventive, curative and rehabilitative activities, and from the social standpoint by supervising the proper integration of the individual in school, at work, and in his or her surroundings.

National Involvement in International Action

In 1985 San Marino acceded to Convention 159 of the International Labour Organisation, on the Vocational Rehabilitation and Employment of the Disabled (Decree No. 56 of 9 May 1985).

Methodology — Types of Legislative Approach to the Equality Concept

Legal provisions for the disabled are contained in a number of different laws, both of a general and a specific nature.

The employment in private undertakings of persons who are handicapped or disabled as a result of accident or occupational disease is governed by Law No. 10 of 29 March 1952. This states that private undertakings employing more than 20 workers and office employees shall be required to take on one disabled or handicapped person for every 20 employees or portion of 20 greater than 10. The provision is applicable to men aged up to 60 years and women aged up to 55 years whose working capacity has been reduced by no less than 40% as a result of accident or occupational disease. It is not applicable to those who have lost all capacity for work or who, in the opinion of the Government Employment Commission, through the nature and degree of their incapacity, may cause damage to the health and safety of their fellow workers or to the security of the plant.

Those with a work disability who seek employment have to submit a request to the Association of Work Handicapped and Disabled, supported by the necessary documentation, including a certificate from the Institute for Insurance against Work Accidents on the degree of their reduced capacity for work. All other disabled and handicapped persons have to submit a similar document from the Government Health Office showing both their general and specific occupational capacities. The Association is responsible for keeping a register of the employable handicapped and disabled, and once every three months sends a copy to the Office of Employment and to the head office of the Institute for Insurance against Work Accidents.

It is the task of the Government Employment Commission, which includes a representative of the Association of Work Handicapped and Disabled, to declare the suitability for work of handicapped and disabled persons for every given occupational category and to secure their employment.

Employers may terminate the working relationship with disabled or handicapped persons whenever, in the opinion of the Institute for Insurance against Work Accidents and of the Government Employment Commission, the degree of disability increases to an extent that prevents the employee from providing the services for which he or she was employed, or when the Commission establishes the existence of a risk to colleagues or to the security of the plant, as mentioned earlier. There is an established appeals procedure against decisions on the degree of reduction of work capacity arrived at by the Institute for Insurance against Work Accidents.

Employers have to provide the Office of Employment twice yearly with information including the total number of their employees and a breakdown by establishment, category and sex. Employers who contravene the provisions of this law are liable to fines. Supervision of the implementation of the provisions is the responsibility of the Inspectorate of Labour.

The obligations of this law were extended to all the civil disabled by Law No. 30 of 23 December 1954.

Review of the Present State of National Legislation

Elimination of discrimination or social prejudice

Educational regulations were reformed by Law No. 60 of 30 July 1980. The State guarantees the right to study and provides the means for doing so, with the aim of overcoming the social conditioning that may lead to prejudice, and combating early exclusion from the educational process. To help attain these goals, the State provides community services, such as canteens, transport and the provision of teaching materials, and contributes by means of educational grants to attendance at institutes and universities outside the territory. Adults are guaranteed the right to study through continuing education, *inter alia* through the establishment of popular cultural courses, supplementary courses, periodic refresher courses, and orientation seminars in specific cultural topics.

Under Article 3 of Law No. 60, disabled persons, where they comply with compulsory education requirements, have the right to attend schools of every type and grade, including the right to higher education.

With this aim in view, schools, together with the minors' service (which forms part of the Social Security Institute, except where covered by specific services and responsibilities) draw up plans every year for integrating disabled pupils, to establish the type of schooling and the educational grouping to which each pupil should be assigned, taking account of the degree and nature of the handicap, an assessment of school age, the capacity of the school to assist, and the levels of collaboration provided by the specialized service. The schools guarantee the participation of disabled pupils in educational and teaching activities, establishing suitable conditions for educational rehabilitation. The specialist team working for the Social Security Institute gives advice on the preparation of work plans, carries out periodic checks, and participates in the team in the educational grouping or institution that discusses the teaching programme. Individual rehabilitative assistance is also provided as part of the minors' service. Where necessary, schools may be assigned specialized or additional personnel, equipment and teaching tools. The employment of personnel to this end is determined annually by the Congress of State, in the light of existing legislation and public grading systems. Materials for training and rehabilitation are provided by the Department of Public Instruction.

Law No. 10 of 13 February 1980 provides for vocational training, which includes vocational qualification courses for those exempted from compulsory education, and vocational qualification and integration courses for persons disabled through accident and illness. Such vocational training courses are of varying duration, depending on their type; they may even last for a number of years, in which case they are broken down into separate training cycles.

The law concerned with building regulations (Law No. 102 of 2 December 1981) contains provisions related to the elimination of obstacles in buildings.

Social reintegration and full participation

A brochure on the integration of the disabled into daily life was issued on the occasion of a conference on the problems of the disabled held in 1981.

There are also regulations governing accommodation for the physically and mentally handicapped, and craft workshops and their non-profit status, and statutes governing the national Disabled Sports Federation.

The prevention of disability

The prevention of accidents at work and work safety and health are governed by Law No. 40 of 2 July 1969.

Preventive measures that are offered to pregnant women through the health system include:

— periodic visits with diagnostic evaluation;

— childbirth preparation courses (respiratory autogenous training, health education);

— an ultrasound examination at the fourth and/or fifth month of pregnancy and at term;

— amniocentesis for older pregnant women;

— abortion on medical grounds;

— birth by Caesarean section;

— neonatal screening (for metabolic conditions).

Systems of income support

The pension system was reformed by Law No. 15 of 11 February 1983. The pension fund established by this Law provides mandatory insurance for the various categories of worker and optional insurance for those who, while not included in such categories, possess residence rights. Accordingly, persons under 65 years may receive a disability pension provided they:

— have at least seven years of contributions equal to a total of 1512 daily contributions, of which at least 432 have been made during the previous three-year period;

— suffer from a disability (a state of disability is deemed to exist when the earning capacity of the insured person in occupations suited to his or her abilities has been permanently reduced by at least 65% as a result of a physical or mental handicap);

— are unemployed;

— were insured at the time of applying for benefit.

An occupational disease pension is paid when: (a) a disease has been contracted which is contained in the list annexed under paragraph A of Law No. 15, (b) the degree of morbidity has been assessed by the Social Security Institute as having begun within the period laid down in the list for each disease and each type of work of which the disease is a consequence, and (c) the disease results in the death of the worker, permanent disability or partial disability of no less than 15%.

The assessment and establishment of degree of disability is provided under Article 21 of Law No. 15 and takes account of permanent disabilities as given in the list annexed under paragraph B of Law No. 15.

Persons of both sexes, resident by birth or for at least five years in the territory of the Republic, may be awarded a welfare pension if the following apply.

1. They have no income from independent work or work as an employee.

2. They have no other income of any type or provenance of an amount equal to or higher than that of the pension itself, apart from optional pension schemes.

3. They are not members or joint members holding licences as, or practising as, or enrolled on the registers of taxpayers listed as members of the free professions.

4. They are considered as being unfit for work.

Persons considered unfit for work are those whose ability to work is recognized by the Social Security Institute as being reduced by at least 65%. Wherever the total income referred to under (2) is less than the amount of the social welfare pension, payments shall be made so as to equal the full pension. Moreover, irrespective of the amount fixed under (2), a full amount shall be paid:

(*a*) to those persons who are considered unfit for work, who cannot move without constant assistance from someone else, or who require constant assistance as they are not capable of looking after their own day-to-day needs;

(*b*) to persons who come under the provisions of (4), and who are in particular financial need, when the spouse, parents or children with whom they live do not engage in activities liable to obligatory insurance, and are not beneficiaries of an ordinary pension paid by any insurance agency, or in receipt of income of any kind equal to or greater than the minimum prevailing payments from the Social Security Institute.

If the pension or income referred to above is less than the minimum provided by law, a supplementary pension is provided to make up the difference. The amount of this supplementary pension should be such that a conventional family is guaranteed a total monthly income equal to the minimum pension paid by the Social Security Institute and to the welfare pension.

Evaluation of Progress in National Legislation

The earliest provisions for the disabled go back to 1952 and Law No. 10 of 29 March on the obligatory employment of the handicapped and disabled in private enterprises. In 1954, this provision was extended to other types of disabled by Law No. 33 of 23 December. Between that date and the mid-1970s no new legislation was introduced; families with a disabled member used their own resources to deal with the problem.

With the development of society and the changes in family structure, increasing demands were made for the State to meet this type of need. Initially, intervention was limited to the provision of economic assistance on a lifetime basis, at first for persons disabled as a result of their occupation, and from 1969 for other types of disabled as well. This law was abrogated with the entry into force of Law No. 15 of 11 February 1983 on pension reform. Previously, the non-occupationally disabled had been granted daily subsidies according to need and to the cost of admission to institutions outside San Marino.

With the establishment of the Social Health Service in 1977, which in turn called for the establishment of new agencies, state intervention on behalf of the disabled increasingly came to be dealt with in San Marino itself.

The activities of the Social Welfare Service, as the institutional agency responsible for problems of disability, took a considerable step forward with the promulgation of laws such as Law No. 10 of 13 February 1980 and Law No. 60 of 30 July 1980, which paid particularly close attention to these problems. The importance of these achievements is striking when one considers the effect of the educational role of schools in general on culture and therefore as a spur to the process of change.

At the same time as the state-run activities, the Disabled Sports Federation was founded; it enjoys the support of many volunteers and has led to a wide-ranging and more effective type of collaboration with sporting groups.

In conclusion, some breakthrough can be noted in the treatment of the problems concerned with disabled persons, but many difficulties still need to be overcome, particularly with regard to integration in the workplace. The work of informing and arousing the awareness of all citizens needs to be continued, with a view to increasing the awareness of the disabled, their problems and their needs, in particular with regard to aspects of the workplace.

A simpler and more comprehensive instrument of law to back up the action conducted by the competent authorities is therefore still needed. The social workers of the Social Health Service have, therefore, drawn up a bill for the reform of obligatory employment of the physically and/or mentally disabled.

The specific aim of this bill is to improve work prospects for young disabled persons looking for their first jobs, and to set this in a broader framework that would bring this social responsibility to the attention of the entire population. The main provisions of the bill can be summarized as follows.

1. Citizens with a reduced working capacity of no less than 40% have a right to be given employment.

2. Private employers are required to include on their staff citizens with a physical and/or mental and/or sensory disability, based on a quota to be established jointly by the various agencies concerned.

3. The offices of state and independent agencies are required to employ (below the grade 4 salary level) citizens with physical and/or mental and/or sensory disabilities, based on a quota to be established jointly among all the various agencies concerned.

4. Those taken on pursuant to this law are to receive the normal payments and benefits.

5. A vocational training contract is to be drawn up for the part-time employment of the worker, designed so that he or she may acquire job qualifications and obtain stable employment.

6. A commission is to be established for integration at the workplace, whose membership is to consist of:

— one representative of the Association of Disabled Citizens

— one instructor from the Vocational Training Centre

— one social assistant from the Social Health Service.

7. The Work Integration Commission (currently being set up) will have attached to it a representative of the employer and a representative of the factory council from the place of work where the disabled individual is to be employed, or a representative of the office or sector of the public administration that the disabled individual is to join. Their tasks will be:

— to develop a training programme;

— to evaluate progress in the acquisition of work skills, social adaptation and adjustment.

8. Those persons referred to in item 1 may participate in all competitions and examinations for employment in the public sector organized by the administration, so long as they are in possession of all the requirements laid down in the announcement of the competition. For this purpose, examination announcements may include special tests to ensure that the above-mentioned persons are able to compete in effective parity with other candidates.

9. The State shall promote the development and establishment of undertakings of the cooperative type, which have as a declared goal the integration in employment of citizens referred to in item 1, who are registered on the obligatory employment lists. Disabled workers working in such cooperative undertakings are entitled to be members of the cooperative and they must not form more than 30% of the personnel.

Spain

General Principles

To paraphrase Federico Sainz de Robles, Chairman of the Spanish Supreme Court of Justice, in the prologue to his book sponsored by the National Institute of Social Services:

> To law corresponds the merit of having first recognized and immediately proclaimed that the disabled is a person, a subject already integrated in the community ... given that the disabled is a person, those norms and techniques which do not consider him/her as such may be rejected ... he/she is just another citizen with specific problems ... it is not a question of establishing a different "status", but of creating the ideal instruments to overcome the difficulties which ... make the process of social integration bitter and sometimes incomprehensible.
>
> If one is to squeeze the essence of the problems of this process, two points will come to light: (a) the necessity of services and facilities which substitute or supplement the handicap itself, and (b) the establishment of a tutelary institution through which such facilities could be applied for.

In Spain, the formal instruments used to ensure that the disabled are treated as persons, that the public authorities take positive action to enable the disabled to achieve full integration and true and effective equality, and that the implementation of positive action through legislation does not discriminate but rather promotes equality and eliminates restrictive barriers, are the legal norms that culminate in the 1978 Constitution. All the above-mentioned principles may be found in the Constitution, specifically in Articles 9.2, 14, 40, 43 and especially and fundamentally in Article 49, according to which the public authorities are to implement a policy of provision, treatment, rehabilitation and integration of the physically, sensorially and

255

psychologically diminished, giving them the special attention they require and the particular protection they need to enjoy the rights given to all citizens.

This is a positive commitment on behalf of the public authorities to achieve real and effective freedom and equality of the individual (Article 9.2), equality in law and before the law and prohibition of discrimination due to personal or social circumstances (Article 14), a public system of social security for all (Article 41), the right to protection of health (Article 43) and the particular care of the disabled (Article 49). Thus, the constitutional and legal framework is entirely sufficient to ensure the implementation of an efficient legal policy concerning the disabled. Title I of the Constitution, in its Chapter III about the governing principles of social and economic policy, sets out the principles applicable to the disabled, particularly in Articles 40, 41, 43 and 49. The corresponding action has been taken with the publication of the fundamental Law No. 13 of 7 April 1982 on Social Integration of Disabled Persons.

Law on Social Integration of Disabled Persons
To coordinate the different types of legislation relating to the disabled that exist in Spain, the Spanish Parliament approved the Law on Social Integration of Disabled Persons on 7 April 1982. This is now the framework of compulsory reference when dealing with the principles of the national policy for the disabled.

The Law requires the Spanish State to develop legislation for the social integration of the disabled, in line with the United Nations Declaration on the Rights of Mentally Retarded Persons adopted in 1971 and the Declaration on the Rights of Disabled Persons adopted in 1975. Enlarging on and specifying the constitutional provisions, the Law establishes that the State is obliged to provide preventive measures, medical and psychological treatment, adequate rehabilitation, education, counselling, work integration, a guarantee of some minimum economic, legal and social rights, and social security. For the efficient achievement of these objectives, central administration, autonomous communities, local corporations, the unions, public entities, organizations and private associations and individuals must participate within their own area of competence (Article 3). The Basque Country, Navarra and the Community of Madrid have already elaborated laws that directly refer to this aspect of the Law.

National Involvement in International Action

In addition to passing the Law on Social Integration of Disabled Persons, which was inspired by the United Nations Declarations on the Rights of Mentally Retarded Persons and on the Rights of Disabled Persons, Spain has subscribed to the Universal Declaration of Human Rights, the International Covenant on Economic, Social and Cultural Rights, the European Social Charter and to Recommendation 99 of the International Labour Organisation on the Vocational Rehabilitation of the Disabled.

Spain is also a member of Rehabilitation International, its national secretariat being organized by the Director of the Social Service for Disabled Persons (National Institute of Social Services, Ministry of Work and Social Security). The National Institute of Social Services publishes, along with the General Secretariat of Rehabilitation International, a liaison bulletin for the Latin American area that is widely distributed among Spanish- and Portuguese-speaking countries.

In collaboration with WHO, the National Institute of Social Services has published the Spanish version of the WHO publication *International classification of impairments, disabilities, and handicaps,*[a] which classifies the consequences of illness, with the intention of progressing to the use of standard terminology in Spanish related to the different aspects of illness and its consequences.

Methodology — Types of Legislative Approach to the Equality Concept

Until the Law on Social Integration of Disabled Persons was passed, Spanish laws were characterized by their plurality. Far from implying a standardized background (it should be noted that the existence of a specific law for the whole group of the disabled might be seen as an indication of its non-legal standardization and true discrimination), this plurality was a source of disconnection, protection gaps, and even unnecessary overprotection in the case of certain groups. The new Law has created a general framework that, although not totally eliminating plurality, will facilitate, as it advances, a functional and legal system for providing for the disabled.

Review of the Present State of National Legislation

This review covers the main aspects of the Law on Social Integration of Disabled Persons, indicating in pertinent cases the present state in the development of norms.

---

[a] *Clasificación internacional de deficiencias, Discapacidades y minusvalías.* Madrid, Instituto Nacional de Servicios Sociales, 1983.

257

The prevention of disability

The introduction of a bill that will establish the basic norms and principles for organizing and coordinating the prevention of disabilities is planned. The Government is also preparing a four-year national plan for the prevention of disabilities. At present, the national plan for the prevention of subnormality is implemented by the Ministry of Health and basically uses coordination and subsidy techniques.

Diagnosis and assessment of handicap

Multiprofessional teams were created by a Royal Decree in 1986 to ensure interdisciplinary care for those who require it, guaranteeing their social integration in the community. The teams' specific functions are the provision of standardized reports for diagnosis, therapy, and the assessment and definition of the assumed handicap for the purpose of access to the benefits, economic rights and services provided for in the legislation.

Systems of income support

A system has been established temporarily to provide social and economic facilities for the disabled. Once the relevant constitutional provisions have been executed, a public system of social security for all citizens, guaranteeing sufficient social assistance and facilities in cases of necessity, will be instituted. The special system includes those disabled persons not covered by the present social security system because they are not in work. Its protective action includes the following facilities: free medical assistance and pharmaceutical facilities; a subsidy to guarantee a minimum income, at present set at Ptas 154 000 (US $1305) per year; a subsidy for help from another person, which at present amounts to Ptas 77 000 (US $650) per year; a subsidy for mobility and compensation for transport expenses; professional rehabilitation; and functional/medical rehabilitation. This system of services has been developed according to Royal Decree No. 383 of 1 February 1984 and its efficiency is being studied to improve its function and increase the extent of protective action and range of coverage.

Rehabilitation of the disabled

The law envisages the establishment of a system of rehabilitation, coordinated with other social, school and work services. Rehabilitation services may include the following aspects: functional/medical rehabilitation to which any person with a functional handicap will be entitled (the process of functional/medical rehabilitation will be supplemented with the supply, adjustment, maintenance and replacement of prostheses, vehicles and other aids where necessary); and psychological counselling and treatment, directed at stimulating the maximum use of residual capacities of the disabled and at functional treatment simultaneously.

As a general principle, the disabled will be integrated into the normal system of education and will receive, where required, the necessary resources and support programmes. The plan and corresponding legislation for the total integration of the disabled into the normal education system, with provisions for the necessary resources, have been issued and implementation began in 1986. Special education will be imparted, temporarily or permanently, to those disabled persons whose integration in the normal system is impossible. It will be carried out in normal, private or public, institutions of the general education system, and will begin as early as each case requires. Its process will be adapted to the psychological development of each individual and will not be subject to strictly chronological criteria. Only when the extent of the handicap makes it absolutely necessary will special education be conducted in specific centres, and these will work in connection with the normal centres.

Professional rehabilitation, other than the pertinent functional/medical rehabilitation, will include career guidance, training, readaptation and re-education.

Integration in work
The policy for employment will have the primary objective of integrating disabled workers into the normal working system or otherwise incorporating them into the production system by means of the special formula of protected work.

The law envisages reserving 2% of jobs for disabled workers in all enterprises with more than 50 workers and guarantees no discrimination in work. It also establishes incentives to encourage the employment of the disabled, such as subsidies or loans for the adjustment of jobs, the elimination of obstacles, the special support of self-employed individuals, and any other measures considered appropriate. Cooperative societies will be specially promoted. In the public sector, the principle of equal opportunities will be declared explicitly.

To guarantee the efficient execution of job integration measures, arrangements have been made for the National Institute of Employment to find jobs for the disabled and for the National Institute of Social Services to guide their professional rehabilitation. The norms for developing the selective employment measures set out in the law have already been established. In those cases where integration into the normal labour market is not possible, the disabled may be employed in special employment centres (when their work capacity exceeds a given level) and in occupational centres.

Finally, for those disabled persons who do not have a paid job and are not able to have one owing to their incapacity, the law envisages a subsidy guaranteeing them a minimum income.

Social services

The objectives of the social services, according to the law, will be to guarantee the disabled the achievement of adequate levels of personal development and integration in the community and to overcome additional discrimination suffered by the disabled living in rural areas. The following social services are particularly important: family counselling, information and advice, care at home, community homes, cultural, sports and occupational activities, and leisure and free time.

Other facets of care for the disabled

The law envisages facilitating mobility and eliminating architectural barriers. These aspects will be the responsibility of the staff in the different services concerned with the care of the disabled. The competent public administration will approve the basic urban and architectural norms to guarantee the accessibility of buildings, roads, parks and gardens for disabled persons. These norms will facilitate the modification of existing buildings and installations and will take account, when promoting officially protected housing, of the construction characteristics needed to allow access to the disabled, reserving at least 3% of living quarters for people with special mobility difficulties.

Personnel in the different services

Personnel will have to be specialized, and the State will take pertinent measures to train the necessary number of different specialists, with the appropriate qualifications, to staff the services adequately. The collaboration of voluntary workers will be encouraged.

Management and financing

To simplify and unite the existing institutions, the administration that plans the general policy of care for the disabled will pay particular attention to: the decentralization of services; the democratic participation, either on their own account or through their legal representatives and professionals in the field, of those who will benefit from the services; the public financing of activities directed at integrated care for the disabled; and the preparation, programming, execution and control of regional plans and the integration of these plans with the

260

general health, educational, labour and social services, and with the national programme of economic and social development.

Financing of the different facilities and services envisaged in the law will be provided by the general state budget and the autonomous communities and local corporations in accordance with their respective competences.

Evaluation of Progress in National Legislation

The proclamation of the Law on Social Integration of Disabled Persons coincided with the International Year of Disabled Persons and therefore implies a fundamental Spanish contribution to the achievement of the objectives set by the Year.

Since its approval, there has been gradual though not always easy progress in developing the norms that will finally facilitate the practical implementation of its clauses. In particular, the special system of social and economic facilities envisaged in the Law is already a reality, although it is limited in the extent of its protection and coverage owing to a period of crisis. It may be substantially improved if the reform of the norms that are at present under study comes about. Norms have also been established for organizing special education and for encouraging employment of the disabled, and professional rehabilitation has progressed, under the responsibility of the National Institute of Social Services. The Institute has, moreover, paid special attention to basic care and social integration programmes by increasing the network of care centres and the variety of treatment offered.

The main difficulties have derived from a lack of resources, which has compelled the Government to plan the development of norms for the legal provisions cautiously, and from the slow progress with the administrative reorganization that the Law itself foresees, in order to unify and coordinate the institutions of care for the disabled. A maximum time limit of 10 years has been established for its full operation. The areas in which the Law has yet to develop norms are architectural barriers, special transport and mobility, and the modernization of electronic, technical, orthopaedic and other materials.

Sweden

Introduction

As laws have to be different because societies are different, a short description of Swedish society will provide some necessary background information. Sweden is a small, highly industrialized country which has not been at war for 170 years. This — at least in part — explains the scope for a number of radical social reforms that have affected disabled persons both directly and indirectly.

Sweden has a strong central government to administer its laws, as well as an extensive system of local government, both at the county and municipal levels. There are 23 county councils and 279 municipalities. They have the right to levy taxes, they have their own elected decision-making bodies, and they are responsible for a large number of public activities and services. Traditionally, these public agencies and commissions at all three levels — central, county council and municipal — are responsible for almost all public services within important sectors such as employment, medical care and social welfare. Private employment agencies are prohibited in Sweden, and there are relatively few private schools and hospitals. In the fields of social welfare and medical care, the tradition of public care goes back as far as the sixteenth century. This has meant that charitable organizations — often working on behalf of disabled persons — have less scope for their objectives than they do in many other countries.

Another important factor is the Swedish tradition of popular movements. The labour movement, the revivalist movement and the temperance movement all have deep popular roots and take part in society's decision-making process. This tradition is also reflected in a strong movement involving and on behalf of the disabled. In the municipalities and counties there are about 1200 associations of disabled people with about 350 000 members. At the national level, there are about 30 associations representing different disability groups.

Disability affects not only the disabled themselves, but also the conditions under which their parents, children and other family members live. In a sense, disabilities affect all human beings. The basis for this approach is that the society has a sense of community among its members, who undertake to bring about developments and improvements within it. Everyone has to make a contribution. Otherwise, should anyone be excluded or isolated, this sense of community breaks down and everyone is poorer.

The work on behalf of disabled persons in Sweden has as its aim that functionally disabled persons shall take part in the communal activities that society provides and live normal lives as far as possible. This is to say that both the environmental superstructure of society and the activities that are pursued by it must be accessible to disabled persons. Those responsible for making policy take the view that the creation of special ventures just for disabled persons is to be avoided as far as possible. The concept underlying work on behalf of disabled persons is usually summarized as: to integrate and to normalize. Full participation and equality, which was the motto for the United Nations International Year of Disabled Persons in 1981, also take pride of place as underlying concepts. To integrate, to normalize, full participation, full equality — all these concepts are in agreement with the Swedish Social Services Act, which sets the tone for the policy that the social services shall further equality in living conditions and active participation in society for everyone.

As the needs of the disabled are many and varied, society must be active in many areas: jobs, financial security, social insurance, housing, social services, mechanical and electronic aids, travel, education, cultural enrichment and medical care. In each of these fields, many meaningful reforms have been achieved over the last 20 years, which have improved conditions for disabled persons. Over the last 10 years, the money earmarked by central government for assistance that directly concerns disabled people has increased almost fivefold. This figure does not take into account the cost of pensions before the normal age of retirement. On top of the central government's allocations are those made by the county councils and municipalities for the care of mentally retarded persons, for other custodial services, for housing, for publicly subsidized transport services, for home-help services, for mechanical and electronic aids, and for rehabilitation. These local government allocations have increased at about the same rate as those of central government.

The State, county councils and municipalities are thus responsible for meeting the various needs of the disabled. The State's responsibility is to prepare and work out laws and regulations through the ministries. Government agencies and their regional and local branches give general instructions on how laws and regulations are to be enforced, and follow developments in society.

The responsibility of county councils and municipalities is to implement the goals that have been formulated in laws and regulations. There has been a trend towards decentralization, implying increased self-government and responsibility for individual county councils and municipalities. County councils are responsible for health and medical care. The municipalities have the ultimate responsibility for providing for the needs of disabled persons: for example, they are responsible for social welfare services, social planning, communications, schools and cultural matters.

Social Services Act

Public social services are established on a basis of democracy and solidarity, with a view to promoting economic and social security, equality of living conditions, and active participation in the life of the community. With due consideration for the responsibility of the individual for his/her own social situation as well as that of others, social services are aimed at liberating and developing the innate resources of individuals and groups. Social service activities are based on respect for the self-determination and privacy of the individual.

According to the Social Services Act, each municipality is responsible for the social services within its boundaries. It is up to the municipality to familiarize itself with local conditions and, through direct contact, to determine who is in need and what measures are to be taken to promote satisfactory living conditions. Although the municipality is ultimately responsible for ensuring that persons residing within its boundaries receive the support and assistance they need, this responsibility does not imply any restriction of the responsibilities incumbent on other authorities.

Every municipality must have a social welfare committee to discharge its duties in the sphere of social services. The duties of the social welfare committee include the following:

— to be familiar with living conditions in the municipality;

— to participate in community planning and to cooperate with other public bodies, organizations, associations and individuals to help secure sound environments in the municipality;

265

— to supply public information about the social services in the municipality;

— to help facilitate good living conditions by providing the necessary impetus;

— to ensure that care and service, information, advice, support, and financial and other assistance are rendered to families and individuals in need.

The social welfare committee should try to ensure that persons who, for physical, mental or other reasons, encounter difficulties in their everyday lives are enabled to participate in the life of the community and to live under the same conditions as others. The committee should help to ensure that the individual has a meaningful occupation and that he or she is provided with accommodation appropriate to the special support needed. It should also provide domestic help and publicly subsidized transport to facilitate the individual's integration into society.

The Social Services Act is an example of a piece of legislation that provides a broad framework for the achievement of a specific goal. In this particular case, municipalities are directed to organize their activities according to their own local circumstances and needs. A law such as this one, which does not set up detailed regulations, gives the agencies responsible — in this case, the social welfare agencies — a great degree of freedom in their work. It also makes it easier to adapt measures to individual wishes and needs. At the same time, there is the risk of different standards in different munici-palities, and of uncertainty about rights and responsibilities. These risks are foreseen in the legislative dispositions connected with the Act. There are, therefore, opportunities to appeal against decisions, and to use the judicial process to obtain a clearer determination of the individual's rights and responsibilities.

Health and Medical Services Act

Another example of a law that provides a framework is the Health and Medical Services Act that came into effect in 1983. The overall goal is good medical services and good health care on the same basis for the whole population. This concept includes preventive measures, which were not a part of the previous law. Another important difference is that the new law deals directly with the individual pa-tient's circumstances. These medical services and health care should:

— be of good quality and cater for the patient's need for security in care and treatment;

266

- be readily accessible;

- be founded on respect for the self-determination and privacy of the patient;

- promote good contacts between the patient and health and medical personnel.

One of the most central points in the new law is that the county councils are made responsible for the total planning of medical services and health care. They are therefore obliged to work together with other bodies concerned with the care of disabled persons. In the legislative dispositions connected with this law, it is assumed that this planning takes into account the individual's immediate milieu.

Care and treatment must as far as possible be designed and conducted in consultation with the patient. The patient must be informed of his or her state of health and of the treatment methods available. If this information cannot be supplied to the patient, it must be supplied to a close relative instead.

Care of the Mentally Retarded Act

In contrast to many other countries, Sweden has no general law to protect the rights of disabled persons. In accordance with moves to integrate the various matters relating to disabled persons into the areas where they belong, special paragraphs concerning disabled persons have been included in certain laws, such as the Building Act and the Social Services Act. In the case of other laws (the Education Act and the Work Environment Act) it is considered self-evident, or it is stated in the legislative dispositions, that disabled persons are covered.

There is one exception to this rule, however, namely the Care of the Mentally Retarded Act, which took effect from 1 July 1986, replacing an existing law. This law contains provisions for special arrangements for the care of the mentally retarded; it also applies to persons who, as a result of brain injury caused by external violence or physical disease, have incurred a significant and lasting intellectual handicap, and to persons with infantile psychosis. The purpose of the special measures of care is to enable mentally retarded persons to live like and with other people. Care arrangements must be aimed at developing the innate resources of the individual, and activities must be founded on respect for the self-determination and privacy of the individual.

267

The special care arrangements comprise:

— personal care, counselling, other personal support and support by a special liaison officer;

— daily activities at day centres or other occupation for persons above school age who are not gainfully employed and are not undergoing training or education;

— short-term stays away from the home, mainly in order to relieve relatives of the tasks of care and supervision, and short-term supervision away from home of school pupils over 12 years old;

— accommodation in family homes or boarding-houses for children and young persons needing to live away from their parental homes;

— group housing accommodation for adults unable to live independently;

— recreational and cultural activities for those in boarding-houses and group housing.

The special care arrangements are the responsibility of the county councils and they are made on behalf of those permanent residents of the county council area who are mentally retarded. The duties of the county council are:

— to obtain close knowledge of the living conditions of the mentally retarded and to work for the comprehensive provision for their needs;

— to supply information concerning the means and ends of activities;

— in association with municipalities in the county council area, to coordinate the activities needed for the mentally retarded and their families, and to take steps to ensure that these activities develop satisfactorily;

— to help to ensure that the mentally retarded are given meaningful occupation by means of gainful employment;

— to collaborate with organizations representing the mentally retarded;

— to help to ensure that public recreational and cultural amenities are made available to the mentally retarded.

Mentally retarded individuals, who are resident in a county council area on a short-term basis only, are given the immediate support and assistance that they require.

Social Insurance

Social insurance forms the largest element of Swedish social welfare policy, which also extends to the health and medical services, welfare services and family benefits of various kinds. Social insurance is defined as including parental, health and dental insurance, partial, basic and supplementary pensions, compulsory occupational injuries insurance, and voluntary unemployment insurance.

All Swedish citizens are insured under the national insurance scheme and all insured persons are registered with a local insurance office from the month in which they reach the age of 16. Within the national insurance scheme, a number of benefits are of special interest to the disabled: the disability pension, the temporary disability pension, the disability allowance and the child care allowance.

The disability pension is intended to provide basic economic security to those aged 16 or over, who have not reached the general retirement age of 65, and who, for medical reasons, such as illness or other reduction in physical or mental performance, cannot support themselves by employment. A disability pension may be granted if work capacity is permanently reduced by at least one half. A full, two thirds or half pension may be paid depending on the extent to which work capacity is reduced. Disability pensions take the form of a basic pension and a supplementary pension, and are taxable income. Decisions regarding disability pensions are made by the social insurance office.

The temporary disability pension is subject to the same rules as the disability pension. It is granted for a limited period and is payable if the reduction in work capacity is not considered to be permanent, but is expected to continue for a considerable period, as a rule a minimum of one year.

The aim of the disability allowance is to give the disabled person financial compensation for the need for help and the extra costs that the disability involves. A person aged 16 or over, who has become disabled before the age of 65, is entitled to a disability allowance. Physical or mental functional capacity should be reduced for a considerable period, as a rule a minimum of one year. The size of the disability allowance depends on how much help is needed and the additional costs incurred. Disability allowances are always paid to the blind, the deaf and those with severely impaired hearing. The

269

disability allowance is not taxable. Decisions regarding the disability allowance are made by the social insurance office.

Child care allowances are paid to parents taking care of children under 16 years of age, who owing to illness, mental retardation or other disabilities require special care and supervision for a considerable period of time. The child care allowance may also include compensation for the additional costs arising from the child's disability. A full or half child care allowance is paid according to the extent of the need for care and the additional costs. The child care allowance is taxable and carries supplementary pension rights for the parent.

Legislation in the Field of the Labour Market

In the sphere of working life, extensive legislative work was carried out in the 1970s to strengthen the position of elderly and disabled individuals on the labour market. The relevant legislation includes, first and foremost, the Security of Employment Act, the Promotion of Employment Act and the Work Environment Act.

The Security of Employment Act
Any dismissals of employees must be "on reasonable grounds". If any employee or his or her trade union believes that a dismissal is not on reasonable grounds, they can take the matter to court. The Act does not contain any detailed description of what are to be regarded as reasonable grounds. As a general rule, illness and reduced work capacity are not regarded as sufficient grounds for dismissal.

The Promotion of Employment Act
This deals, among other things, with measures to promote the employment of elderly employees and employees with reduced work capacity. Adjustment groups are supposed to exist at all workplaces with at least 50 employees. There is a three-way collaboration in each adjustment group between management, the trade union and the employment service. Their most important task is to help arrange employment for older people and the disabled. In practice, however, the groups mainly work with transfers of existing employees to suitable jobs at the workplace to prevent them from being "squeezed out" through their inability to cope. The aim is that transfers of current employees should be handled between management and the trade union, while the adjustment groups should spend more of their time working to improve the opportunities for the disabled and older people to enter the work force.

270

The Work Environment Act
Regulations concerning the state of the work environment, general obligations for employers and employees, the disposition of working hours, and cooperation between employers and employees are contained in the Work Environment Act. One statutory provision with a particularly important bearing on employment prospects for disabled persons is that the employer must give consideration to the particular aptitudes of each employee for the work in hand. In the planning and arrangement of work due regard must be taken of the fact that individual persons differ in their aptitudes to perform tasks.

Economic assistance
Money to finance measures designed to make it easier for disabled persons to obtain or retain employment is allocated by the Government and Parliament within the framework of labour market policy. Wage subsidies are paid to employers hiring persons with reduced work capacity who would be unable to find employment in the open labour market without such subsidies. Grants are obtainable towards the cost of working aids needed by a disabled person in order to do a job, or towards the cost of alterations and other workplace adjustments. Grants are also payable towards the cost of a work assistant or a vehicle for travelling to and from work.

Legislation in the Field of Education

The vast majority of pupils with educational difficulties and handicaps now attend ordinary schools and are taught together with the other pupils. Integration and coordinated remedial teaching are the concepts that express how the teaching of pupils with educational difficulties and handicaps is organized. The integration of pupils with handicaps and the coordination of special supportive measures with ordinary teaching have gone so far that it is very difficult today to draw dividing lines between the various sorts of pupil, with one exception: it has not been found possible to integrate deaf children in ordinary classes.

Individualization within the framework of the class, and access to special teaching, are important aspects of the attempt to create the right conditions for a course of study suitable to the circumstances and needs of handicapped pupils.

For the more severely handicapped categories of pupil, extraordinary resources must be available if they are to enjoy an education equivalent to that offered to ordinary pupils. Under the new system of government subsidy to the comprehensive school, which was introduced on 1 July 1978, the special allocation of resources to remedial teaching has disappeared. The local authorities and the schools now decide for themselves how to make use of so-called reinforcement resources.

Legislation concerning Building Policy and Traffic Planning

The objective of Swedish housing policy is to provide the whole population with sound, well planned and practical dwellings of a high standard and at a reasonable cost. In the planning of housing, special regard should be paid to the needs of the elderly and the disabled.

The Building Code incorporates regulations concerning the accessibility and utility of buildings for individuals with disabilities. The chief rule (paragraph 42a), which came into force in 1966, is that permanent housing, public rooms and working quarters should be so designed that they are accessible to, and can be used by, persons with impaired locomotor function or sense of locality. Nevertheless, certain exceptions are permitted. Conversions, too, are regulated by the Building Code. Those parts of a building that are affected by the alterations must meet reasonable requirements for adjustment to the needs of the disabled.

Opportunities for independent, integrated housing for the disabled do not depend only on the dwellings' technical design. It is important that the environment, including the communications systems, functions well.

A special law, which came into force on 1 January 1980, prescribes that the authority responsible for supervising public transport and the agencies operating such traffic shall ensure that the transport is adapted to meet the needs of the disabled. The direct responsibility for executing adaptations for the benefit of disabled passengers lies with the various traffic offices and carriers. A traffic authority, the Transport Council, was established in 1979, to coordinate the adjustment of the public transport system to the needs of the disabled, and to issue the necessary detailed regulations.

Conclusions

Local self-government is one of the cornerstones of the Swedish Constitution. The decentralized decision-making that this has made possible has meant a great deal for development in the field of provisions for the disabled.

The Local Government Act is pre-eminently a reaffirmation of the principle of local democracy and can be seen as the result of the general debate conducted during the 1960s and 1970s about increased citizen participation. The Act lays down that municipalities and county councils shall conduct their own affairs. The meaning of their own affairs is not directly explained in the Act, but it is conveyed by the drafting documents and is to a great extent determined by precedent. This results in a flexible system that can be smoothly adjusted in response to social development.

Special powers emanate from special enactments governing certain responsibilities that local authorities have to discharge on behalf of the Government and Parliament. Legislation of this kind provides, for example, that municipal authorities should give disabled children priority in the allocation of preschool places; and that public assistance is given to all persons in need thereof. Similarly it is the duty of a county council to care for sick persons in their area.

The different acts are largely, by nature, framework legislation, setting out no more than basic principles, which can then be implemented with specific directives. Criteria are thus constant and fundamental in character in that only objectives and guiding principles are laid down. Accordingly, there is leeway for the implementation of directives from sources other than the Government and the central administrative authorities. Framework legislation, as an expedient, has been used in Sweden first and foremost to give direction to those areas with which the municipalities and the county councils are charged, such as schools, social services and health care.

Framework legislation has a number of advantages — flexibility, improvements in administration, and ease of coordination — that make it possible to pay due regard to local needs and circumstances. This means that greater allowance can be made for the needs and desires of the individual than is possible with legislation containing highly detailed regulations.

Framework legislation also raises some essential questions, such as the risk of an unmanageable number of directives emanating at the lower levels, the problems of interpretation and giving direction, the problem of legal rights, questions of constitutionality, and uncertainty as to lines of authority and fiscal responsibility. Framework legislation therefore entails risks, one such being that of discrepancies of implementation and resource accumulation between different municipalities and county councils, another being that the needs of minority groups, such as the disabled, will not be considered.

The State can use special state grants to influence activities that it wants established throughout the country but via local government. They are also a tool for reducing discrepancies between different local authorities.

To ensure that the intentions of framework legislation are fulfilled at the local level, evaluations should, ideally, be undertaken at intervals. At present such an evaluation is being carried out of the implementation of the Health and Medical Services Act.

Switzerland

General Principles

This report is based on extracts from a commemorative report, *1960–1985. 25 ans d'assurance d'invalidité,* produced by the Federal Social Insurance Office to mark 25 years of disability insurance. When considering the relationship between disability insurance and other forms of social insurance, it has to be remembered, first of all, that the different branches of the Swiss insurance system were set up at different times and under different social, economic and political conditions. Although they share points of similarity, they do not reflect a general coordinated approach. The legislator has therefore been faced with two particularly important problems: to fill in the gaps in the system, and to prevent any duplication of benefits between the different branches of social security. It may reasonably be claimed that this task, undertaken only recently, is well on the way to completion.

Disabled persons are covered by disability insurance:

— from birth to the age of majority if they suffer from a congenital disease;

— from the age of majority onwards, if their disability (whether congenital or acquired) has reached a stable state.

Disability insurance covers the medical treatment of those under the age of majority. Once the disabled are over that age, disability insurance covers their rehabilitation and the restoration of their earning capacity, while their medical treatment becomes the responsibility of sickness and accident insurance.

Before the Federal Disability Insurance Act came into force in 1960, it was unusual for sickness insurance offices to assume

275

responsibility for the treatment of congenital diseases. This anomaly has now been remedied and insured minors are entitled to receive all necessary medical assistance. The qualifying conditions are relatively simple. The congenital disease must have been present at birth, even if it only manifests itself later, and it must appear in the list drawn up by the Federal Council. This list, which is included in the Congenital Diseases Order, has been repeatedly amended over the years. The efficacy of the treatment administered, in simple and adequate form, must be recognized by medical science. The entitlement to benefit starts as soon as the need for treatment has been professionally diagnosed; it ends when the treatment is complete or at the latest when the insured person reaches majority.

In persons who have reached their majority, disability insurance applies the same criteria to congenital diseases as to other pathological conditions and states that cause disability. The medical rehabilitation that is covered by disability insurance is concerned not with treating the condition as such, but with achieving a substantial and durable improvement in the disabled person's earning capacity or preventing any appreciable decrease in earning capacity.

The first requirement for the implementation of rehabilitation measures is the existence of a disability (that is, an injury to health that substantially and durably reduces the working and thus earning capacity) or the threat of an imminent disability. The second requirement is the presence of a disease that has reached a stationary state, that is, a disease that is no longer advancing. The likelihood of the rehabilitation succeeding is not an adequate criterion for determining whether the case should benefit under disability insurance or under sickness and accident insurance.

Judicial practice has adopted as a demarcation criterion a changing pathological state, a definition that is by no means clear cut to the medical practitioner. If, however, the envisaged measure would be equally appropriate whether the insured person is engaged in remunerative activity or not, the treatment will not generally be regarded as a rehabilitation measure under disability insurance, but as medical treatment under sickness and accident insurance. This does not mean, however, that only those who are earning can benefit from rehabilitation under disability insurance. A housewife could be eligible for a rehabilitation measure if one of the conditions, such as a disability or a relatively stable pathological state, was met. Measures taken to treat injuries, infections or internal diseases, on the other hand, are outside the scope of disability insurance. This applies equally to treatment intended in principle to save life. Finally, the Act requires a substantial and durable improvement in earning capacity, thus rendering all minor cases ineligible for benefit under disability insurance.

Although the entitlement of children and adolescents to benefits under disability insurance is relatively simple to determine, this is not always the case for adults. Refusals often give rise to claims and appeals to the courts, involving long and complicated legal proceedings that may necessitate the calling of expert witnesses. It is hardly surprising that, in order to avoid such disputes, the idea has been mooted of excluding medical measures from the scope of disability insurance and including them in normal sickness insurance benefit. Would this be a step forward? From the point of view of administrative and judicial procedures it certainly would, but it has to be remembered that the disability insurance system has the advantage of not imposing on the insured any expenses or any waiting time. The social aspects of the question have therefore to be carefully weighed.

Disability Insurance and Education

In spite of the progress made in therapeutic education, there were only a limited number of special training establishments in Switzerland when disability insurance was first introduced.

Special schooling measures
Special education and instruction measures were available at that time only to disabled children who were capable of improving their technical and intellectual knowledge, for example, in the field of writing or arithmetic. Those who could not were merely regarded as unsuitable for any form of training. Initially, disability insurance paid Sw.fr. 3 (US $1.85) daily to these children for boarding expenses and up to Sw.fr. 3 (US $1.85) daily for home care depending on the severity of the handicap. It very soon emerged, however, that even children regarded as unsuitable for training could achieve remarkable progress and greatly improve their manual skills as a result of suitable systematic training. In most cases this increase in manual skills enabled them to perform fairly well everyday activities such as eating, washing and dressing, meeting minimum requirements of hygiene and cleanliness, and making contact with those about them.

The first revision of the Federal Disability Insurance Act, which came into force on 1 January 1968, was mainly concerned with the implementation of medical education measures and special training for the disabled. This made it possible to provide the disabled, in record time, with medico-educational institutions, special schools and suitably qualified staff.

The idea of educational therapy measures was also included in this first revision of the Act. This concept was understood to mean individual measures that were not included either in school education in the strict sense or in medical treatment, such as lip-reading and auditory training for deaf children, corrective voice training for serious elocution disorders and special gymnastic exercises to develop the motor capacity of children suffering from severe mental retardation or sensory disorders. Remarkable progress has been made with educational therapy measures for the training of very young children with serious mental or physical handicaps. This could not have been achieved without the extended range of benefits under disability insurance.

The Federal Act allows the special training benefits to be paid under disability insurance up to the age of 20 if necessary. This flexibility has proved exceptionally valuable, since experience has shown that the need for special schooling extends well beyond the normal schooling period. It also made it possible to meet a very large number of requests at a time when special training facilities were still limited.

Quality of instruction

Very large sums of money are spent under disability insurance on the special training of the young, both in the form of grants to insured persons and directly on the construction, equipment and operation of special schools. Every precaution is taken to ensure that these resources are used effectively to provide the best possible special schooling for disabled children. Insurance grants are therefore only made to special schools recognized by the Federal Social Insurance Office in conjunction with the cantonal authorities. Only institutions that provide special schooling for children whose deficiencies prevent them attending state schools are regarded as special schools according to the disability insurance definition. These institutions may be privately run or managed by associations, foundations or public establishments under the cantonal or district authority. They must all, however, comply with the rules and regulations issued by the competent cantonal authority. The management, training and educational staff must have received a form of educational and therapeutic training recognized by the cantonal authorities.

Grants from disability insurance enabled exceptionally rapid progress to be made with the construction of special schools and the training of disabled children and young persons during the 1960s and up to the middle of the 1970s. By about 1975, the number of vacancies was sufficient to meet virtually all requirements. Development was then slowed down to cover priority aims, filling any regional gaps and providing vacancies for special categories of adolescent, such as those suffering from very severe and multiple disabilities.

Training of specialist staff
The introduction of disability insurance imparted great impetus to the development and diversification of specialist staff training institutes, catering for specialist teachers and instructors, teaching therapists, logopaedic teachers and special class teachers. As was to be expected, disability insurance played an active part right from the start in all training activities, promoting and financially supporting the initial, advanced and refresher training of specialist staff. Basic training was given in normal centres such as the universities, therapeutic training faculties, training institutes and colleges, whereas advanced and refresher training courses were run by associations and organizations responsible for aid to the disabled.

Disability Insurance and Professional Training

The professional integration of the disabled has always occupied a paramount position in disability insurance. Right from the start rehabilitation was aimed wherever possible at professional integration. This approach has not changed fundamentally during the 25 years of disability insurance.

Vocational guidance and professional training
The choice of a suitable profession is particularly difficult to make where professional opportunities are restricted by a physical or mental handicap or a psychological deficiency. Specialist vocational services are therefore available in regional disability insurance offices for the vocational guidance of the disabled. All insured persons who, as a result of an infirmity or disability, have difficulty in choosing or exercising a profession are entitled to vocational guidance, based on a detailed examination of their capabilities and manual and intellectual aptitudes. This vocational guidance is not confined to rehabilitation measures in the restricted sense of the term. It is also intended to enable disability insurance commissions to assess whether and under what conditions the insured person is capable of rehabilitation.

The vocational guidance and professional training counsellors in the regional offices are also responsible for supervising the professional training of the disabled and for direct liaison with employers on their reclassification and employment. These complementary tasks mean that their knowledge of vocational guidance is enriched by direct experience of professional training and the labour market. It has proved particularly effective during periods of recession.

Whereas the vocational guidance and employment of the disabled is the responsibility of the disability insurance services, professional training in the strict sense is left to outside organizations. The number of disabled persons unable to undergo training alongside the healthy was found to be relatively high. Disability insurance therefore decided to cater for them by establishing special rehabilitation centres run by private philanthropic institutions. The very wide range of training courses is thus able to meet any requirements that may arise, ranging from introductory courses in minor, relatively simple activities to highly specialized instruction, for example, in the fields of microelectronics or data processing.

Disability insurance assumes responsibility for vocational training expenses in so far as the necessity for training is occasioned by disability. Thus the cost of initial training, which a non-disabled person might equally be expected to undergo and pay for, would not be reimbursed. Conversely, where a disability prevents someone from pursuing a normal remunerative activity, the expenses of the vocational retraining will be met in full.

Daily wage allowance

The daily wage allowance counts as a substitute income and is paid to a disabled person attending a course of medical or professional rehabilitation. This concept of an earned wage is highly significant. The aim of the legislation is to build a bridge between the earning capacity before the disability occurred and what can be earned after completion of the rehabilitation course. Preference has been given to a daily allowance, payable for a clearly determined period, rather than a disability pension that gives the impression of a continuing benefit. The daily wage allowance is intended to cover the normal living expenses of the insured person and his or her family. The priority given to rehabilitation is emphasized by the daily allowance being paid at a higher rate than the disability pension.

The right of disabled persons undergoing initial professional training and of insured minors, who have not yet engaged in remunerative activity, to the daily wage allowance was deliberately excluded at the drafting stage of the Disability Insurance Act. The motive for this was that adolescents should be supported by their parents and in any case apprentices were not paid a salary in the normal sense of the word. Circumstances have, however, changed considerably since that time and apprentices are now paid an appreciable salary, depending on age and profession. It is therefore only fair that disabled young persons should be paid during training and it would be wrong to try to reduce the financial costs to a minimum. At the same time it is generally recognized that everything must be done to prevent the allowances paid to disabled persons, particularly the young, becoming permanent. The revised draft of the Act is intended to correct a regulation that was not very happily conceived in the first place.

Disability Insurance and Employment of the Disabled

Recruitment in the private sector

Rehabilitation takes precedence over a pension. This key slogan, conceived right from the start of disability insurance, was intended to secure for each disabled person his or her place in normal economic life, depending on his or her physical, psychological and mental capabilities. Gradually, owing to the untiring efforts of regional offices, the appeals of associations for the disabled, the provision of special equipment at the workplace, and to an upturn in the economy, the labour market has been opened to a steadily increasing number of disabled persons.

The recent recession has appreciably increased difficulties over recruitment, reintroducing an element of realism. After 25 years of varying and to some extent contradictory experience, a more stable situation has now been arrived at, from the point of view both of disabled applicants and of their potential employers.

Protected workshops

The disabled person who cannot be integrated into the free economy still has the right to perform a remunerative activity appropriate to his or her restricted working capacity. It was therefore necessary to establish protected workshops capable of meeting the needs of the disabled, by providing the necessary protection appropriate to their restricted movements and their low production rates and concentration levels.

When disability insurance first came into being, workshops for the disabled were very few, covering very restricted fields of activity. The measures taken by highly dynamic private and public organizations have to a large extent filled these gaps gradually in all regions of Switzerland. The range of potential activities has increased steadily, covering the production of articles in wood, metal, fabrics, wool, terracotta and plastics, and of mass-produced articles, as well as agriculture and horticulture. There has also been a steady increase in the categories of disabled person employed: the physically disabled, persons with sensory, mental and psychological disorders, alcoholics and drug addicts. Each of these categories can now find some perfectly natural entrée into community life.

Obviously these workshops could not be self-supporting, and disability insurance undertook to contribute to their support right from the start. Taking advantage of this assistance, which has been progressively adapted to meet their needs, protected workshops have been able to play an important part in the production system and provide the disabled with appropriate remuneration.

Therapeutic workshops

Whatever their degree of incapacity, all disabled persons may look forward to obtaining suitable employment that follows on from their special schooling. This aim, which has been pursued by all organizations providing assistance to the disabled, could not be fulfilled in the initial stages of disability insurance. Over the years, it became apparent that some form of simple employment, even one of no economic value, was vital for persons with very serious physical and mental handicaps. As a result of the setting up of specially designed establishments, either independent or based on protected workshops, disabled persons need no longer live in institutions that do not meet their specific needs, such as psychiatric clinics or asylums intended for elderly persons whose faculties have deteriorated. These therapeutic workshops can only operate with large-scale financial aid from disability insurance to cover the costs arising out of the disability of the workers, in particular staff costs.

The future

Disability insurance has made a major financial contribution to the establishment and operation of these protected and therapeutic workshops, but both national and regional organizations have also played their part. Rather unexpectedly, protected workshops were not faced with unsurmountable difficulties during the recession. The wide range of work carried out, the ability to adapt the production programme very rapidly and the continuing search for new product ranges enabled these workshops to maintain normal working schedules and wage levels. The recession did however bring back from the free labour market into the protected system a number of disabled workers who had become redundant.

What are the prospects for the future? Although the trend of technological progress has been towards replacing the human being by the machine, managers of protected workshops do not believe that this will exert a major influence on their work, since they believe there will always be simple tasks that have to be entrusted to human beings merely because they are simple. Obviously the future of these workshops can only be guaranteed if the three financial sponsors maintain and indeed increase their support: private sources, the disability insurance system and the public authorities.

Disability Insurance and Social Integration

Those responsible for disability insurance have always been convinced that, as in the sphere of work, every effort should be made to guarantee the disabled a place in society where they can, as far as possible, play their part in everyday life. The primary aim is therefore to allow disabled persons to remain for as long as possible in their natural environment, that is, to look for and promote every possible means of accommodating them in the normal social system, while providing the advice and assistance necessary for their particular situation.

Social services
When the Disability Insurance Act came into force, many organizations were already active in providing assistance to the disabled. Rather than paying out individual social integration benefits, the decision was taken to make use of the services of these organizations, providing them with financial assistance to perform their tasks better than before and to extend the scope of their social integration measures.

As a result the increased assistance to the disabled since 1960 has been more than encouraging. The pioneers in this field, such as Pro Infirmis, the Swiss Association for the Disabled and other associations catering for persons suffering from sensory or physical disabilities, have expanded their activities to meet the needs and new tasks resulting from a more up-to-date attitude to the disabled. The past 25 years have also seen the establishment of many organizations at the national, regional and cantonal levels, to assist disability categories that had been largely neglected in the past, such as those with a cerebromotor defect, paraplegics and the mentally and psychologically handicapped. Today any disabled person can count on the support of an organization to stand up resolutely for his or her interests.

These organizations have not confined themselves to advising the disabled and assisting them in a wide range of situations. They have also assumed responsibility for organizing all types of course to develop their physical skills and to promote sporting and social activities, including leisure activities. They have also organized courses for close relatives of the disabled. They act as an effective spokesperson when dealing with authority and it is due to them that, since 1984, the costs of transport to facilitate contact between severely disabled persons and their immediate families have been borne by disability insurance.

Homes for the disabled

In a system that recommends and encourages social integration, it is reasonable to ask whether homes for the disabled still have any *raison d'être*. Many regard them merely as a means of getting the disabled out of the way, a form of segregation. It remains true that a protected habitat is still indispensable for a large number of disabled persons.

When the disability insurance system was started, homes were only provided for disabled persons in connection with the exercise of a remunerative activity or professional training. The contribution of the insurance system in this field was restricted to the subsidized construction of homes to reduce the amount of rent charged. This situation had to be modified once it became clear that the overall management of particular categories of disabled person, in particular those suffering from mental and multiple handicaps, could only be successful if some form of protected accommodation were available.

From 1973 onwards, the home formed part of the overall requirement for all categories of disabled person, whether undergoing professional training, or engaged in remunerative activity under normal economic conditions, in a protected workshop or in a therapeutic workshop. It was no longer sufficient for disability insurance to subsidize home construction, and in addition a major financial contribution was made to cover operating expenses.

The actual concept of the home also changed considerably. Losing the traditional image of a refuge, the home began to offer a wide range of opportunities, taking into account the specific needs and the degree of independence of the disabled person. Homes for the disabled now provide accommodation *en pension,* consisting of larger or smaller independent groups, and small independent communities interconnected at the administrative and service level. Such homes may be located in an urban or rural environment, directly attached to a protected workshop or independent. Bearing in mind the special needs of certain disabled persons, it is reasonable to say that diversity has become the basic rule when establishing homes for the disabled.

The number of homes available on the national scale and even more in individual regions is still insufficient and funds are required from private sources, from the disability insurance system and from the public authorities. The time has not yet come to restrict, let alone eliminate, disability insurance assistance in this field.

Disability Insurance and Pensions

Rightly or wrongly, even though in almost all cases it represents a failure of rehabilitation measures, the disability pension exercises some form of fascination over Swiss and foreign insured persons suffering from a physical or mental disability. It is hardly surprising therefore that pensions, taken overall, were payable to 131 000 beneficiaries in 1984 (excluding the members of their families) and amounted to Sw.fr. 1784 million (US$ 1108 million), or almost two thirds of the total disability insurance disbursements.

The disability insurance pension as a measure of the loss of earning capacity

A disability pension is paid to insured persons whose loss of earning capacity — not to be confused with their unfitness for work — has reached 50%. A pension may also be paid, where the loss of earning capacity reaches $33^1/_3\%$, to persons with a very low income. Persons in these two categories are entitled to a 50% disability pension. The full disability pension is payable in cases where the loss of earnings exceeds $66^2/_3\%$. An inability to carry out normal work replaces the concept of a loss of earning capacity in the case of persons not engaged in remunerative activities.

Right from the start, determining the level of disability has always been the most delicate and controversial task of the services responsible for implementing the law. The principle adopted is to determine the ratio between the income the insured could have earned in the absence of a disability and that which he or she can be reasonably expected to earn after completion of any necessary rehabilitation measures, based on a balanced situation on the labour market.

The Act accordingly imposes very strict requirements for the assessment of the disability level. It would not have been surprising if, in spite of the instructions issued by the Federal Social Insurance Office, the 100–150 persons responsible for making decisions on pension applications had arrived at different assessments in individual cases. A recent analysis of decisions by cantonal disability insurance commissions, however, revealed that with few exceptions, the proportion of pension approvals was remarkably constant in relation to the populations concerned. More detailed random checks showed that the basic principles had never been contravened.

The task of the experts has on occasion been complicated by the obligation to take into account a balanced situation on the labour market — an idea that has been taken up in recent years in other social legislation. So much so that there has been a move in some quarters for its deletion. But, apart from the fact that this provision may afford protection to the disabled worker in a booming economy, its deletion would certainly give rise to abuses, especially during periods of recession. There would be a great temptation to attribute a reduction or loss of earning capacity to a decrease in personal working ability rather than to a general reduction in the number of workplaces. Furthermore, omission of the reference to the labour market would add weight to the medical aspect at the expense of the economic in the examination of particular cases, which would not always be desirable.

The aim of a more finely graduated scale of payment for disability pensions

For several years now, organizations providing assistance to the disabled and more recently public authorities at the local level have drawn the attention of the federal authorities to the disadvantages of an insufficiently finely graduated scale in the payment of pensions (in the form of half pensions or complete pensions) and have asked that the possibility of a more refined graduation be examined.

A pensioner whose disability level has been assessed as 70% (who, in consequence, receives a complete disability pension) is in danger of being put on a half pension in the event of a slight increase in earnings sufficient to reduce his or her disability level below $66^2/_3\%$. At the same time, the loss of the half pension is only too often far from compensated for by the increase in the salary earned. This may be an incentive for the pensioner not to work too hard or at least not to earn too much so as to avoid the possibility of losing his or her pension. A more finely graduated pension scale would mitigate this phenomenon without eliminating it. A decision to introduce quarter pensions would cost disability insurance a further Sw.fr. 70 million (US $43.5 million) annually.

A new regulation, currently under discussion in the Federal Chambers, provides for the replacement of the pension awarded to borderline cases by a quarter pension, the half pension being paid between 50% and 65% disability, a three-quarter pension between 65% and 80% disability and the full pension above 80% disability.

This rapid survey of some of the fundamental aspects of the problem of disability pensions highlights the importance of the improvements that have been made to the initial system. Others will doubtless follow within the limits of available financial resources as the essential step of coordination with other social insurance systems is taken.

Allowance for the severely disabled

This allowance was paid initially to insured persons in case of need, that is, where their income failed to reach a threshold level. Payment of the allowance was often refused, however, to disabled persons in a medico-educational establishment or in a home for the disabled. Since 1968, the allowance has been transformed into a conventional insurance benefit, payable only to disabled persons domiciled in Switzerland, who are over 18 and in permanent need of assistance and personal supervision in the performance of everyday activities (Article 42 of the Disability Pension Act). An exhaustive list of these activities, such as dressing, eating and washing, is given in the administrative regulations. These activities include establishing contact with those around the disabled person through such means as writing, reading or attending cultural functions. Since disabilities interfere to a varying extent with participation in such activities, it was logical for the allowance to be graduated as a function of the seriousness of the handicap. The degree of invalidity was therefore assessed as severe, moderate or low, the corresponding allowances being 80%, 50% and 20% of the normal minimum old age pension (Sw.fr. 690 (US $430) monthly in 1985).

Far-reaching changes have taken place in Swiss society during the past 25 years. It has become a major consumer of goods and services, with greatly increased emphasis on leisure. The world of the disabled, up to now out of the mainstream of these social transformations, is now directly exposed to them. The disabled have become aware of their right to integration in society. Campaigns have also sensitized public opinion to their problems, preparing the way for fundamental changes of attitude. It is only necessary to compare the old hostels and asylums to which, for lack of financial resources, the severely disabled, whether mentally or physically, were relegated like lepers, with the modern establishments for the disabled. The latter, which are adequately fitted out and staffed by properly trained teams, provide the disabled with employment appropriate to their disabilities and suitable leisure activities. As their remaining faculties blossom out, the disabled learn to master their handicap, acquire a new independence and find a measure of happiness and dignity in the human community of which they now form part.

It goes without saying that the operating costs of such establishments are no longer comparable with those of the past. The question to be asked is whether the present allowance for severe disability, the benefits of which are beyond dispute, is still commensurate with today's needs. Would it not be right to envisage in some cases moving up from the present practice of a fraction to a multiple of the normal old age pension for serious cases of severe disability, such as 120% or even 150%?

Disability Insurance, Its Services and Procedures

When disability insurance was introduced in 1960, the guiding principle was that it should as far as possible be integrated in the retirement and life insurance system, a system that had proved its worth, consisting of compensation offices throughout the country and a headquarters in Geneva.

The functions of contribution collection and the payment of pensions and daily wage allowances were therefore taken on by the compensation offices in parallel with similar operations on behalf of the retirement and life insurance system and in accordance with the system for loss of earnings allowances.

Disability insurance services

To enable disability insurance to examine properly and resolve the very wide range of problems resulting from disability, specialist services were set up responsible for the assessment of disability and the determination and monitoring of appropriate rehabilitation measures. On the other hand, disability insurance was not given any staff of its own for the implementation of the medical treatment prescribed or for education or vocational training. These areas were covered by close collaboration with the private sector, with doctors, dentists, pharmacists, hospital staff, paramedical personnel, rehabilitation centres, special schools and professional training establishments. This division of labour has been fully satisfactory.

Disability insurance commissions

The driving force of the whole disability insurance organization was provided by the disability insurance commissions in each of the 26 cantons, and two further special commissions, one for the staff of the federal administration and federal establishments and the other for insured persons resident abroad. Each disability insurance commission consists of five members: one doctor, one lawyer, one rehabilitation specialist, one person familiar with the labour market and vocational training, and one social assistant. At least one of the members has to be a woman, in the absence of a specialist on questions affecting schools and education.

Disability insurance commissions are called on to decide on all applications for benefits, to clarify and define insured persons'

288

opportunities for integration, to determine and monitor suitable special training and rehabilitation measures, and to assess the degree of disability to be used as a criterion for the granting of a disability pension and in appropriate cases an allowance for helpless disability. Initially, the commissions dealt with some 15 000 cases a year. By 1983, this figure had risen to 171 000. With no increase in staff, this has inevitably resulted in delays, exacerbated by the increasing complexity of cases and the worsening recession. The International Year of Disabled Persons served as a spur to simplify the procedures, to speed up decisions and deal with them in a more humane manner. Although all these measures have proved effective, the administrative machine still moves too slowly. Further significant improvements are to be made at the next revision of the Act. The goodwill and dedicated attitude of all concerned are a pledge that these improvements will really be made.

Disability insurance regional offices

To provide specially qualified persons to carry out the functions of vocational guidance and advise on the professional integration of disabled persons, the Disability Insurance Act envisaged the establishment of regional disability insurance offices. Thirteen regional offices exist at present, each covering one or more cantons. The grouping together of several small cantons in an economic region increases the chances of finding employment to suit an insured person's particular handicap. The regional offices assess people's professional capabilities and aptitudes, recommend the necessary rehabilitation measures to disability insurance commissions and, after approval, monitor and follow up their implementation.

Disability Insurance and Its Financial Structure

Disability insurance is financed on the basis of a system of allocated expenses. This means that all expenses in one year must in principle be covered by the receipts for the same year. No provision has therefore been made for the establishment of a capital accumulation fund. Fluctuations in the amount of both expenses and receipts are inevitable, however, and they are allowed for by a joint compensation fund operated by retirement and life insurance and disability insurance.

The general resources available to disability insurance consist of insured persons' and employers' contributions, contributions by the public authorities and the proceeds of legal claims against third parties. The obligation to pay contributions to disability insurance is governed by the system in force for retirement and life insurance. The same persons are required to pay contributions in both cases, irrespective of whether they are eligible for benefits from disability insurance. Any exceptions to the obligation to pay apply to both categories of contribution. No alternative provision has been made, even for the severely disabled who are unable to carry out any remunerative activity. In the same way the Retirement and Life Insurance Act applies, by analogy, to the contribution rates assessed for employees, employers and self-employed persons.

All employers required to pay retirement and life insurance contributions are simultaneously liable for a disability insurance contribution equivalent to the employee's own contribution. Since 1 July 1975 the contribution of all insured persons has been assessed as 1% of their income. Salaried employees, however, are only liable for half their contribution, namely 0.5%, whereas the self-employed pay the whole 1% contribution themselves. Insured persons not engaged in any remunerative activity pay a disability insurance contribution of Sw.fr. 25 to Sw.fr. 1000 (US $15.5 to US $620) depending on their assets or capitalized income in the form of a pension. Daily wage allowances and disability pensions are not included for calculation of the contribution.

Whereas insured persons' contributions are assessed in relation to their income, contributions from the public authorities are based on annual expenditure. The Act provides that 50% of the annual expenditure of disability insurance shall in principle be borne by the public authorities. The federal authority is responsible for three quarters and the cantonal authorities for one quarter of the contributions by the public authorities, that is, 37.5% and 12.5% of the total expenditure, respectively.

Changes in expenditure
The percentages for the principal categories of expenditure — cash benefits (pensions, allowances and compensation), costs of individual measures and grants to institutions — have varied little over the years. Cash benefits, for example, account every year for about two thirds of the total expenditure.

Disability insurance, as has been seen, pays out the same types of pension as the retirement and life insurance, namely single pensions, pensions for married couples, complementary pensions for young married couples and orphans' pensions. The 121 857 beneficiaries of single pensions, representing 55% of all beneficiaries, were responsible for 70% of the total expenditure on pensions.

Various rehabilitation measures account for one sixth of all disability insurance expenditure. The lion's share goes to medical measures and expenses incurred in the special training of helplessly disabled minors. The proportion of the expenditure allocated to rehabilitation measures is one of the highest on the international scale and is a good illustration of the basic rule in disability insurance that wherever possible rehabilitation takes precedence over a disability pension.

The number of disabled persons receiving benefits has increased continuously in recent years. There are three main reasons for this increase: the wider conditions for the granting of benefits, the greater life expectancy of disabled persons, and the increasing proportion of disabled persons in the older age groups. These trends will become even more marked in coming years.

Disability Insurance and Other Forms of Social Insurance

Disability insurance and retirement and life insurance

Disability insurance is closely linked with retirement and life insurance both in respect of the material law applicable to these two forms of insurance and in their organization. This is very clearly reflected in the fact that numerous passages in the Disability Insurance Act claim validity by analogy with the provisions of the Retirement and Life Insurance Act. The calculation and amounts of disability pensions correspond to those of retirement and life insurance pensions, while the latter Act guarantees that, where a disability pension is replaced by an old age pension, insured persons will not find themselves at a disadvantage as a result of the relatively low contributions that they paid as a disabled person. At the same time, the rights acquired in the retirement and life insurance system remain valid even where disability or supplementary assistance has been paid. The opposite may also occur as, for example, when payments of supplementary assistance are reimbursed by the retirement insurance system.

Professional Retirement, Life and Disability Insurance Act

The Federal Act on Professional Retirement, Life and Disability Insurance, in force since 1 January 1985, has been carefully coordinated with disability insurance in respect of disability benefits; it grants disabled salaried workers a status largely equivalent to that of their non-disabled colleagues. Disabled salaried workers engaged in remunerative activity are treated as follows: if their disability level is less than 50% and their income at least Sw.fr. 16 560 (US $10 285), they are automatically subject to full insurance cover; in the case of a disability level between 50% and $66^2/_3\%$, they are insured provided that their income is at least Sw.fr. 8280 (US $5143). Persons with a disability level in excess of $66^2/_3\%$ are not eligible for this insurance. Disability levels identical with those obtaining in disability insurance confer eligibility by analogy for the benefits under Professional Retirement, Life and Disability Insurance. Thus, a person suffering from at least $66^2/_3\%$ disability will receive a full disability pension; a half-pension is applicable to disability levels of at least 50%.

When considering the exclusion from insurance not only of persons having a disability level in excess of $66^2/_3\%$, but also those earning less than Sw.fr. 16 560 (US $10 286) or Sw.fr. 8280 (US $5143) and subject to the disability levels specified above, the aim of the second criterion should not be forgotten, namely to enable elderly salaried workers to maintain their normal standard of living, in addition to covering their vital needs on the basis of the first criterion. This standard is of course already ensured by retirement and life insurance pensions, but the situation of persons working in protected workshops, in particular, could still be improved by the special provisions contained in the statutes or regulations of insurance institutions.

Disability insurance and sickness insurance

There has been some uncertainty about the obligations of these two insurance systems towards insured persons in respect of medical rehabilitation measures, in accordance with the Disability Insurance Act, Article 12. It was therefore proposed, at the latest partial revision of the Sickness Insurance Act, to annul this Article 12. The competence of disability insurance would then be restricted to medical measures for the treatment of congenital diseases in accordance with its Article 13. This would put an end to the innumerable arguments, reports and expert opinions that hold up administrative and judicial procedures.

With regard to pensions, disability insurance is responsible for ensuring that no overpayment is made during the period covered by the payment of daily allowances under the sickness insurance system. The Disability Insurance Act (Article 29, paragraph 1) provides that the right to a pension shall only arise after an insured person has been at least 50% unfit for work for 360 days without any appreciable interruption. Pensions paid as a result of sickness account for more than 70% of all disability insurance pensions.

Disability insurance and unemployment insurance

Disability insurance makes good losses of earnings due to any prolonged illness of the insured, while unemployment insurance is concerned with the loss of work and earning capacity as a result of the economic situation. There is, therefore, a clear demarcation line between the competence of these two insurance systems, which has been confirmed by court decisions. This demarcation line did not alter when the new unemployment insurance regime came into force on 1 January 1984, improving the status of the disabled in respect of benefits. Persons receiving a full disability pension, for example, can now be considered for employment, if a vacancy can be obtained for them on the labour market appropriate to their particular handicap. It is no longer necessary for the disabled to be eligible for employment in order to benefit from courses to counter unemployment, organized by the unemployment insurance system. They are entitled, in their capacity as insured persons who are difficult to employ, to attend refresher courses subsidized by the unemployment insurance system.

Disabled persons working in protected workshops are now required to pay contributions, having been excluded under the old system as unsuitable for employment. This will entitle them to draw unemployment insurance benefits if they are once again capable of working in the open labour market. Unemployment insurance has therefore accepted the principle of paying provisional benefits. It is argued that — on the assumption of a balanced labour market situation — a disabled person who is not manifestly incapable of employment, and who has applied to disability insurance, is deemed to be suitable for employment until disability insurance has reached a decision on his or her case. There is therefore no question of prejudging the outcome of the disability insurance assessment of a person's fitness for work and earning capacity.

This finding brings out clearly the many points of contact between the two insurance systems. The following concepts are in fact common to both systems: "suitability for employment", "balanced situation of the labour market" or "work that may be reasonably required", or again "rehabilitation measures that may be reasonably required". Obviously these concepts have to be applied in the same way in both systems: for example, to prevent disability insurance deciding that an insured person is suitable for employment, while unemployment insurance refuses to pay his or her benefits on the grounds of his or her not being suitable.

Another point is the importance of coordinating the activities of the executive organs of the two insurance systems, in order to prevent the interests of the insured being prejudiced either by duplication or by gaps between the two systems.

Disability Insurance and Foreign Nationals

At the beginning of 1985, some 942 000 foreign nationals were established on Swiss territory. The retirement and life insurance/disability insurance central registry, which has records of the names of all persons paying or having paid contributions or receiving pensions, includes more than 7 million Swiss citizens and 6 million foreigners (although with often considerable fluctuation in the latter figure) originating from 170 different countries. All these foreigners are also entitled to benefit from protection under disability insurance. It is therefore necessary that their employers or others in a position of responsibility should be sufficiently familiar with disability insurance to provide them with any information or advice they need.

Turkey

General Principles

In line with the principle of equality, the disabled in Turkey enjoy the same rights and duties as all other Turkish nationals under the Constitution and the law. In addition, the Constitution and relevant legislation contain some protective provisions that take account of the special position of disabled groups.

Article 17 of the Constitution states that everyone shall enjoy the right to live and pursue self-improvement, physically and morally. The physical integrity of the individual may not be violated except under medical necessity or in cases prescribed by law; the individual shall not be subject to scientific or medical experiments without his or her consent.

Article 49 states that everyone has the right and duty to work; the State shall take the necessary measures to raise the standard of living of workers, to protect workers and improve the general conditions of labour, and to create economic conditions conducive to abolishing unemployment. The State shall facilitate and promote measures to ensure peaceful worker–management relations and introduce measures to protect the principle of equality at work.

Article 50 of the Constitution stipulates that no one can be employed in work that is not compatible with their age, sex and capabilities, and that the young and women, as well as those who have a physical or mental disability, shall receive special protection.

Article 61 safeguards the social rights of the disabled. It stipulates that the State shall take steps to ensure the protection of the disabled and promote their integration into social life; the elderly, too, shall be protected by the State. State assistance to the elderly and other rights and privileges to be provided to them shall be regulated by law. The State shall take steps to rehabilitate children in need of protection. To achieve these aims, the State shall establish the necessary organizations or facilities, or arrange for their establishment by other bodies.

The national policy concerning disabled persons in Turkey is based on the following principles, with due regard to the fact that human resources constitute a vital element of development:

— development of the educational and material status of the population, with expansion of the health, education, housing and nutrition services, and social security and social assistance schemes;

— adoption of measures for the protection, training and development of the family, which is of primary importance for the integration of the individual into society, and is a sound institution in a material and spiritual sense;

— adoption of training measures for the implementation of family planning services in conjunction with other health services with a view to protecting, in particular, the health of mother and child;

— provision of a supply of teachers and other personnel for the education of both retarded and gifted children who require special training, as well as children with sight, hearing, speech or orthopaedic disabilities, and socially disturbed and chronically sick children; and an increase in the number of appropriate institutions to provide education for a higher proportion of the disabled;

— development of standards for safety at work and workers' health and cooperation with the relevant trained technical personnel, so that measures can be taken to reduce the current work accident rate to the level of developed countries, and expansion of the related supervision facilities;

— promotion of the physical and mental health of the people by providing health services to all in a balanced, continuous and effective manner that ensures that all members of society make the utmost use of health services;

— gradual conversion of curative health services into preventive health services, expansion of the latter across the country in a sufficient and balanced manner and, to that effect, establishment of the necessary infrastructure, personnel and equipment;

— reorganization and expansion of social assistance programmes to meet the requirements of children, the disabled and the elderly who are in need of protection, health care and assistance, and ensuring that these groups are accorded priority in the implementation of such programmes;

— exertion of every effort to ensure that the disabled can integrate into society in a productive way, by providing therapy and training at medical and occupational rehabilitation centres.

Coordination mechanisms

The Law on Associations (No. 2908) requires the various national associations of the disabled now functioning separately to unite in the form of federations for each category of disability. Consequently, federations have been organized and work is under way on the creation of a confederation. Each federation will be responsible for coordinating the plans, programmes and activities of all the associations under its umbrella, and for monitoring such activities.

Meanwhile, a National Coordination Board for the Protection of the Disabled has been set up and named as a standing body affiliated to the Ministry, in compliance with the Law on the Organization and Duties of the Ministry of Labour and Social Security (No. 3146, Article 27). Under the chairmanship of the Minister of Labour and Social Security, this Board is composed of one representative each from the Prime Minister's Office, the Ministries of the Interior, Defence, Foreign Affairs, Finance and Customs, Education, Youth and Sports, Public Works and Resettlement, Health and Social Assistance, Transport and Communications, and Labour and Social Security, the State Planning Organization, the Radio and Television Corporation, the State Institute of Statistics, the Employment Agency, and the Confederation of the Disabled. The universities are also represented. The Board is assigned by law to:

— ensure the adoption of preventive and curative measures for disabilities;

— ensure that the disabled have proper access to social, medical and occupational rehabilitation, to economic and cultural resources, and to employment opportunities;

— achieve coordination among and cooperate with all public and private, national and international institutions and organizations that render services to the disabled.

297

Fifth Five-Year Development Plan (1985–1989)
The following guidelines and policies have been laid down in the social services, assistance and social welfare section of the Fifth Five-Year Development Plan (1985–1989) in connection with the health and social rights of disabled persons in Turkey.

Social service programmes will be rearranged and expanded to respond to the requirements of the disabled, the elderly, families, children and others who are in need. The principal goal in the provision of social services will be to alleviate and prevent financial, moral and social difficulties, and to improve and raise the living standards of families and individuals. In the implementation of social service programmes, priority will be given to children, the disabled and the elderly in need.

Educational institutions that provide special education services for children with sight, hearing, speech and orthopaedic defects, and for mentally handicapped children will be improved and their numbers increased to the level necessary to meet requirements.

The activities of public organizations and institutions and non-governmental organizations active in the field of social services will be coordinated to ensure the most efficient use of available resources.

The counselling and formal education services required in major cities and slum areas will be provided in an integrated fashion in accordance with social service guidelines.

The joint activities of organizations concerned with the employment of the disabled and the improvement of their economic, social and psychological situation will be reviewed and rendered more effective. Legislative and planning work to ensure that social services and assistance are not only oriented towards those in need, but also used as a tool in the distribution of improved welfare will be completed during the plan term.

Services will be rendered in an integrated manner under the auspices and supervision of the State. Since they are rendered on a voluntary basis, voluntary contributions from the people will be encouraged, and the public will be kept informed of progress in reaching target populations.

Development programme (1985)
The measures designed for disabled persons in the development programme prepared by the State Planning Organization for 1985 were to:

— develop social assistance services and increase their effectiveness, thus extending assistance to the family rather than giving priority to the so-called institutional services;

— ensure that the disabled make proper use of economic, social, cultural, educational and employment facilities, with due regard to the nature of their disability, and to ensure their recovery and rehabilitation;

— expand the special education services for those with sight, hearing and speech defects, the orthopaedically disabled and the mentally handicapped, which are provided by the Ministry of Education, Youth and Sports and which unfortunately currently reach only a few of those who need them;

— encourage guidance and research centres and other social service and education institutions to ensure that those children who are in need of protection are given priority and that disabled children receive special education.

A draft law will be prepared to replace Law No. 3457, which came into force in 1938, with a view to minimizing accidents at work and maximizing the efficiency of labour while laying down guidelines for preliminary and on-the-job training of workers.

The jobs that the disabled can perform will be defined with respect to various categories of disability, and this information will be made public.

National Involvement in International Action

Turkey is in cooperation with such international organizations as the United Nations, the International Labour Organisation, the Food and Agriculture Organization of the United Nations, the United Nations Children's Fund, the United Nations Department of Narcotic Drugs, the United Nations Development Programme and the Council of Europe. Turkey's activities are pursued in accordance with the basic guidelines of these organizations.

Turkey endorsed 1981 as the International Year of Disabled Persons and 1983–1992 as the Decade of Disabled Persons. Consequently, activities concerning the disabled have been intensified and positive decisions have been taken in the interests of the disabled.

Turkey is also a member of certain specialized organizations that render services for the disabled: the International Federation of the Blind, the World Council for the Welfare of the Blind, the World Federation of the Deaf, and the International Federation of Disabled Workers and Civilian Handicapped. Furthermore, relevant non-governmental organizations within the country keep in constant contact with their foreign counterparts, taking joint decisions and working on their implementation.

Methodology — Types of Legislative Approach to the Equality Concept

While legal provisions for disabled persons are contained in a number of different laws, a certain degree of harmony has been achieved among them.

Current legislation covers the employment of the disabled (Labour Law No. 1475, and Law No. 657) and provides for the statutory allocation of jobs to the disabled and for conditions of employment.

Disabilities have been classified, and the disabled are eligible for reductions in tax obligations (Law No. 193, as amended by Law No. 2361) and for early retirement benefits under the Social Security Law (No. 506) and the State Pension Fund Law (No. 5434) in accordance with that classification.

Legislative work is under way to improve the status of the disabled and to protect their rights. The National Coordination Board for the Protection of the Disabled, set up as an affiliate to the Ministry of Labour and Social Security, has launched activities under a ten-year programme in the following six main areas:

— the rehabilitation and education of the disabled;

— public relations and promotion;

— problems relating to buildings, facilities, traffic and other daily affairs;

— legislation and related arrangements;

— coordination with associations and organizations concerned with the disabled;

— definition and population census of the disabled.

A manpower training and rehabilitation department has been established within the General Directorate of Employment with a view to increasing qualified manpower and ensuring the occupational rehabilitation of the disabled.

There is no legislation that addresses itself to particular categories of disabled person, such as the mentally disabled or the blind, or specifically safeguards the rights of the disabled, and there are no plans to that end.

Review of the Present State of National Legislation

Turkey's national legislation consists of various laws of a protective nature, directly or indirectly related to the care, protection, rehabilitation, employment of and assistance to the disabled. There are also a number of laws covering medical measures aimed at the prevention of disabilities.

In addition to the aims outlined on pp. 295–299, the current emphasis is on the establishment and expansion of occupational rehabilitation centres with the aim of promoting the integration of disabled persons into social and professional life, and of medical rehabilitation centres for improving the functional self-sufficiency of the individual. The rehabilitation centres of faculties of medicine of those universities that have adequate training and education facilities, and the rehabilitation department or services of various hospitals, are used for this purpose. Cooperation among several ministries continues, and the services of some specialized institutions, such as foundations and associations active in the rehabilitation of people with certain categories of disability, are also employed.

Elimination of discrimination or social prejudice
There is no single law to protect the disabled against discrimination and abuse, and no single agency has been assigned the responsibility of ensuring the elimination of such prejudice. As described on pp. 295–296, however, the disabled enjoy the same rights under the Constitution as other Turkish nationals. Furthermore, provisions under a number of different laws, described on the following pages, are aimed at ensuring the protection of and assistance to the disabled in specific areas.

Social reintegration and full participation
The Law on Protection of Children and Social Services (No. 2828, Article 4) stipulates that special care and rehabilitation services are to be provided to the disabled, to ensure that they are able to be self-sufficient in society and can become productive, and special care and rehabilitation centres will be established for that purpose. The Social Services and Child Protection Agency, which is responsible for those services, is also required to draw up guidelines of social assistance and services in line with policies and targets, to prepare and implement work plans and programmes, and to ensure coordination and cooperation between relevant ministries, organizations and institutions on behalf of the Ministry of Health and Social Assistance. The regulations concerning the employment of the disabled and ex-convicts state that the Employment Agency should cooperate with and use the technical services of medical and occupational rehabilitation centres.

The Ministry of Health and Social Assistance currently has three rehabilitation centres, located in Ankara, Istanbul and Kasamonu, and five mental health and psychiatric hospitals. A further four rehabilitation centres, the Altinokta Rehabilitation Centre for the Blind in Emirgan, Istanbul, the Ankara Rehabilitation Centre for the Blind, the Enver Bakioglu Rehabilitation Centre for Trainable Children and Adults with Mental Defects in Izmir, and the Erol Sabanci Training and Rehabilitation Centre for Spastic Children in Istanbul function under cooperation protocols with the Ministry.

The Social Security Law (No. 506, Article 122) states that persons in receipt of benefits for permanent invalidity or disability whose working capabilities could be developed should be retrained by the Social Security Agency, with the purpose of employment either in their own field or a new one.

The Labour Law (No. 1475, Article 25) covers the question of employment of the disabled. Allocation of 2% of jobs to the disabled is obligatory for all employers. Further, various regulations and bye-laws provide that the disabled can only be employed in jobs that are compatible with their professional, physical and mental qualifications and may not aggravate their disabilities, and define the special conditions to which they are subject, including wages and training. Law No. 657 (Article 50) stipulates that the disabled have to take special examinations for employment.

The National Coordination Board for the Protection of the Disabled has submitted draft legislation to the relevant authorities aimed at facilitating the daily life of disabled persons. It would require the installation of handrails, ramps and other facilities to allow greater access for the physically disabled to such premises as post offices, hospitals, government buildings, schools, market places, bus and airport terminals and train stations. It also suggests that where more than one elevator is installed, one should be large enough to accommodate wheelchairs, and that specially designed washrooms and special parking areas should be provided for the disabled. Plans for new buildings should incorporate these modifications. The Board has also recommended special pedestrian ways for the disabled and slopes by pavements, and high-frequency sound alarms for the blind adjacent to traffic signals at crossroads.

In accordance with the Law on Children Requiring Special Education (No. 2916), children who are blind, deaf, dumb, have orthopaedic or other physical disabilities, or who are mentally handicapped and require special education are trained and educated at schools designated by the Ministry of Education, Youth and Sports, which are appropriately staffed and equipped. Furthermore, special classes created in primary schools are aimed at educating handicapped children, thus preventing their isolation from society. A preschool education and research centre has been established for children with hearing defects, and libraries have been set up for the blind.

Competitions, exhibitions and summer camps are organized for the disabled at different locations every year for sports and cultural activities. In addition, literacy and occupational courses have been offered to disabled adults to train them in such fields as tailoring, knitting, switchboard operation, typing, carpentry, ceramic crafts and carpet weaving, to ensure their full participation in society.

The prevention of disability.

In Turkey, there is a growing awareness of the importance of health. Topics such as the development of protective measures, new techniques and first aid, disability (how and why it may come about, its types), the rehabilitation of the disabled, the importance of protective treatment and immunization before and after birth, the improvement of health facilities, the provision of adequate manpower in the health sector, accidents at work, at home or in the street and ways of avoiding them, the provision of qualified security personnel, and the continuation of development-oriented research in all these areas are explained to the Turkish people via the mass media, conferences, and religious training and preaching. The public are also informed that intra-family marriages, unbalanced nutrition and the unnecessary use of medicines may lead to disability.

Various organizations have developed protection programmes against dangers that may lead to disability in a number of fields. Training programmes sponsored by the Ministry of Health and Social Assistance on mother and child care, nutrition, family planning, environmental health and contagious diseases, encourage parents to raise their children in a healthy way.

These activities are in accordance with the Sanitation Law (No. 1593, Article 1) which stipulates that the State shall struggle against all diseases and other hazardous factors that are detrimental to the health of the nation and shall improve health conditions and provide medical and social assistance to the people.

Law No. 224 concerning the provision of health services defines these services as medical activities to eliminate various factors that are hazardous to human health, to free society from the effects of such factors, to cure disease, and to rehabilitate people whose physical and mental capabilities have been reduced. The Law calls for the provision of these services within the framework of a programme. Efforts are being made to strengthen and expand mother and child care services, and to improve services for the treatment of the disabled and of diseases and injuries that may result in disability, in general and specialized hospitals and medical rehabilitation centres.

One of the main causes of disability in Turkey is traffic accidents — they cause some 15 000–20 000 deaths and 50 000 injuries annually. To reduce this toll, preventive activities need to be stepped up and regional emergency and traumatology hospitals set up. Some deterrent provisions are being added to the Traffic Law with the aim of reducing traffic accidents and improving safety. The public are kept informed about this topic via radio and television announcements. The Ministry of the Interior provides training programmes on traffic accident prevention for the mass media, and the Ministry of Education, Youth and Sports holds traffic accident prevention courses in primary schools.

Systems of income support
A law that entered into force in 1946 established insurance for job accidents, occupational diseases, other diseases and pregnancy. Subsequently, legislation was introduced to provide insurance for old age, disability and death. Insurance services subject to a series of laws were integrated under the Social Security Law (No. 506) enacted in 1965.

People who are employed at business premises covered by the Social Security Agency and who have lost part or all of their working capacity as a result of an accident at work or an occupational disease are eligible for temporary or permanent disability benefit, health assistance and rehabilitation assistance.

The State Pension Fund (Law No. 5434) provides health assistance for its members and their dependants in addition to various insurances, and shortens the tenure of service in cases where a member is disabled or becomes unable to work as a result of an incurable disease. Those who are entitled to early retirement for reasons of disability receive a disability allowance.

The Income Tax Law (No. 193, Article 31) as amended by Law No. 2361, classifies disabilities and provides for a disability allowance, thus enabling income tax payments to be reduced.

The Social Security Law (No. 506, Article 60) provides that those who are defined as disabled under Law No. 193, Article 31 can benefit from early retirement, provided that they have been covered by the social security scheme for 15 years and have paid social security premiums for at least 3600 days. An amendment to the State Pension Fund (Law No. 5434) allows for early retirement for state employees provided that they have actively worked for 15 years and they can certify that they have lost 40% of their work capacity.

With a view to protecting workers against accidents and occupational diseases, the Social Security Agency is authorized by the

304

Social Security Law to conduct inspections at the workplace, request its members to undergo health examinations whenever it is deemed necessary and adopt appropriate preventive health measures.

The provision (Article 73) that the whole of the insurance premium for occupational accidents and diseases shall be paid by the employer offers financial support to workers by freeing them from the obligation of paying such premiums. Jobs have been classified according to the danger involved, and these classes have in turn been divided into categories as to the specific work conditions and safety measures required.

Health care and treatment services for those employed under Law No. 506 or No. 5434 are provided by the State. Of the health insurance premium of 11% of the wage, 5% is paid by the wage-earner and 6% by the employer. The health assistance provided in this context is aimed at protecting the health of the worker, helping him or her to regain working capacity and promoting the ability to be self-sufficient.

There are no additional benefits in Turkey such as a disability insurance or family allowance. Nevertheless, Turkish nationals who can certify, by means of a health board report, that they are disabled to the extent of being unable to survive without external help, and who cannot be provided with appropriate jobs receive a certain monthly benefit under Law No. 2022 (1 July 1976). They also enjoy free health care services at state hospitals. Meanwhile, organizations such as the Red Crescent, the Social Services and Child Protection Agency and the tuberculosis hospitals help to ease the living conditions of the disabled by providing material and moral support.

An amendment made to the Customs Law (No. 1615) provides that live tissues, machinery and equipment and medicines may be imported in the name of the sick or disabled with the consent of the Ministry of Health and Social Assistance.

Under the Bag-Kur Law (No. 1479), artisans and craftsmen and other self-employed workers (provided they are Bag-Kur members) and their families are eligible for disability, old-age and death insurance. In addition, there are various private insurance facilities.

At this stage, there is no general health insurance to protect the health of the entire population, and there is no unemployment insurance.

Evaluation of Progress in National Legislation

As a direct consequence of the International Year of Disabled Persons, 1981, there have been a number of legislative developments in Turkey.

The National Coordination Board for the Protection of the Disabled has been established, and provincial coordination boards have also been set up. Disability has been defined and the disabled population has been counted. This has allowed classification of the disabled and determination of the numbers of disabled persons in each category. Census guidelines were laid down in connection with the 1985 population census.

Provisions have been added to the Labour Law to ensure recruitment of the disabled, and the relevant legislation has been amended to allow the disabled to pay lower taxes and to grant early retirement rights to disabled workers and state employees.

The Traffic Law has been amended to raise fines to discouraging levels.

Measures have been taken to ensure accessibility of public buildings and towns.

Measures have been taken for the prevention of disability-creating accidents and diseases, and mother and child care services have been strengthened and expanded. Activities have been accelerated for the creation of medical and occupational rehabilitation centres.

The final stage has been reached in the activities to unite organizations for the various disability groups in federations, and these, in turn, in a confederation.

Special schools have been set up for the disabled in addition to special classes in regular schools. Libraries, and literacy and craft courses have been organized.

In reviewing the achievements since 1981, it cannot be said that all the problems facing the disabled have been solved, but it is equally clear that considerable progress has been made by keeping the matter continuously in the limelight. Naturally, some difficulties have been encountered in this process, which may be summarized as follows:

— the means of communication and the mass media have proved to be inadequate in disseminating information about the disabled throughout the country;

— financial resources are insufficient to build the road network necessary to prevent traffic accidents and subsequent loss of life and property, to set up emergency aid and traumatology centres on highways, and to procure the necessary am-"bulances, helicopters, telephones and other equipment;

— employers are reluctant to employ the required number of disabled despite legislative obligations to that effect.

Through a more considerate and realistic approach, however, and with due care for human affection and prosperity in the struggle to ensure a better life for the disabled, Turkey is determined to overcome all these difficulties.

Union of
Soviet Socialist Republics

General Principles

The principle enshrined in the Constitution (Fundamental Law) of the USSR of creating progressively more favourable conditions for the fullest possible development of the personality is guaranteed by the political and economic system of the country and the basic directions of social development and culture. The State has set itself the task of extending the real opportunities for the exercise by all citizens of their creative powers, capabilities and gifts irrespective of sex, age, nationality, state of health and working capacity.

The general principles of the state policy on disability are set out in Article 43 of the 1977 Constitution, which states that citizens of the USSR have the right to material security in old age, in sickness and in the event of a complete or partial loss of fitness for work. This right is guaranteed by the payment by the State and collective farms of a pension in relation to age and disability, by the organization of work for citizens who have partially lost their fitness for work, and by the provision of care for the old and the disabled.

The organization of activities for the social integration of the disabled in the life of society is the responsibility of the state social security services, working in close cooperation with the trade unions and the standing commissions on health and social security of the Soviets of People's Deputies.

The volume of work undertaken by these commissions and active groups of experts, co-opted for the solution of complex problems, is increasing all the time. In addition to monitoring the activity of sectoral organs, these standing commissions regularly take the necessary steps, in conjunction with these organs and other sectoral commissions, to ensure an ever more effective system and the operational elimination of any defects.

309

An extensive network of scientific research institutes has been set up in the USSR to study disability problems in the principal regions of the country.

Social organizations, such as associations for the blind and deaf, are actively engaged in organizing social assistance to blind and deaf persons in the Union Republics.

National Involvement in International Action

The Soviet Union complies punctiliously with the basic provisions of the Universal Declaration of Human Rights, the International Covenant on Economic, Social and Cultural Rights, the resolutions, world programmes of action and other United Nations documents and agreements, as well as those of intergovernmental organizations, relating to the health of the disabled.

Methodology — Types of Legislative Approach to the Equality Concept

All measures carried out in the Soviet Union to protect the health of the disabled rest on a solid legal base, thus significantly extending the opportunities for assistance promulgated in the Fundamental Law of the country. The system of health and social legislation for the disabled includes a large number of statutory instruments, ranging from official acts of the USSR, which enjoy ultimate force, to decrees, orders and instructions by the relevant state and social organizations. The legal basis of social assistance to the disabled is therefore to be found in a wide range of laws, including the Soviet Constitution, the legislation of the USSR and Union Republics, and orders issued by the administrative authorities with general and special competence in this field, and by the trade unions.

In the Soviet Union, the disabled take their place as fully equal members of society and are not subject to any form of discrimination. There is no question of the general population displaying a negative attitude to the disabled who, for the most part, live side by side with those who are fit for work and actively participate in the development of society on the basis of currently valid legislative acts.

Soviet citizens with a long-term or permanent, complete or partial loss of the capacity to work as a result of illness, accident, mutilation or defective development (disabled persons) enjoy to the full the socioeconomic, political and personal rights and freedoms enshrined in the Constitution of the USSR (Article 39) and in Soviet legislation.

The fundamental social rights, enjoyed by disabled persons on an equal footing with other Soviet citizens, are the right to work (Article 40), the right to leisure (Article 41), the right to health (Article 42), the right to material security in the event of illness or a complete or partial loss of fitness for work (Article 43), the right to housing (Article 44) and other rights. Under Soviet legislation, in addition to the general range of fundamental rights and freedoms, disabled persons enjoy additional privileges and opportunities for study and the acquisition of special skills, a special workplace organization and the provision of housing, everyday services and social and cultural facilities.

An effective system operates to guarantee the rights of citizens, including the right of the disabled to health. All Soviet citizens enjoy the right to the protection of the courts against actions infringing their honour and dignity, life and health, and their personal freedom and property (Article 57 of the Constitution).

There is no need for a special committee to examine cases of discrimination against the disabled in the USSR, since any restriction imposed on the disabled in the provision of services or opportunities, and any unjust, intentional or unintentional refusal of such services or opportunities to persons who have lost their capacity to work may be referred to the courts in accordance with Article 58 of the Constitution, and any letter, complaint or proposal shall be examined by the strictly specified procedure and within the periods laid down by the law.

Review of the Present State of National Legislation

Soviet legislation includes a wide range of regulatory acts to ensure that the necessary measures are taken for the social integration of disabled persons and to promote their full participation in the life of society. The Socialist State provides those who have lost their capacity to work with extensive opportunities to participate in the production process, thus obtaining satisfaction, which is their right, and enhancing their general wellbeing.

Social reintegration and full participation
Social and medical rehabilitation occupies an important place in the category of measures aimed at ensuring the social integration of the disabled. Therapeutic techniques and social and medical measures for restoring the capacity for work have been developed by Soviet science and are incorporated in a specially designed system. This system has been given final shape in the relevant legislative documents, approved by the ministries of health of the USSR and

311

Union Republics, the ministries of social security and the All-Union Trade Union Congress. The principal elements in this system are an advanced course of treatment before an examination by the special expert committee (VTEK) and during the period of disability, regular prophylactic inspections (through dispensaries), and the diagnosis and elimination of conditions interfering with the work or working capacity of the disabled, as specified in the conclusions of the VTEK. Greater use is being made every year of far-reaching therapeutic and prophylactic facilities, including treatment at sanatoria and spas.

The special expert committee has a very important part to play in assessing the state of health of the disabled and the extent of their loss of capacity to work, establishing the relevant disability group and causes of the disability, and determining the conditions and form of work or profession open to the disabled. These committees also verify the proper employment of disabled persons at the workplace and cooperate in restoring the working capacity of the disabled. Article 50 of the Fundamental Principles of Health Legislation provides that the conclusions of the special expert committee on the working conditions of the disabled and the nature of the work done by them are binding on the management of enterprises, institutions and organizations.

Persons with a restricted capacity to work enjoy the general entitlement of all citizens to free qualified medical care (Article 42 of the Constitution).

Medicines and prostheses

The supply of medicines and prostheses is an important element in the care of the disabled. Hospital treatment is available free of charge to all Soviet citizens. The supply of medicines to patients free of charge, or with a 50% or 20% discount on the cost price, has become increasingly common in recent years. Certain population groups and disease categories are entitled to the provision of free medicines during outpatient treatment in accordance with Special Decree No. 97 of the Council of Ministers of the USSR of 28 January 1983. They include, in the first place, designated invalids of the Second World War and, on an equal footing, disabled persons in general; the eligible disease categories include those leading to prolonged unfitness for work (such as tumours and haematological diseases, diabetes, and tuberculosis). Medicines are also supplied free of charge to patients suffering from schizophrenia and epilepsy, groups I and II psychiatrically disabled persons and those working in the therapeutic/production workshops of psychiatric and psychoneurological institutions.

The provision of prostheses is an important means of compensating for organic functions that have been lost or destroyed, thus restoring to the disabled their capacity to perform socially useful work. Section 54 of the Fundamental Principles of Health Legislation lays down. that, where necessary, citizens shall be provided with prostheses, orthopaedic and corrective devices, hearing aids, physiotherapeutic equipment and special means of conveyance. The categories of disabled person entitled to the supply of these products and equipment free of charge or at reduced rates are specified in the health legislation. The detailed procedure for the supply of prosthetic aids is laid down in the regulations adopted by the competent authorities in the field of health and social security responsible for the provision of prostheses and orthopaedic services.

Housing and physical environment

One of the most important elements in promoting the social integration of the disabled and their full participation in the life of society is the creation of favourable conditions in their immediate environment, including the home. The right of Soviet citizens to housing, enshrined in the 1977 Constitution (Article 44), has been given clear legal implementation in the Fundamental Principles of Housing Legislation, approved during the Fifth Session of the Supreme Soviet of the USSR at its tenth meeting on 24 June 1981. The relevant legislation expressly stipulates the priority provision of housing to improve the living conditions of invalids of the Second World War, groups I and II work-disabled and military service-disabled persons and also patients suffering from serious chronic diseases (Article 20 of the Fundamental Principles of Housing Legislation).

In addition to the priority allocation of housing, disabled persons are entitled to an allowance for the payment of communal charges, to interest-free loans for the construction of private dwellings, with relief from land charges, interest-free loans for capital repairs to dwellings, the provision of essential materials for the construction and repair of dwellings, advantageous admission to allotment associations (cooperatives), and exemption from the payment of interest on loans from the Soviet Bank of Building and Construction (*Stroibank*) and the State Bank (*Gosbank*) granted for the building of houses by housing construction cooperatives. These entitlements are in accordance with the Fundamental Principles of Housing Legislation (which came into force on 1 January 1982), the Order on Allowances for Invalids of the Great Patriotic War and the Families of Perished Servicemen (approved by Order No. 209 of the Council of Ministers of the USSR of 23 February 1981) and the Order on Housing

Construction Cooperatives (Order No. 765 of the Council of Ministers of the USSR of 19 August 1982).

Independent living

Disabled persons enjoy a wide range of privileges in their everyday life under Soviet legislation. Invalids of the Second World War and group I disabled persons are entitled to priority in the installation of a telephone. In addition, the practice has become progressively more widespread in recent years of providing home help for disabled persons to cover domestic and similar tasks, and the delivery of food and medicines. Over and above these privileges set out in legal regulations, various organizational forms of assistance are provided for persons with a restricted capacity for work (for example, assistance from the relevant enterprise, institution or social organization).

Transport

Special privileges and advantages on public transport are available to facilitate movement by the disabled. These privileges enable them to participate actively in socially useful work, and help them to organize their leisure and rest periods and to maintain extensive social relations and contacts.

Transport concessions for disabled persons are laid down in legal regulations at the All-Union and Union Republic levels, and by the local and sectoral authorities. Existing regulations make provision for two forms of transport concession: priorities and advantages in the use of public transport, and the provision of special means of transport. Most disabled persons are entitled to travel free on all forms of city transport. In some disabled categories, this right is extended to railway and water transport and local bus services. In addition, they are entitled to a 50% reduction on season tickets and railway tickets.

Another social service available to the disabled is the provision, on medical prescription, of a means of transport and its replacement when worn out, facilities for technical servicing and the supply of replacement parts. Invalid vehicles are provided (free of charge, with an 80% reduction, or on a priority basis), special servicing points are set up for disabled vehicles and allowances paid covering, in full or in part, petrol, repairs and technical servicing. Local authorities give disabled persons priority in the allocation of spaces in garages for general use, permit the construction of garages in the immediate vicinity of their dwellings and provide practical assistance in the building and assembly of garages. Driving instruction for cars and motorcycles is provided free of charge to disabled persons, financed from the resources allocated to social security services for the training and introduction to the workplace of disabled persons.

Working life and vocational rehabilitation

Social and work rehabilitation is one of the most important means of promoting the social integration of the disabled and as far as possible their reincorporation in the life of society. Measures to promote rehabilitation in the social and work environment are designed to restore their previous skills to disabled persons who have in part lost their capacity to work or to teach them new skills and methods of work, so as to permit their active participation in creative work.

The legal measures relating to rehabilitation of the disabled in the social and work environment pay particular attention to professional training (particularly requalification) and specialized employment. The fundamental principle has been adopted in Soviet legislation that work, compatible with disabled persons' state of health, facilitates the process of adjustment, enhances the moral and material state of the disabled and satisfies their natural human desire for work activity.

Specialized employment is a vital element in helping the disabled, and social and medical legislation places particular emphasis on the restoration and strengthening of the health and fitness for work of disabled persons, irrespective of the extent to which it has been lost and even if only a minimum working capacity remains. If the working conditions, the nature and extent of the pathological condition, and the work prognosis permit, disabled persons can safely return to work, often with great benefit to their health. In the important field of specialized employment for the partially disabled, a wide range of measures has been taken to prepare their return to work, carefully planning their production activities and providing assistance with work and living problems, thus increasing the productivity of work and raising the professional status of the disabled person. The main emphasis in this case is on the retention and restoration of the health and working capacity of the disabled.

The organizational and legal basis of the specialized employment of the disabled in the Soviet Union includes a number of different legal guarantees that figure primarily in the Constitution (Article 43 expressly guarantees the right to work and the right of partially disabled persons to specialized employment). The legal aspect of one of the constituent elements of the specialized employment of the disabled, namely vocational guidance, emphasizes the need for an expert medical recommendation in regard to specialized employment. The need for vocational guidance derives from the right of disabled persons to specialized employment and the obligation on the relevant services to provide the necessary conditions for them to exercise that right. Recommendations about work not only include a scientifically based work prognosis but also constitute a form of professional guidance that has legal force. The reason for this is that these recommendations are legally binding on the managers of enterprises.

The procedure for the specialized employment of the disabled is governed by the Fundamental Principles of Labour Legislation (Article 66), the labour codes of the Union Republics, government orders and the instructions issued by sectoral management services on the use of disabled labour. Under existing regulations, the specialized employment of disabled workers and salaried employees will normally be arranged in the same enterprises or organizations in which they suffered partial disablement. If the conditions in these enterprises are unsuitable, the management of the enterprise is required to assist the disabled person to obtain specialized employment in other enterprises, taking into account the recommendations of the special expert committee.

Disabled persons whose state of health dictates special working conditions are given specialized employment in special enterprises, workshops or sectors, intended to cater solely for the work of the disabled. Disabled persons with visual or hearing defects are found specialized employment by the social security services in conjunction with the associations for the blind and deaf in training/production units, state enterprises, institutions, organizations and collective farms.

Particular attention is paid in the Soviet Union to invalids of the Second World War. Specialized employment has been found for them with the aim of reintegrating them in the work environment. Medicoprophylactic and social measures are carried out on a planned basis to restore their working capacity. War-wounded and other categories of disabled person enjoy a wide range of privileges, including a special system of services.

Soviet legislation gives disabled persons the right to specialized employment in all enterprises, institutions and organizations, provided they are found suitable for the particular work according to the recommendation of the special expert committee. Such persons are entitled to specialist courses at professional training establishments and technical colleges.

One of the most important elements in work rehabilitation is vocational training to enable the disabled to return to work in their previous profession or to be retrained in a new profession. Vocational training is given in the enterprise itself, in technical schools

316

or in secondary specialized schools run by the social security services (or in technical colleges, technical schools or teaching/production combines), in teaching/production enterprises and training schools run by associations for the blind and deaf, and also in general higher and middle teaching establishments and in general professional training establishments. The training given in these establishments is governed by legislation (Article 83 of the Fundamental Principles of Labour Legislation).

The principle of the free vocational training of all citizens including the disabled is enshrined in the Constitution. Disabled persons are moreover granted a scholarship during training, plus the established wage, and after completion of training they are guaranteed work to acquire professional experience. During training as boarders in technical training establishments, disabled persons are fully maintained by the State (provided with clothing, food, hostel accommodation, and social, cultural and other facilities).

The correct choice of profession, depending on the state of health, nature of the disease, interests and educational level of the disabled person, largely depends on an effective information service (which should make use of the daily press, radio and television).

In recent years an increase has occurred in some towns in the Soviet Union in the number of training institutes catering for the need to restore working capacity and with facilities for combined teaching and production activities. Through these, partially disabled persons acquire new skills, an independent attitude to life and work, and the ability to help themselves.

A network of technical and professional boarding establishments for invalids has been set up in which students are fully supported by the State and prepared at the same time for a return to work activity. By the end of the course students have acquired a special qualification, attested by an appropriate certificate.

Cultural activities

The social integration of the disabled into the life of society includes, of course, the cultural aspect. The ability to play a full part in the cultural life of the country has a profound effect on their general condition and mood, promoting a feeling of health and stimulating them to play an active part in the performance of socially useful work. Once in work, the disabled enjoy all the social and cultural advantages available to other workers. Homes for the disabled and the elderly have their own clubs, libraries, cinemas and other facilities, and creative activities are organized within the group. Lectures, recreational evenings and artistic performances are held regularly for

317

persons with a diminished capacity to work. Persons disabled during military service are given priority when booking at theatres, cinemas and concerts. Voluntary societies, such as associations for the blind and deaf, play an important part in organizing social and cultural functions for the disabled.

The prevention of disability
The Soviet State attaches paramount importance to the prevention of disability and a wide range of political, economic and social measures, including of course legislative measures, have been undertaken to this end.

Environmental protection
Soviet legislation on environmental protection is made up of statutory regulations and standards, which lay down the procedure and conditions governing environmental protection in the USSR, the activities of state organizations in environmental protection, the rights and obligations of those who make use of the environment and their liability in the event of contravention of environmental regulations.

The Constitution sets out clearly the fundamental aims of the economic policy of the USSR with its emphasis on protecting the interests of present and future generations, so as to maintain and foster health and prevent disease and any loss of working capacity. At the same time a number of articles in the Constitution (Articles 18, 73, 131 and 147) lay down in detail the rights and obligations of state services and directorates in respect of environmental protection, while Article 67 propounds the obligations of Soviet citizens to preserve nature and natural resources.

Important provisions regarding the protection of individual elements in the natural environment or individual aspects of environmental activity are contained in the basic legal documents that acquire force from the Constitution of the USSR, for example the All-Union Fundamental Principles of Legislation, the Union Republic Codes or other special laws. Some of the more important legal enactments regarding the creation of a healthy natural environment are: the Fundamental Principles of Land Legislation of the USSR and Union Republics (1968); the Fundamental Principles of Water Legislation of the USSR and Union Republics (1970); the Fundamental Principles of Legislation on Mineral Resources of the USSR and Union Republics (1975); the Fundamental Principles of Timber Legislation of the USSR and Union Republics (1977); the forestry codes of the Union Republics; the Atmospheric Air Protection Act (1980); and the Act on the Protection and Utilization of the Animal World (1980). Some provisions of other statutes are concerned with environmental protection, for example Article 21 of the Fundamental Principles of Health Legislation of the USSR and Union Republics, which prohibits the commissioning of new or modified factories, workshops, workshop sections, plants and other objects, which are not equipped with facilities for the effective purification, decontamination and trapping of harmful effluents, wastes and discharges. The third part of this Article empowers units of the hygiene and epidemiological service to prohibit or temporarily suspend the operation of installations if their effluents, wastes or discharges are liable to be injurious to human health.

In implementation of the guaranteed right of Soviet citizens to the protection of their health, Article 42 of the Constitution calls for the development and perfecting of safety and industrial health techniques, including measures for purification of the environment. These measures are aimed at producing an environment favourable to human health (Article 18), covering the protection both of nature and of the living and working environment.

Disease prevention and health promotion
One of the priority aims of the Soviet State is to improve the health of the population and prevent disease. The resolution of the Central Committee of the Communist Party of the Soviet Union and of the Council of Ministers of the USSR of 19 August 1981, concerning additional measures to intensify the protection of the population's health, sets out the principal directions to be followed in improving the public health system, including first and foremost the institution of prophylactic measures. In implementation of this resolution, a complex programme of work has been evolved to intensify disease prevention and maintain the health of the Soviet population over the period 1985–1990. This programme provides for:

(*a*) a further improvement in working conditions and work safety, together with the implementation of health hygiene measures to reduce the level of temporary unfitness for work, occupational disease, production accidents and disability and to raise the health level of the working environment;

(*b*) a greater emphasis on the health education of the population, building up social pressure against drunkenness and other harmful habits that reduce working capacity and adversely affect a person's state of health;

(*c*) the development of facilities for active recreation among the population, the organization of large-scale physical culture and sport, expanding and increasing at the same time the effective use of sanatoria and preventive health centres, tourist and sporting installations and other institutions to promote the health of the population.

The development of preventive medicine is inseparably linked with the achievement of a higher level of health education among the population, especially in regard to the prevention of disability. Health education in the Soviet Union is a means of imparting knowledge on the subject of medicine and health; its implementation is a state responsibility, based on a proper scientific foundation.

The dissemination of information on the prevention of disability, on risk factors to the population, detailed discussion of disability questions and greater knowledge of the importance of vaccination is carried out through popular publications and journals, and radio and television programmes (for example, the popular science journal *Health* (*Zdorov'e*) has a circulation of 16 million copies).

Ample state support is available for scientific research on disability prevention. This problem is being studied independently in five special institutes, with particular emphasis on the fitness for work and specialized employment of the disabled (in Moscow, Leningrad, Rostov-on-Don and other cities), in three research institutes on prostheses, in medical institutes, in labour institutes under the auspices of the State Committee of Labour, and in scientific research institutions under various directorates.

Systems of income support

Measures in support of the disabled are mainly financed from the following sources within the social security system: social security in the form of direct allocations from the national budget; state social insurance of workers, salaried employees and some other persons; social insurance of collective farm workers; social security of collective farm workers, drawn from the central Union social security fund for collective farm workers; and special funds of social organizations (individual collective farm funds, artistic, literary and musical funds, and the Cinematograph Association fund). The main source of finance is social security in the form of direct allocations from the national budget. This allows for the provision of disability pensions, numerous forms of monthly and lump sum disability allowances, the maintenance of partially disabled persons in specialized homes, the training for work and specialized employment of disabled and other persons, and the treatment of the disabled in institutions under the national health system.

Evaluation of Progress in National Legislation

Revision and amendment of the social and medical health legislation for the protection of the disabled has been actively pursued since 1981, the International Year of Disabled Persons. In this connection various measures were passed by the Council of Ministers of the USSR alone, such as the Regulation on Benefits for Invalids of the Great Patriotic War and the Families of Servicemen Who Were Killed, increases in the minimum pension levels and other pension provisions, and further measures to enhance the social security of the population. In 1983, resolutions were adopted concerning the procedure for confirming sickness certificates entitling persons suffering from these diseases to priority housing, the free issue of medicines to various categories of outpatient, and the provision of means of transport to disabled workers, salaried employees and collective farm workers as well as to persons disabled from childhood. In 1984, further measures were passed concerning allowances under state social insurance, and approval of the rules for compensation to be paid by enterprises, institutions and organizations for injuries to workers or salaried employees causing disability or damage to health affecting the discharge of their work responsibilities.

Further progress on the prevention of disability and the more effective social integration of disabled persons into the life of the community will necessitate amendment of the social and medical health legislation for protection of the health of the disabled. One possible approach would be to draft a general legal enactment covering all the basic statutory regulations on different aspects of the position of the disabled in society, sociomedical and labour rehabilitation and other questions.

The successes achieved in the USSR in economic and social development, the improvement in working and living conditions, the greater prosperity of workers and the achievements of the public health service have raised the level of health of the people, reduced the number of accidents and occupational diseases, eradicated some previously widespread infectious diseases, and cut back the general level of disability (improvements have been recorded, for example, in regard to tuberculosis, psychiatric disorders, and diseases of the central nervous system and respiratory and alimentary tracts).

United Kingdom

General Principles

In the United Kingdom, disability policies and services have evolved over several decades, dating back to the creation of the National Health Service in 1948, the creation of national insurance schemes for income support, and beyond. Employment provisions for disabled people have developed mainly from the Disabled Persons (Employment) Act of 1944.

The United Kingdom has no single policy statement or national plan embracing all aspects of services for disabled people. Present needs are too diverse and complex to be embraced in one blueprint. Comprehensive health, personal social and income support services have already been established. The present requirements are to refine and develop these services as resources permit, to ensure flexibility in accommodating changing perceptions of needs and techniques, and to promote opportunities for disabled people in wider "mainstream" provision such as in education, housing, transport, and employment. All policy considerations are guided by the basic goals that disabled people should be enabled to live as independently and normally as possible, in their own homes or in other accommodation in the community if practicable, and with the maximum opportunities for full participation and integration in the life of the community.

The United Kingdom has no written constitution and no formal statement of aims for any group in the community.

In the main, this report refers to legislative and administrative practice in England & Wales. Although in many areas of provision separate legislative and administrative arrangements apply in Scotland and Northern Ireland, broadly similar services and policies have been adopted in each of the home countries.

In England & Wales, statutory responsibility for planning and maintaining health and personal social services is vested in district health authorities and directly elected local authorities, and for education in local education authorities. In Scotland, health services are maintained by area health boards, and personal social services are the responsibility of social work departments of the regional and island councils, which are also responsible for education services. In Northern Ireland, health and personal social services are the responsibility of local health and social services boards, and education services are administered by local education and library boards.

Each agency has a responsibility to identify and meet the health, welfare or educational needs of its local community. Disabled people have also been identified in national guidelines as one of the priority groups to be given special attention, for example, in the policy document *Care in action* distributed to all health and local authorities in England in 1981. A review of all government department programmes for disabled people in the immediate wake of the International Year of Disabled Persons was set out in the United Kingdom Government's publication *IYDP and after — the UK response,* which was published in 1982.

Coordination of services is essential. For example, in England & Wales, the Government has given extra powers and funds to health and local authorities specifically to promote the joint planning and coordination of services at the local level, and to encourage closer planning and service provision with nongovernmental voluntary and disability organizations.

Since 1974, successive United Kingdom governments have included a minister to take special responsibility for disabled people.

National Involvement in International Action

The United Kingdom Government has supported and participated in a wide range of international initiatives on behalf of disabled people. It supported and sponsored the United Nations resolution proclaiming 1981 the International Year of Disabled Persons, and funded the four independent national committees established in the United Kingdom to promote the Year and its events. The contribution of government departments to the Year's activities are set out in the report *IYDP and after — the UK response.*

The United Kingdom endorses the World Programme of Action, which, as a member of the United Nations Advisory Committee, it helped to draft. The United Kingdom has also endorsed the main principles of Rehabilitation International's Charter for the 80s, which the Prime Minister accepted on behalf of the Government in November 1981. The Government helps fund the independent Royal Association of Disability and Rehabilitation in its role as principal United Kingdom affiliate to Rehabilitation International.

The United Kingdom adopted the Council of Europe's 1984 resolution on a coherent policy for the rehabilitation of disabled people, and supported the 1981 Council of Ministers resolution on a European Community programme for the social integration of disabled people, which was adopted during the United Kingdom's Presidency of the Council. (For further information on this programme, see the details already mentioned under the Belgian contribution, pp. 33–37.)

The International Year of Disabled Persons in 1981 drew attention to the fact that much disability could be avoided if existing health care systems were developed to provide the mass delivery of curative and preventive measures already available. Such measures include the mass removal of cataracts in mobile camps, the treatment of trachoma, immunization, the prevention of vitamin-A deficiency by supplementation and modification of agricultural programmes to grow vegetables rich in vitamin A, and the prevention of goitre by the addition of iodine to salt in goitre-endemic areas. To examine how these measures might be applied more widely, an international group of scientists, health specialists, and politicians met in Leeds Castle, Kent, in November 1981. Their recommendations were presented to the United Nations General Assembly the following month. The result was the setting up of IMPACT, a campaign promoted by the United Nations Development Programme, the United Nations Children's Fund and WHO to prevent disability in developing countries; IMPACT foundations are now being established in a number of countries.

The United Kingdom participated in the Second European Ministers of Health Conference in April 1985 and was party to the agreement reached at the Conference on a European strategy for the development of community-based programmes designed to reduce the level and extent of disability arising from mental illnesses.

The United Kingdom is taking an active part in discussions within the European Community on the protection of workers from the risks of exposure to noise at work.

Methodology — Types of Legislative Approach to the Equality Concept

Disabled people have the same fundamental and civil rights as any other United Kingdom citizen. The purpose of state intervention is to ensure that they can take a full part in the life of the community to the maximum extent possible. This is achieved by ensuring that general health and welfare services are available (for example through the National Health Service and the National Assistance Acts), that the educational and employment opportunities available to them are extended (the Education Acts 1944 and 1981, the Disabled Persons (Employment) Acts), or that particular services or benefits are provided for them as individuals to meet their needs (the Chronically Sick and Disabled Persons Act 1970, and social security legislation).

The Government is not convinced that the goal of integration and equality can be particularly advanced by any all-embracing or generalized law proclaiming the rights of disabled people. The Government also believes that the widely varying needs of the different categories of disabled person, and the many different circumstances in which opportunities for disabled people should be sought and the practical difficulties which may beset them, are too complex for any single measure. Ill-prepared legislation can be a costly, inflexible, and ineffective tool. Rather the Government believes that the best way forward is to enhance awareness of the needs and abilities of disabled people, to place the emphasis in health and welfare provision on supporting disabled people within the community wherever practicable rather than in separate institutions, and to identify specific practical problems that may hinder integration and seek to remedy them, where necessary by legislative measures when these can be properly focused and effective. One example of legislation specifically geared to certain special needs of disabled people is the Mental Health Act 1983 which, in amending the previous 1959 legislation, carefully defines the limited circumstances in which a mentally disordered person may be compulsorily admitted to hospital and the safeguards that attend to those few patients and the treatment they may receive. Other measures have sought to preserve or extend opportunities for disabled people by incorporating clauses requiring special attention to their needs in legislation on specific services, such as in the Telecommunications Act 1984 or the London Regional Transport Act 1984. Regulations first made in 1980 require companies employing more than 250 workers to include a policy statement about their employment of disabled people in their annual reports.

Review of the Present State of National Legislation

Elimination of discrimination or social prejudice
Some disabled people and disability organizations favour the introduction of anti-discrimination legislation to protect disabled people's

interests. This view is not shared by all disabled people, however, and others feel that the best way forward is not through generalized legislation but by continuing to work to change people's attitudes towards disability. The Government is also not convinced of the need for, or value of, generalized anti-discrimination legislation. In its judgement, there is a lack of sufficient evidence of problems of unjustified discrimination, as opposed to areas of ignorance or mis-understanding, of a type amenable to legislative solution. Any such legislation would face formidable problems of definition; it would need to make provision for programmes of positive discrimination in favour of disabled people; and it would lead to additional complex and costly bureaucracy to ensure compliance with and enforcement of its provision. Several proposed anti-discrimination bills have been introduced and debated in Parliament, but have failed to attract sufficient support to progress. The present Minister for the Disabled has indicated his willingness to keep the matter under review.

Social integration and full participation

Physical rehabilitation

The Government provides a number of rehabilitation services de-signed to enable physically disabled people to lead independent lives, at home whenever possible.

In England & Wales, these services include demonstration centres in rehabilitation, which act as focal points for the development, demonstration and dissemination of skills covering all facets of rehabilitation. Thus, in addition to high standards of service, they offer training opportunities for all categories of staff involved in rehabilitation both in hospital and in the community.

Rehabilitation activities are also carried out in hospitals and in the community, that is, in health centres, schools, residential homes and patients' own homes, through coordinated work by a range of pro-fessional workers.

In the field of rehabilitation of the speech impaired, a small network of communication aids centres have been established in association with the Royal Association for Disablement and Re-habilitation. The aim of these centres is to help find solutions to the problems of the speech impaired and to develop and spread good practice. The centres are staffed by speech therapists and have on display a range of communication aids and an information bank. They are open to other therapists to enable them to learn about the aids in question, either informally or through courses organized by the centre. Patients can be referred to the centre for assessment and, where appropriate, for provision of an aid to take home. It is also

327

anticipated that the centres will fulfil a valuable purpose by developing skills in evaluating the different aids on the market and formulating judgements on their suitability for different patient groups.

Technical aids

Aids may be provided to enable disabled people to live in the community and to participate in various activities. Central government agencies directly provide artificial limbs, wheelchairs, aids for war pensioners, and environmental control and typewriter systems for very severely disabled people, as well as aids to enable disabled people to obtain or retain suitable employment. Under the National Health Service Act 1977, aids to medical treatment and nursing care may be provided through the National Health Service. In cases where they establish need, local authority social services departments have a duty under the Chronically Sick and Disabled Persons Act 1970 to provide the necessary aids to assist disabled people with everyday tasks such as washing, dressing and cooking. Also, under the Education Act 1944, local education authorities may provide aids and equipment required by disabled schoolchildren and students for use in schools and colleges.

Various development projects and expert groups are considering the use of new technology and its implications for disabled people, including developments in telecommunications and how they can benefit users with impaired hearing.

Housing

Section 3 of the Chronically Sick and Disabled Persons Act 1970 gives local authorities the responsibility, when considering the housing needs and conditions of their districts, to consider the special housing needs of chronically sick and disabled people. Needs are met by the provision of wheelchair dwellings (specially designed housing to allow full access to and within a dwelling for a person confined to a wheelchair), mobility dwellings (ordinary housing made convenient for disabled people to live in or visit), by adaptations to the existing housing stock, and by the provision of certain sheltered or warden-assisted housing.

Applicants under the Housing Acts 1974 and 1980 for improvement or intermediate grants for house adaptations, to meet the requirements of a disabled occupant, are exempt from the normal requirements relating to the age of the dwelling, and from the normal rateable value limits that apply in other cases. Priority rate grants, under the home improvement grant system, have been extended to cover the adaptation of dwellings for disabled people. The higher grant rate under the homes insulation scheme, provided by the Homes Insulation Act 1978, is payable for applications made, or authorized

328

to be made, by a person on a low income who personally, or one of whose dependants, is severely disabled.

People who are vulnerable because of mental or physical disabilities come within the priority category of homeless people for whom local authorities must secure accommodation under the Housing (Homeless Persons) Act 1977.

A film *Housing for the disabled* and an accompanying information pack were produced by the Government in 1981, and shown to local authorities and voluntary bodies to publicize the housing options available for disabled people.

In addition, a number of important government housing reports and guides have been issued. *Organising house adaptations for disabled people* reviews the practices of local authorities in England & Wales in the management of house adaptations and makes recommendations aimed at improving the service they provide. *Housing for mentally ill and mentally handicapped people* gives a profile of the amount and type of housing accommodation provided by local authorities, housing associations and voluntary bodies, and also reviews how the different types of accommodation are organized, managed and used. *Housing services for disabled people* is a guidance manual for local authorities wishing to issue consumer advisory booklets.

Access

The Government recognizes the importance of working to remove physical barriers to make environments accessible to all. On 1 August 1985 an amendment to the Building Regulations came into operation, which introduced the first enforceable requirement that new buildings, and sanitary conveniences if provided within them, should be accessible to disabled people. The Building (Fourth Amendment) Regulations 1985 apply to new offices, shops, new single-storey factories, educational establishments and single-storey public buildings. The Regulations are the first step in a phased programme to require all new public buildings to be accessible to disabled people.

The Government has also encouraged the establishment of access groups or committees. For example the Access Committee for England was established in 1984, with government funding, to provide a national focal point on issues of access for all disabled people, to offer support to local access groups, and to promote an accessible environment. The Committee includes representatives of all professions who help shape the physical environment, building operators, and disabled people. A growing number of local authorities are designating access officers to coordinate consideration of access issues.

Transport

The Government recognizes that for disabled people personal mobility is essential if they are to have the opportunity to lead independent lives and participate fully in society. A range of measures has therefore been introduced to meet the needs of disabled people in both public and personal transport.

The Transport Act 1968 gives all county and district councils powers to provide concessionary bus fares for disabled people and most local authorities operate such schemes, although there is a wide variation in the concession offered. The Government does not, however, believe that it would be justified in legislating for reduced fares nationally because it considers that local authorities themselves are best placed to assess the needs of local residents in the light of available resources. Similar powers to provide concessionary fares are contained in the London Regional Transport Act 1984, which also places a specific duty on the transport authority in London to have due regard to the transport needs of disabled and elderly people. In addition, the Act requires the authority to include in its annual report to the Secretary of State for Transport a statement of what it has achieved in terms of securing provision for disabled people in the public transport services and facilities provided for Greater London.

To assist disabled people who drive a vehicle or travel as a passenger, the Chronically Sick and Disabled Persons Act 1970 introduced the Orange Badge Scheme. Under this scheme a vehicle driven by a disabled person or with a disabled person as a passenger and displaying the Orange Badge is permitted to park free at meter bays and in other areas where parking restrictions apply.

Under the same Act, disabled people are permitted to use invalid carriages on the footway providing the vehicle complies with prescribed requirements. These requirements are minimal and relate only to the maximum speed, weight, braking system and lighting of the vehicle.

For many young disabled people, transport can often prove a major obstacle to finding employment and to getting to and from their place of work. The Government therefore included in the Motor Vehicles (Driving Licences) Regulations 1981 a provision whereby disabled people receiving the mobility allowance may apply for a provisional driving licence to drive a car at 16 years of age, instead of the minimum age of 17 years specified for able-bodied people.

In addition to these legislative measures, the Department of Transport has a large programme of research and development aimed at improving transport facilities and the urban environment for disabled people.

330

Working life and vocational rehabilitation and training
The public employment and training services, including those intended for disabled people, are provided by the Manpower Services Commission in Great Britain, and by the Department of Economic Development in Northern Ireland. These services are available, as appropriate, to all categories of disabled person who are capable of some form of meaningful work, irrespective of the nature or cause of the disability. Special provision is made for those who require the conditions of sheltered employment.

Disabled people are able to benefit from the full range of employment and training services available to able-bodied people. These include skill training for both young people and adults, help with finding jobs in the ordinary labour market and participation in temporary employment schemes. In addition, there is a flexible range of assistance to help disabled people to prepare for and obtain suitable employment and to help reduce any obstacles to employment caused by their disability. This includes specialist help from Disablement Resettlement Officers, occupational assessment and work preparation, relaxed entry conditions for mainstream training, some residential training provision, the provision of special aids to employment, grants for the adaptation of premises and equipment, financial assistance with the extra costs of travel to work, grants to employers towards the costs of wages of disabled people for a trial period, help towards the costs of employing personal readers to help the blind, and help for disabled people to set up their own business if they are unable to work in open or sheltered employment.

The Disabled Persons (Employment) Acts established a quota scheme under which employers with 20 or more workers have a duty to employ a 3% quota of registered disabled people and enable entry into certain occupations to be reserved for registered disabled people. Employment under sheltered conditions is provided for under these Acts for the minority of disabled people who are unable, because of the severity of their disability, to get or keep jobs in the ordinary labour market.

These same Acts established the National Advisory Council on Employment of Disabled People which advises the Secretary of State for Employment on matters concerning the employment of disabled people, and a number of committees for the employment of disabled people which advise on such issues at the local level. Both the Council and each committee have an independent chairman, equal numbers of members representing employers' and workers' organizations respectively, and a number of other members with a direct interest in the employment of disabled people.

A major initiative to improve the employment position of disabled people was the introduction in 1984 of a Code of Good Practice on the Employment of Disabled People. The Code encourages the adoption of positive policies on all aspects of the employment of disabled people and provides practical guidance on how such policies might be implemented.

The Government's urban programme supports a range of schemes designed to tap the potential skills of disabled people through commercial enterprise.

Social services
Local authority social service departments provide a variety of services for physically and mentally handicapped people designed to enable them to live as independently as possible in their own homes, and provide residential care for those requiring more intensive care.

Under the Chronically Sick and Disabled Persons Act 1970, local authority social services departments have a duty to know about the number and needs of disabled and chronically sick people living in their areas (the blind, the deaf, the substantially and permanently handicapped, and the mentally disordered), to arrange for them to be provided with any practical assistance they need, and to supply them with information on the services available.

Domiciliary services include those provided by occupational therapists, who advise disabled people and their families on the problems arising from their disability; social workers; home helps, who give assistance with domestic tasks; and the meals-on-wheels service, which provides hot midday meals for people unable to prepare their own food. These services are supplemented by free home nursing and nursing supplies, and visits by health visitors, provided under the National Health Service. Authorities may make adaptations to disabled people's homes, such as ramps for wheelchairs, wider doorways, ground-floor bathrooms, hoists, and special switches, taps and door handles. Increasing use is being made by disabled home owners of local authority improvement grants to enable them to adapt their homes. Assistance may also be given where necessary with the installation of a telephone or a television set.

To assist with social rehabilitation and adjustment to disability, many authorities run day centres providing occupational, social, educational and recreational activities, and they may also organize special holidays. Adult training centres provide further education and social and work training for those mentally handicapped people who are unable to enter open or sheltered employment. Free or subsidized travel is available on public transport in some parts of the country.

Increasing thought is being given to the needs of the families of disabled people and the need to organize services for the disabled person, such as attendance at day centres or the provision of short-term respite care, in such a way as to give the maximum help and support to their normal carers. Some local authorities are also experimenting with the organization and content of services in order to give support to those severely disabled people who may wish to live independently, for example through greater and more flexible use of care attendants.

For many of these services, local authorities work closely with local voluntary workers and organizations of and for disabled people. Many such organizations will receive grant support from their local authority, and some may be "commissioned" by the local authority to provide a particular item of service. The Government is keen to promote such partnerships between the statutory and voluntary sectors, and encourages local authorities to plan and work with relevant local disability groups. Central government departments similarly work in collaboration with national voluntary organizations of and for disabled people, and a range of central grant schemes are operated to assist their activities. Particular emphasis is given to support for the work of voluntary organizations in the fields of help for carers, information and advice, the promotion of self-help groups, and the promotion of employment opportunities.

In England & Wales, health authorities also have powers to give some financial support to the development of community services for disabled people by local authorities and voluntary organizations.

The Government provides assistance to families caring for severely handicapped children through the Family Fund. The Fund was set up in 1973 and is administered by an independent trust. It helps families with the cost of certain essentials related to the particular problem of caring for severely handicapped children at home, which are not normally covered by other services. In 1984/1985, £5.43 million (US $8.97 million) was allocated to families by the Fund.

Education

In England & Wales, the Education Act 1981 requires that children with special educational needs should be educated in an ordinary school, subject to the wishes of the parents, assurance that the child is able to receive the special educational provision required, the provision of efficient education for the children with whom he or she will be educated, and the efficient use of resources.

In Scotland, the principle that handicapped children should, if possible, be integrated into ordinary schools was set out in a Scottish Education Department Circular in 1955. There is no specific requirement to integrate children with special educational needs under the Education (Scotland) Act 1981, but the earliest principles still apply and parents enjoy the same right to express a preference for a particular school as parents of non-handicapped children. In Northern Ireland, the Education (Northern Ireland) Order 1984 established in law the principle that children with special educational needs should be integrated into ordinary schools, so far as that is compatible with their receiving the special educational provision required, the provision of efficient education for other children in the schools, and the efficient use of resources.

In the United Kingdom, integration is understood to take place at three levels: locational, social and functional. Locational integration is simply the placement of a child with special educational needs in a unit or class for disabled children in a mainstream school, or in a special school that shares the same site as an ordinary school. Social integration occurs when the children in the unit/class mix with mainstream children for a range of nonacademic activities, and functional integration occurs when children with special educational needs follow courses, or elements of courses, with their peer group with any necessary support they require. The objective is to ensure the achievement of all three aspects. All integrated placements are assumed to satisfy the full definition of integration.

Cultural activities
The government-funded Arts Council Grant helps several acting companies with special needs, notably the British Theatre of the Deaf, Graece and Strathcona.

The Arts Council has drafted a Code of Good Practice for employment of the disabled, which it will be commending to all its clients.

Existing legislation states that provision should be made for the disabled in museums and galleries. The publicly funded institutions are aware of the problem of providing access to and facilitating the use of the museums by the disabled, and they are adapting their premises within the constraints of the existing buildings and budgets.

A recent report by a committee funded by the Carnegie Trust (*The Attenborough report*) made sweeping recommendations about wider provision for the disabled, which are being actively considered by ministers. The Carnegie Trust also sponsored the production of *Arts for everyone,* a practical manual of guidance on arts provision for those suffering from every kind of disability.

Public library authorities are conscious of the special needs of disabled readers and work in close liaison with social services departments and the voluntary sector. All library authorities provide domiciliary library services for people unable through permanent or temporary disability to visit library service points. Some authorities have purchased specialized vehicles to serve the disabled at home or to enable them to use a scheduled mobile library service. Others have invested in specialized computer equipment such as the Kurtzweil reading machine to make their collections accessible to the blind and provide information and referral.

Leisure and sport
Central government assistance for sport and recreation for all, including disabled people, is channelled through national and regional sports councils. Both the Government and the councils are concerned to promote wider opportunities for active recreation for all including the disabled and to encourage integration with the more able-bodied wherever appropriate. The Government provides the councils with an annual grant-in-aid to help achieve these aims and objectives.

The sports councils encourage and grant aid to local authorities and others to provide access to new and existing facilities for disabled people; grants may be withheld unless facilities comply with access requirements. Governing bodies of sports are encouraged to include disabled people in their activities and ensure coaching is available. The councils publish a wide range of useful information on facility requirements and sports and recreation provision for disabled people.

The councils work closely with the British Sports Association for the Disabled (BSAD), the national development and coordinating body which, through its regional organization, actively promotes opportunities for participation and competition. Sports Council funding is available for administration and development work and for training and participation of national teams abroad. The United Kingdom Sports Association for People with Mental Handicap, a member of BSAD, also receives a grant from the Department of the Environment towards its administrative costs.

To coincide with the International Year of Disabled Persons the Sports Council, in cooperation with BSAD, mounted a United Kingdom campaign to raise public awareness of the value of sports for the disabled, to increase participation, to help integration with the more able-bodied, and encourage disabled people to become more involved in the organization of sport and recreation. The initiatives associated with the Year are being actively pursued.

The countryside offers an important and enjoyable source of recreation for a large part of the community, including disabled people. The Wildlife and Countryside Act 1981 requires that grants given by the Nature Conservancy Council for buildings open to the public take account of the access needs of disabled people. The Act also requires that the Countryside Commission include a statement in its annual report of action taken to promote enjoyment of the country-side by disabled people. The Commission publishes information on informal countryside recreation for disabled people.

The Government's urban programme supports a wide range of innovative activities designed to aid disabled people in the inner cities and urban areas. Many of the projects funded through the programme are concerned with providing the community, especially disadvantaged groups such as the disabled, with opportunities for sport and recreation. Since 1979, the levels of support for pro-grammes for the disabled have increased significantly, both in ab-solute terms and as a percentage of the programme as a whole.

The prevention of disability

Road safety

The Government attaches the highest priority to reducing casualties on the road and has introduced in the Transport Act 1981 the most substantial piece of road safety legislation for nearly a decade. The main features of the Act have been to tighten up the law on drinking and driving, provide motorcyclists with stronger incentives to take proper training, and implement compulsory seat-belt wearing by drivers and front-seat passengers in cars. A number of important new regulations have also been introduced to make standards of vehicle construction and use even more stringent.

The Department of Transport's publicity, which includes press, radio and television coverage, offers guidance to all road users. Because of the high cost of advertising and the many other claims on its resources, the Department's principal effort in the publicity field has in the past concentrated on those areas likely to produce the maximum benefit in terms of casualty savings. Recent campaigns have included child pedestrian safety, bicycle safety, and drinking and driving.

Consumer safety

The Department of Trade and Industry's Consumer Safety Unit is responsible for the safety of all consumer products used in and around the home which are not specifically the concern of other government departments (For example, the Department of Health and Social Security deals with medicines and drugs, the Ministry of Agriculture deals with food).

The Unit's home safety activities take various forms, including:

— the investigation of complaints;

— the preparation of safety regulations, including the incor-poration of European Community directives and participation

336

in the operation of voluntary safety standards on which regulations may subsequently be based;

— research including the collection of data on accidents involving products; and

— publicity on accident prevention.

Investigation of complaints. Complaints about products that are alleged to be unsafe are notified via local authorities, consumer and safety organizations, and direct from members of the public. Expert advice is obtained from the Unit's technical adviser, and from outside bodies where appropriate, and whenever necessary the complaints are taken up with the manufacturer concerned. This action is taken in order to secure appropriate modifications and improvements, and to have unsatisfactory products withdrawn from sale if the degree of hazard warrants this.

Legislation. As and when necessary, regulations imposing requirements (such as those relating to such matters as composition, design, packaging and labelling) for consumer products have been made under the Consumer Protection Act 1961 (as amended by the Consumer Protection Act 1971). Under this Act it is an offence to sell or hold for sale a product that does not comply with any regulations in force. The powers in the Consumer Protection Acts 1961 and 1971 were refashioned and extended by the Consumer Protection Act 1978, which widened the range of requirements that could be laid down in safety regulations, gave new powers to the Secretary of State to prohibit the supply of goods and to require suppliers to issue warnings, and made changes to the powers of enforcement authorities. Existing enforcement powers are to be strengthened further, with particular regard to identifying and halting the supply of unsafe goods before they reach the shops. It is also proposed to impose a general duty on all suppliers to ensure that their goods are safe in accordance with sound modern standards of safety.

The European Community Directive on product liability was adopted on 25 July 1985. It will make producers and importers throughout the Community strictly liable for damage caused by unsafe products. Member States have up to three years in which to implement the Directive.

Research. The Unit's home accident surveillance system has been in operation since October 1976 and now has over 600 000 cases in its data bank. Data on accidents in and around the home are collected from a rotating sample of 20 hospitals located throughout

337

England & Wales and analysed centrally. The system's main purpose is to provide information on accidents involving consumer goods, so that the extent of the involvement of each type of product can be ascertained. This is helpful in identifying the need for improvements in safety standards and in deciding the content of future regulations. It is also of assistance in assessing the adequacy of safety instructions on products and in planning accident prevention publicity campaigns. The system regularly provides information to other government departments, as well as to manufacturers and organizations such as the British Standards Institution, the Consumer Association and the Royal Society for the Prevention of Accidents.

Detailed studies of particular hazards presented by products are undertaken from time to time.

Publicity. Home safety publicity is undertaken by both central and local government and by voluntary organizations. The Department relies primarily on short television films and radio tapes produced on its behalf by the Central Office of Information. A number of these films are currently held by the British Broadcasting Corporation and the independent broadcasting companies and are shown from time to time during breaks between programmes. The Royal Society for the Prevention of Accidents, which receives a grant-in-aid from the Department of Trade and Industry, produces a wide variety of posters and leaflets on the subject of home safety.

Health education
The Government has taken every opportunity to stress the importance of prevention and health education and places particular importance on initiatives against coronary heart disease, smoking and the misuse of drugs. The major risk factors for coronary heart disease are smoking and diet, and there has been considerable work in both these areas. Among other initiatives that the Government is taking to tackle the problem of smoking is an important new pilot campaign using the media to discourage smoking among teenagers. Practical guidance for families on a sensible healthy diet has been published. On drug misuse, the Government is currently undertaking a campaign of information and education to discourage the misuse of drugs by young people.

The Health Education Council, which is almost wholly government-funded, has a number of long-term programmes on major health issues where sustained education activity is needed — smoking, dental health and activities designed to encourage the sensible use of alcohol are included. It also develops the role of health professionals and teachers as health educators. Increasingly the Council has established links with the National Health Service so that a coordinated effort can be made in putting across the health education message that prevention can often avoid illness, disability and even sometimes early death. Increasingly also, there is health authority support for prevention and health education, and marked progress towards the goal of a health education unit for each health authority, and the concept of multidisciplinary regional health promotion groups has become firmly established.

Prenatal and postnatal care

The Government has reaffirmed (in its policy document *Care in action*) the priority it attaches to the reduction of perinatal mortality and the prevention of associated handicaps by improvements in the maternity and neonatal services. A Maternity Services Advisory Committee was set up in 1981 to advise the Government on various aspects of maternity and neonatal care. The Committee produced a comprehensive series of reports on good practice. The first report on prenatal care emphasizes the importance of good health and early and regular prenatal class attendance in helping to ensure a trouble-free pregnancy and the birth of a healthy baby. The third report on postnatal and neonatal care provides a detailed chapter on the diagnosis and care of babies born with a malformation or risk of handicap, and provides health authorities with a checklist of action. Advances in technology have also led to improved screening equipment, for example to detect congenital hearing defects in the first four weeks of life. The Health Education Council recently launched its *Pregnancy book*. This book, issued free of charge, contains up-to-date advice on health before pregnancy, becoming pregnant, prenatal care and care during childbirth, presented in a way that should interest and inform would-be parents from different social and cultural backgrounds. This book adds to the health education material already available in a way that should help significantly in the progress being made in reducing perinatal mortality and handicap.

Vaccination

Considerable importance is attached to immunization against infectious diseases as part of the United Kingdom's strategy in the field of prevention. High vaccination uptake rates have been achieved against a range of childhood diseases including tetanus, poliomyelitis, tuberculosis and diphtheria. Nationally coordinated initiatives aimed at improving vaccination rates have been launched. In particular, the National Rubella Campaign was launched in November 1983 and is being carried forward by the National Rubella Council, under the patronage of the Princess of Wales. It was aimed at increasing uptake among schoolgirls in the 10–14 years age group to 95% and among non-immune adult women of childbearing age to 90% by 1986. The campaign objective is to make a significant advance towards the elimination of the congenital rubella syndrome.

Research on the prevention of disability and rehabilitation development

In England, the Department of Health and Social Security currently funds a number of research training fellowships in occupational therapy and physiotherapy. Also funded are research units whose work is wholly or partly concerned with disability and a number of single research projects.

The areas of research currently funded are:

— rehabilitation for physical disability (a comparative study between hospital and community provision);

— communication aids provision;

— basic investigative studies of musculoskeletal physiology and of the mechanical factors involved in orthopaedic conditions and treatment, with special reference to orthotics;

— blindness (a survey of blind people in Birmingham, mobility problems of the visually handicapped, low vision training);

— deafness (evaluation trials on a neonatal auditory response cradle);

— physiotherapy (non-specific factors influencing the process of recovery in patients with physical disability of recent onset; an evaluation of different methods of treating shoulder pain in patients with hemiplegia; a study of methods of assessing and measuring pain, and of limitation of movement, in patients with musculoskeletal conditions; research advisory service);

— mental handicap and rehabilitation (development of procedures and teaching manuals for assessing communication abilities in mentally handicapped people, developmental research concerned with the maintenance of appropriate staff–client interaction in small residential facilities);

— informal care (the financial needs and circumstances of informal carers, the service needs of disabled people and their informal carers).

Additional research in some of these areas is carried out by the Medical Research Council.

Systems of income support

There is a wide range of social security benefits for which the long-term sick and the disabled can qualify. There are different qualifying conditions for each of these benefits, of which some are linked to the payment of contributions, some are non-contributory, and some are based on a means test.

In general, entitlement to a benefit is not based on the nature of the disability, but on the way in which a person's everyday life is affected by it. For example, those who are long-term sick and incapable of work can qualify for invalidity benefit or a severe disability allowance; people who need a lot of care and attention may qualify for an attendance allowance; those who have difficulty in walking may qualify for a mobility allowance; those whose income is below a certain level may qualify for supplementary benefit and housing benefit. There are separate schemes for people who are disabled through work or war injuries.

Children do not normally qualify for benefits in their own right although additions to benefit can be paid for them to an adult claimant. The exceptions are the attendance allowance, which can be paid from the age of two, and the mobility allowance from the age of five. They can claim other benefits from the age of 16 years.

Disabled people can also claim benefits that are not provided specifically for them, such as unemployment benefit, on the same basis as other claimants.

The Government's long-term aim is to work towards a more coherent system of disability benefits, and a major survey of disability is now being undertaken to provide information on which the development of policy can be based.

Evaluation of Progress in National Legislation

This report has already referred to the implementation of several examples of legislative action on behalf of disabled people since the International Year of Disabled Persons. Such a list can include the Education Act 1981 (implemented in 1983), the Disabled Persons Act 1981 (which dealt with highways, parking and access requirements), the 1985 access amendment to the Building Regulations, and the inclusion of special provisions for disabled people in the 1984 Telecommunications Act and the London Regional Transport Act.

The major constraint on new measures is the need to consider the practical resource implications. International and national economic circumstances have necessitated careful control of public expenditure. Additional spending resources can only be freed by switching

341

resources from other objectives, by greater efficiency, or by generating greater national wealth through improved commercial performance. Resources are already subject to growing pressures, for example through the growth in the number of elderly and disabled people because of demographic changes, and the growing cost and scope of new medical techniques. There also remains scope for improved coordination of services, and of increased public awareness of the needs, aspirations and abilities of disabled people.

The United Kingdom Government seeks to monitor the effects of all its legislative and other policies, but the success of policies aimed at improving the social integration of disabled people is very difficult to judge by any comprehensive and objective measures. Certain measures do point to encouraging progress, for example units in hospitals for younger disabled people are being used more intensively, reflecting in part their increased use for short-stay patients. Statistics in England indicate a doubling of the number of patients treated per available bed since 1978. A similar pattern is seen in local authority provision, where 79% of all admissions to residential homes in England in 1982–1983 were for short-stay care — a proportional increase of nearly a quarter since 1978–1979.

Despite progress to date there is clearly still much scope for improvement in the design and effectiveness of services, in the structure of income provision, and in the range of choice and opportunities for the disabled, particularly severely or multi-handicapped people, to "normalize" their lives as far as practicable. The Government will continue to seek cooperation and planning between statutory agencies and with voluntary organizations, to promote the concept of care in the community, to pledge the maximum practicable resources for health and welfare services, and to seek further improvements through programmes of research and policy development. Some examples are given below.

The Government is funding research projects aimed at evaluating the cost-effectiveness of different models of community care for people previously in long-stay hospitals.

The Government is monitoring the progress of implementation of the 1981 Education Act in England by means of a centrally funded research project, which is looking at policy and procedures in local education authorities. Other projects, also centrally funded, are looking at resources for integration and a modular approach to inservice training for teachers of children with special educational needs. In Scotland, a research project has taken place on the implications of parental choice of school for the provision made for children with visual impairment. This project is about to be followed by a more general study across the spectrum of impairment, on the policies and practice of education authorities in identifying and making provision for special educational needs. In addition, the Scottish Council for Research in Education is exploring the range of opportunities for education and training open to young people aged 16–18 years.

The Government is currently considering the recommendations of a working party set up by the Manpower Services Commission to examine ways of improving the effectiveness of the quota scheme for employment (see p. 331). The effectiveness of the Code of Good Practice on the Employment of Disabled People will be evaluated once employers have had sufficient time to implement the guidance it contains — that is, in about 2–3 years' time. One of the main elements of the European Community's programme for the social integration of disabled people (see p. 325) is the establishment of a network of district projects within Member States. Their objectives include finding ways to improve the coordination of existing services for disabled people at the local level and the dissemination of information about those services. Two of these district projects are currently taking place in the United Kingdom.

The Government's aim is to move towards a more coherent system of social security benefits and it has produced a consultation document following a review of some of the areas of benefit provision. Benefits specifically for sick and disabled people were not included in this review, but the first major survey for some 16 years has been commissioned to obtain up-to-date information about the extent and effects of disability. The results of this survey will enable these benefits to be reviewed in their turn. The information obtained from the survey of disability will also be helpful in the planning of services to meet the needs of disabled people. Meanwhile, the importance attached by the Government to the special needs of disabled people is reflected in the proposals made relating to the benefits already reviewed. The structure of the proposed means-tested income support scheme includes a special premium for long-term sick and disabled people, which will also be reflected in the new simpler housing benefit arrangements. A more generous disregard of their earnings will also be applied in this proposed income support scheme.

Yugoslavia

General Principles

In Yugoslavia, great importance has always been attached to social care for the disabled, beginning with care for victims of war as early as the first days of the National Liberation War and the Socialist Revolution. The approach is based on linking the social position of the disabled with the status of the individual in production, in society, and within socioeconomic development. It proceeds from clearly defined principles and attitudes contained in the Constitution of the Socialist Federal Republic of Yugoslavia, the constitutions of the republics and autonomous provinces (eight federal units), the Associated Labour Act, and numerous other legal and political programme documents. Thus care for the disabled is the moral and constitutional obligation of society. Society should create conditions for the rehabilitation and protection of the disabled and their integration into society. This is the basic precondition for the exercise of human and civil rights and is a direct expression of the profoundly human content of self-management socialism. Accordingly, the Yugoslav approach to disability encompasses the status of the disabled in society with its sociopolitical aspect, as well as the prevention of disability, with its humanitarian, social, legal and economic aspects and the rehabilitation and care of the disabled and their integration into all fields of social life and work.

The major objective of this concern of society is to prevent disability through various different measures and with maximum efficiency. Where it cannot be prevented, the objective is to prepare the disabled, through appropriate programmes, measures and activities based on their remaining faculties, for independent life and work, thus enabling them to feel and become useful, equal members

345

of the social community. For the disabled who cannot be rehabilitated for specific reasons, the social community ensures their social
and economic security and other appropriate forms of protection.

In implementing these social principles, the system of disability
prevention and rehabilitation, care for the disabled, and their integration has been continuously updated. Various measures have been
taken to continue the promotion of the social status of the disabled
and to create equal opportunities for them. These measures have been
integrated in the development plans of planning bodies at all levels
and important results have been achieved in all these fields.

In this sense, the establishment and continuous development of a
broad and well developed legal basis, which regulates the prevention
of disability, the rehabilitation and protection of the disabled, and
their integration, their status and their rights, are of special importance and play a significant role. This legal basis includes a large
number of federal and (in accordance with the Yugoslav
constitutional system) republican and provincial laws. A typical
aspect of the Yugoslav system of self-management is also the increasing number of regulations issued by organizations of associated
labour, communities of interest, local communities and communes.
With the further development of this legislation and the adoption of
the 1974 Constitution and self-management regulations, the opportunities for the rehabilitation and protection of disabled children, young
persons and adults have been broadened. This has enabled them not
only to benefit from a wide range of specific rights and forms of
protection, but has also created conditions for their integration into
all forms of life and work and for equal opportunities in society.

The 1974 Constitution contains a number of provisions related to
the disabled, examples of which are given below:

— the social community shall create conditions for the vocational rehabilitation of citizens who are not fully able to
  work and for their adequate employment (Article 159, paragraph 4);

— citizens who are not able to work and have no means of
  support shall be entitled to assistance from the social community (Article 189);

— the right of workers to social security shall be ensured through
  obligatory insurance based on the principles of reciprocity
  and solidarity, on their past employment in self-management
  communities of interest, and on contributions collected
  from their personal incomes and from the income of the

346

organizations of associated labour in which they work (Article 163, paragraph 1);

— disabled war veterans shall be entitled to vocational rehabilitation, disability benefits and other forms of care (Article 187, paragraph 2).

The constitutions of the federal units also contain a number of provisions on the disabled. Programmes of activities beneficial to the disabled, including legal provisions, also exist at the federal, republican, provincial and local levels.

The proclamation of the International Year of Disabled Persons, 1981 and of the United Nations Decade of Disabled Persons, 1983–1992 gave Yugoslavia yet another chance to analyse the situation comprehensively, initiate further measures and activities to promote the position of the disabled, and focus the attention of society on the needs of the disabled, especially as regards legislation and development plans. Accordingly, all the activities carried out during the Year and the Decade are consistent with the policies and principles already adopted. Many activities are carried out at the grassroots level.

As early as 1980, the Federal Executive Council (the Government of Yugoslavia) established the Yugoslav Committee for the International Year of Disabled Persons. Corresponding committees were also set up in all the federal units. At the end of the Year, the Yugoslav Committee and the committees in the federal units became standing coordinating bodies for the United Nations Decade of Disabled Persons, responsible for coordinating and organizing activities in the country and cooperating at the international level with specialized agencies of the United Nations, international organizations and appropriate bodies established in other countries.

The Committee has a programme for the Decade and adopts annual working plans. It consists of a chairman and 18 members of which three are representatives of the Assembly of the Socialist Federal Republic and federal administrative bodies, seven represent organizations of the disabled, and eight are representatives of socio-political and social organizations and of self-management communities of interest at the federal level. The chairmen of the corresponding committees of the federal units are *ex officio* members of the Committee.

The Chairman of the Committee is the President of the Federal Committee for Labour, Health and Social Welfare, who is a member of the Government of Yugoslavia. Technical and other services for the Committee are rendered by the staff of the Federal Committee for Labour, Health and Social Welfare.

National Involvement in International Action

In Yugoslavia, great importance is attached to the implementation of numerous international instruments (charters, declarations of rights and resolutions) that relate to the disabled and have been adopted by the United Nations or intergovernmental organizations, and to which the country has acceded. Yugoslavia cooperates successfully with all the organizations of the United Nations system and other intergovernmental organizations active in this field.

The preparation and implementation of the World Programme of Action concerning disabled persons should particularly be emphasized. Yugoslavia was an active member of the United Nations Advisory Committee for the International Year, which prepared the draft of this Programme. After its adoption by the United Nations General Assembly, Yugoslavia established the Technical Cooperation Support Service for the rehabilitation of the disabled. The Service includes all Yugoslav rehabilitation institutions, and since 1982 it has been successfully preparing and executing projects and programmes in this field in cooperation with the United Nations Centre for Social Development and Humanitarian Affairs in Vienna.

Special attention has been given to the role of and cooperation with nongovernmental organizations of and for the disabled, both at national and international levels. For a number of years, Yugoslavia has been cooperating with numerous nongovernmental international organizations such as the World Federation of the Deaf, the World Council for the Welfare of the Blind, the International League of Societies for Persons with Mental Handicap, Disabled People's International, Rehabilitation International and the International Federation of Disabled Workers and Civilian Handicapped.

Methodology — Types of Legislative Approach to the Equality Concept

The promotion of the status and care of the disabled, as well as the continuous improvement of measures, methods and forms of rehabilitation and integration, have always been one of the main orientations of Yugoslavia's socialist self-management society. Over the past few years, the legal basis for this has developed into a ramified network of legal provisions and enactments that is constantly expanding and improving. This is due, in particular, to the fast development of enactments by organizations of associated

348

labour and communities of interest concerning social activities with a self-management emphasis.

Legal approaches to regulating these issues have changed and improved over the years. The present situation is characterized by the following. No uniform federal law on the disabled covers all the disabled irrespective of the category, characteristics or type of disability, although such general laws exist in some federal units. These matters are regulated by laws that can be divided into four main groups:

(*a*) laws that regulate the status of the four main categories of disabled according to their characteristics (for example laws on: retirement and disability insurance regulating the status and rights of disabled workers, disabled members of the armed forces whether disabled in war or peace, civilians disabled during the war, and other disabled persons not falling under any of the categories mentioned);

(*b*) specific laws that deal with a particular field or form of rehabilitation and care for the disabled (for example laws on: the special education of disabled children and young persons, the classification of disabled children and young persons, protective workshops for the vocational rehabilitation and employment of the disabled, and special benefits for blind persons and persons who accompany them in public transport);

(*c*) laws regulating certain fields of significance for the status and care of the disabled (for example laws on: health, health insurance and health care, labour relations, employment, safety at work, social welfare, child care and children's allowances, and marriage and family relations);

(*d*) laws containing certain provisions for disabled persons, their rehabilitation and their integration (for example laws on: urban development, housing, construction, public utilities and transport, including provisions aimed at removing barriers to the integration of disabled persons; tariffs with provisions to exempt disabled persons from customs when importing orthopaedic and other appliances, as well as to exempt institutions when importing machines and equipment for rehabilitation; taxation with provisions to exempt disabled persons from taxes on income from certain activities or when importing cars, and to exempt rehabilitation institutions from taxes on their products; and additional rights, such as allowances for assistance and care for certain categories of severely disabled person, such as those whose disability is over 70%, the blind, and persons suffering from muscular dystrophy).

Review of the Present State of National Legislation

Elimination of discrimination or social prejudice
Measures taken to eliminate the major prejudices against disabled persons, and to enable their integration in the life of the community include, for instance:

- numerous laws expressly stating that the disabled enjoy equal rights (such as those on elementary and vocational training, preschool coverage and labour relations);

- legislative measures in some republics and autonomous provinces to reduce the possibility of discrimination through architectural standards and town planning regulations to prevent architectural and other urban barriers, and to eliminate these barriers for severely disabled persons during the construction of public buildings and flats;

- legislative measures ensuring health care, child care and social welfare, vocational training and rehabilitation, education and upbringing, employment, the protection of self-management rights, and recreational and sports activities, in other words, ensuring that the disabled enjoy the same rights as all the other working people of the country.

Social reintegration and full participation
These measures include the following:

- the right to compulsory forms of health care, diagnosis and adequate medical treatment, through physical medicine and rehabilitation, free orthopaedic appliances, medical instruments and necessary supplies;

- the special obligations of communes in the field of housing for disabled persons;

- transport facilities for certain persons (the blind) and various concessions granted by transport companies for several groups of disabled persons and their attendants;

— the inclusion of the time spent on vocational rehabilitation in the length of service, and a reduced number of years of service required for retirement for some categories of severely disabled persons;

— special social welfare rights, such as allowances 50% higher for disabled children;

— cultural, art, sports and recreation activities organized by societies of the disabled and of their parents, as they participate in the formulation and implementation of the system of rehabilitation and protection;

— the stimulation of self-help and independent living, envisaged by all the above-mentioned regulations and measures;

— laws on elementary education and the training of mentally or physically handicapped children and young persons in the framework of normal education; disabled children unable to attend normal classes are educated in normal schools through work in groups or special classes with adapted programmes, aids and appliances, or in special schools and institutions, depending on the degree of impairment; in addition to the law on elementary education, laws on secondary education and vocational training have also been adopted.

The education of disabled children and young people is an integral part of the educational system. They are trained for work in various organizations: organizations of associated labour in the field of education, upbringing and social welfare, organizations of associated labour in the economy, and protection organizations. Training and education depend on the type and degree of the handicap, and special forms of training are organized.

Before being included in the system of education and training, disabled children are classified according to the category and degree of their handicap in line with rules on classifying and registering mentally and physically handicapped children. These rules specify the procedure for identifying such children, with precise criteria for their classification, and for sending them to adequate educational institutions. After completing their education and vocational rehabilitation, and until they take on an adequate job, disabled children are entitled to compensation.

Disabled persons are employed in a normal working environment, if possible, depending on their working abilities and health condition. An important role is played by organizations for the rehabilitation and employment of the disabled, that is, the so-called protective workshops, which employ disabled persons under special conditions.

The prevention of disability

Disability prevention is one of the basic and primary tasks of society. Numerous legislative measures, self-management regulations and development plans envisage measures for the prevention of disability, including the education of the public (children and adults) to protect them from various risks and dangers causing disability, the development of prenatal and postnatal control and the promotion of knowledge of the importance of vaccination, the development of appropriate health services, the establishment and implementation of safety measures at work and on roads and in other public places, the stimulation of research in the field of disability prevention, and the development of rehabilitation.

Systems of income support

Laws on retirement and disability insurance specify the rights of beneficiaries still capable of working as: the right to work half the working hours at least in the jobs and tasks undertaken before the disability occurred, the right to be transferred to other jobs and tasks with full working hours, the right to retraining if necessary, and the right to appropriate monetary compensation when exercising these rights. The laws also regulate the right to professional rehabilitation of the children of insured persons and beneficiaries, as well as children receiving dependants' pensions who, through normal education, cannot be trained to live and work on their own owing to mental or physical impairment. These children are entitled to compensation for travel expenses while exercising their right to rehabilitation. The rehabilitation of disabled children is carried out in special organizations, where children and young people with mental and physical handicaps attend preschool, elementary and secondary school institutions and receive vocational training according to their abilities and talents.

Disabled persons who are not capable of working are entitled to the following allowances and services. They receive a disability pension. The full health care ensured for all disabled persons includes monetary compensation as well as detection, observation, diagnosis, medical and other rehabilitation, therapy, hospital treatment, orthopaedic and other appliances. The laws on child care prescribe that disabled children are entitled to the following forms of

352

child care: enrolment in institutions for preschool education and day care in other families, organized rest and recreation, and the organized use of free time. These or other special laws specify the right to an allowance for children depending on the material standing of the parents, this allowance being 50% or more higher than the normal child allowance. This right lasts until rehabilitation is completed, or for life if no conditions for rehabilitation exist. Laws in the field of social welfare ensure the following rights for disabled persons: financial aid (regular or lump sum aid), allowances for dependants, allowances for education and training, allowances for external care and assistance, training for work and aid during that time, home care and help at home, and day care.

Disabled civilian war victims have the following rights: a civilian's pension (a fixed monthly amount), an allowance for external care and assistance, additional monetary aid, an allowance for another family member incapable of working, and health care and rehabilitation.

Disabled war veterans have the following rights: pension and disability allowances, allowances for external care and assistance, orthopaedic allowances, health care with monetary compensation, treatment in spas and resorts, and other additional rights.

Evaluation of Progress in National Legislation

As mentioned above, following the International Year of Disabled Persons and during the United Nations Decade of Disabled Persons, great progress has been achieved in the field of legislation pertaining to disabled persons. This is reflected not only in the updating of existing laws and the passing of new ones, but primarily in the incorporation of new approaches, measures and methods, and the inclusion of new rights for disabled persons, aimed at ensuring their rehabilitation and integration, and at creating equal opportunities for them in life, work and society. The difficulties in the implementation of these social objectives have primarily been of an economic nature. The developments in the legal field have had a highly positive impact on the successful social integration of disabled persons and on the creation of equal opportunities for the disabled.

In view of the results achieved, the experiences gained, and the measures taken and planned for the future in this field, the Yugoslav Committee for the International Year of Disabled Persons in its final report (adopted by the Yugoslav Government) charted the main courses of action for the promotion of legislative measures and self-management regulations in this sphere. The main course of action should be the constant revision of these regulations, to bring them into line with the development of modern disability prevention, rehabilitation and protection, in compliance with changes in the needs of disabled persons, and with the realistic opportunities of the social community, with the active participation of disabled persons and their organizations.

Work on the elaboration of a comprehensive analysis of legislative measures and self-management regulations in this sphere is under way, and will include a review of the development, situation and problems, as well as proposals for future activities. This analysis, which is being prepared by the Yugoslav Committee for the Decade of Disabled Persons in cooperation with a large number of bodies and organizations, institutions and experts, should make a great contribution to the attainment of the objectives in this field.